MW00658927

THE CAMBRIDGE CO[…]
ELIZABETH BI[…]

Elizabeth Bishop is increasingly recognized as one of the twentieth century's most important and original poets. Initially celebrated for the minute detail of her descriptions, what John Ashbery memorably called her "thinginess," Bishop's reputation has risen dramatically since her death, in part owing to the publication of new work, including letters, stories, and visual art, as well as a controversial volume of uncollected poems, drafts, and fragments. This *Companion to Elizabeth Bishop* engages with key debates surrounding the interpretation and reception of Bishop's published and unpublished writing in relation to questions of biography, the natural world, and politics. Individual chapters focus on well-known texts such as *North & South, Questions of Travel*, and *Geography III*, while offering fresh readings of the significance of Nova Scotia, Massachusetts, and Brazil to Bishop's life and work. With a chronology and guide to further reading, this volume explores the full range of Bishop's artistic achievements and the extent to which the posthumous publications have contributed to her enduring popularity.

ANGUS CLEGHORN is professor of English and Liberal Studies at Seneca College, Toronto. Since 2004, he has served as the editor of the *Elizabeth Bishop Bulletin* for the Elizabeth Bishop Society. He has published articles on Bishop and Wallace Stevens, as well as the book *Wallace Stevens' Poetics: The Neglected Rhetoric* (2000); guest-edited two issues of the *Wallace Stevens Journal* (1999, 2006); and co-edited the volume *Elizabeth Bishop in the Twenty-First Century: Reading the New Editions* (2012).

JONATHAN ELLIS is senior lecturer in American Literature at the University of Sheffield, England. He is the author of *Art and Memory in the Work of Elizabeth Bishop* (2006), as well as articles on Michael Donaghy, Paul Muldoon, Sylvia Plath, and Anne Stevenson. His next book, for which he received a British Academy Research Development Award in 2008, is on twentieth-century letter writing. He is currently editing a collection of essays on poets' letters, *Letter Writing Among Poets: From William Wordsworth to Elizabeth Bishop*.

A complete list of books in the series is at the back of this book.

THE CAMBRIDGE
COMPANION TO

ELIZABETH BISHOP

THE CAMBRIDGE COMPANION TO
ELIZABETH BISHOP

Edited by

ANGUS CLEGHORN
Seneca College

JONATHAN ELLIS
University of Sheffield

CAMBRIDGE
UNIVERSITY PRESS

CAMBRIDGE
UNIVERSITY PRESS

32 Avenue of the Americas, New York, NY 10013-2473, USA

Cambridge University Press is part of the University of Cambridge.

It furthers the University's mission by disseminating knowledge in the pursuit of education, learning, and research at the highest international levels of excellence.

www.cambridge.org
Information on this title: www.cambridge.org/9781107672543

First published 2014

Printed in the United States of America

A catalog record for this publication is available from the British Library.

Library of Congress Cataloging in Publication Data
Cleghorn, Angus J. and Ellis, Jonathan S.
The Cambridge Companion to Elizabeth Bishop / Angus Cleghorn, Seneca College; Jonathan Ellis, University of Sheffield.
pages cm. – (Cambridge Companions to Literature)
Includes bibliographical references and index.
ISBN 978-1-107-02940-8 (hardback) –
ISBN 978-1-107-67254-3 (pbk.)
1. Bishop, Elizabeth, 1911–1979 – Criticism and interpretation. I. Cleghorn, Angus, 1966– II. Ellis, Jonathan, 1975– III. Title.
PS3503.I785Z59 2014
811′.54–dc23 2013027355

ISBN 978-1-107-02940-8 Hardback
ISBN 978-1-107-67254-3 Paperback

CONTENTS

FIGURES

CONTRIBUTORS

STEVEN GOULD AXELROD is distinguished professor of English at the University of California, Riverside. He is the author of *Robert Lowell: Life and Art* (1978), *Robert Lowell: A Reference Guide* (1982), and *Sylvia Plath: The Wound and the Cure of Words* (1990). He is the editor or co-editor of *Robert Lowell: Essays on the Poetry* (1986); *Critical Essays on Wallace Stevens* (1988); *Critical Essays on William Carlos Williams* (1995); *The Critical Response to Robert Lowell* (1998); *The New Anthology of American Poetry, Volume 1, Beginnings to 1900* (2002); *The New Anthology of American Poetry, Volume 2, 1900–1950* (2005); and *The New Anthology of American Poetry, Volume 3, 1950–Present* (2012). He has also published more than sixty scholarly articles in such journals as *American Literature*, *American Quarterly*, and *Contemporary Literature*.

SANDRA BARRY is a poet, independent scholar, and freelance editor. She is the author of *Elizabeth Bishop: An Archival Guide to Her Life in Nova Scotia* (1996) and *Elizabeth Bishop: Nova Scotia's "Home-Made" Poet* (2011) and co-editor of *Divisions of the Heart: Elizabeth Bishop and the Art of Memory and Place* (2001). She is co-founder and past president of the Elizabeth Bishop Society of Nova Scotia and a co-owner and the administrator of the Elizabeth Bishop House in Great Village, Nova Scotia.

ANGUS CLEGHORN is professor of English and Liberal Studies at Seneca College in Toronto. Since 2004, he has served as the editor of the *Elizabeth Bishop Bulletin* for the Elizabeth Bishop Society. He has published articles on Bishop and Stevens, as well as the book *Wallace Stevens' Poetics: The Neglected Rhetoric* (2000), and he has guest-edited two issues of the *Wallace Stevens Journal* (1999, 2006) and co-edited the volume *Elizabeth Bishop in the Twenty-First Century: Reading the New Editions* (2012).

BONNIE COSTELLO is professor of English at Boston University. She is the author of numerous articles on modern poetry and five books, including *Elizabeth Bishop: Questions of Mastery* (1991). Her most recent books are *Shifting Ground: Reinventing Landscape in Modern American Poetry* (2003) and *Planets on*

Tables: Poetry, Still Life and the Turning World (2008). She was the general editor for *The Selected Letters of Marianne Moore* (1997). Costello is currently at work on *Private Faces in Public Places: Lyric and the First Person Plural*, for which she was awarded a Cullman/American Council of Learned Societies fellowship for 2011–2012. She has been a Fellow of the American Academy of Arts and Sciences since 2004.

JONATHAN ELLIS is senior lecturer in American Literature at the University of Sheffield, England. He is the author of *Art and Memory in the Work of Elizabeth Bishop* (2006), as well as articles on Michael Donaghy, Paul Muldoon, Sylvia Plath, and Anne Stevenson. His next book, for which he received a British Academy Research Development Award in 2008, is on twentieth-century letter writing. He is currently editing a collection of essays on poets' letters, *Letter Writing Among Poets: From William Wordsworth to Elizabeth Bishop*.

LORRIE GOLDENSOHN'S 1992 book, *Elizabeth Bishop: The Biography of a Poetry*, was nominated for a Pulitzer Prize and contained discussion of "It is marvellous to wake up together," a previously unknown Bishop poem that Goldensohn discovered in Brazil. Goldensohn's *Dismantling Glory: Twentieth Century English and American Soldier Poetry* received nomination for a Book Critics Circle Award in 2003, while *Choice Magazine* selected her anthology, *American War Poetry*, as one of their Best Critical Books of 2006. She has published articles, essays, and reviews in prominent journals for several decades. Grants have supported her literary criticism: two from the National Endowment for the Humanities, as well as two Fulbright awards, the latter both during and after her retirement from Vassar College.

BETHANY HICOK is associate professor of English at Westminster College in Pennsylvania. She is the author of *Degrees of Freedom: American Women Poets and the Women's College, 1905–1955* (2008), which focuses on the poetry of Marianne Moore, Elizabeth Bishop, and Sylvia Plath. She is also co-editor (with Thomas Travisano and Angus Cleghorn) of a collection of essays, *Elizabeth Bishop in the Twenty-First Century* (2012). She is currently working on a book on Elizabeth Bishop in Brazil.

BARBARA PAGE is professor of English (retired) at Vassar College, as well as the former acting dean of faculty. She is the author of essays on Elizabeth Bishop and the Bishop Papers at Vassar, including "Shifting Islands: The Manuscripts of Elizabeth Bishop," "Off-Beat Claves, Oblique Realities: The Key West Notebooks of Elizabeth Bishop," "Elizabeth Bishop and Postmodernism," and "Elizabeth Bishop: Stops, Starts, and Dreamy Divigations." She is co-author, with novelist and translator Carmen Oliveira, of a book in progress, *Elizabeth Bishop in Brazil*.

SIOBHAN PHILLIPS is an assistant professor of English at Dickinson College and the author of *The Poetics of the Everyday: Creative Repetition in Modern American*

Verse (2010). Her poems and essays have appeared in *PMLA*, *Twentieth Century Literature*, *Literary Imagination*, *Yale Review*, *Southwest Review*, *The Hudson Review*, and other journals. She has degrees from Yale, Oxford, and the University of East Anglia, and she is a former junior Fellow at the Harvard Society of Fellows.

SUSAN ROSENBAUM is an associate professor of English at the University of Georgia, where she teaches twentieth-century American poetry. She is the author of *Professing Sincerity: Modern Lyric Poetry, Commercial Culture, and the Crisis in Reading* (2007), as well as essays on Elizabeth Bishop, Mina Loy, and the poets of the New York School. She is currently completing a book titled *Exquisite Corpse: American Poetry, Surrealism, and the Museum of Modern Art, 1920–70*, for which she received a National Endowment for the Humanities fellowship.

PEGGY SAMUELS is professor of English at Drew University in Madison, NJ. She is the author of *Deep Skin: Elizabeth Bishop and Visual Art* (2010), as well as a range of articles on John Milton and Andrew Marvell. She is currently researching the Geraldine R. Dodge Poetry Festival archive.

LLOYD SCHWARTZ has taught at Boston State College, Queens College, and Harvard University and is currently Frederick S. Troy Professor of English at the University of Massachusetts in Boston. He is co-editor of *Elizabeth Bishop and Her Art* (1983) and the Library of America's *Elizabeth Bishop: Poems, Prose, and Letters* (2008) and the editor of *Elizabeth Bishop: Prose* (2011). His most recent book of poems is *Cairo Traffic* (2000). His poems, articles, and reviews have appeared in *The New Yorker, The Atlantic, Vanity Fair, The New Republic, The Paris Review,* and *The Best American Poetry*. In 1994, he was awarded the Pulitzer Prize for criticism. He recently released a book collection of his radio pieces, *Music In – and On – the Air*.

THOMAS TRAVISANO is professor and chair of English at Hartwick College. Along with numerous articles on modern and contemporary literature, Travisano is the author of *Elizabeth Bishop: Her Artistic Development* (1988) and *Midcentury Quartet: Bishop, Lowell, Jarrell, Berryman and the Making of a Postmodern Aesthetic* (1999). He also served as the principal editor of *Words in Air: The Complete Correspondence Between Elizabeth Bishop and Robert Lowell* (2008), as co-editor of *Gendered Modernisms: American Women Poets and Their Readers* (1996) and *Elizabeth Bishop in the Twenty-First Century: Reading the New Editions*, and as co-editor of the three-volume *New Anthology of American Poetry*. He is the founding president of the Elizabeth Bishop Society and a senior advisor to the Robert Lowell Society.

KIRSTIN HOTELLING ZONA is the author of *Marianne Moore, Elizabeth Bishop, and May Swenson: The Feminist Poetics of Self-Restraint* (2002) and editor of *Dear Elizabeth: Five Poems and Three Letters from May Swenson to Elizabeth*

Bishop (2000). She has published numerous essays on contemporary poets and poetics in journals such as *Modernism/Modernity*, *Twentieth Century Literature*, and *ISLE*. Her poetry has appeared in a wide range of journals and anthologies, including, most recently, the *Cincinnati Review*, the *Southwest Review*, *Columbia*, the *Georgetown Review*, the *Mississippi Review*, and *Beloit Poetry Journal*. Zona lives with her husband and two children in Maine and Illinois where she is an associate professor at Illinois State University. She is the editor of the *Spoon River Poetry Review* and co-host of *Poetry Radio* on WGLT, a local National Public Radio affiliate station.

ACKNOWLEDGMENTS

Thanks to the contributors to this book for the good grace and patience with which they responded to two editors reading their work. We did not anticipate bringing Elizabeth Bishop's "two looks" to life quite so literally. In addition to their contributions to this book, Steven Gould Axelrod, Sandra Barry, Susan Rosenbaum, and Thomas Travisano gave us invaluable advice on the Chronology and the Introduction. Moreover, we would like to thank Thomas Travisano for stimulating this book by organizing the conference sessions that brought us together where we originally discussed this project. The volume draws on and is indebted to the critical insights of at least two generations of Bishop scholars, many of whom are cited here. The book would not have happened without the enthusiasm of Ray Ryan and Louis Gulino at Cambridge University Press or the external readers who responded positively to our initial proposal.

Angus Cleghorn is grateful to students and colleagues at Seneca College and Trent University who have made valuable insights in lively discussions of Bishop's writing. Thanks to Claire Moane in the School of English and Liberal Studies at Seneca College for supporting the travel grants to Brazil, San Francisco, and Boston to pursue research and dialogue. Many scholars and enthusiasts in the Elizabeth Bishop Society have broadened my knowledge since I began editing the *Elizabeth Bishop Bulletin* in 2004. Thanks to my wife, Julie, and sons, Andrew and Simon, for making life full and enjoyable.

Jonathan Ellis is particularly grateful to the British Academy for a research award that gave him time to begin thinking about this project and to the University of Sheffield for granting him research leave to finish it. Without Jamie McKendrick and Angela Leighton, I may never have found my way to Bishop in the first place. Katrina Mayson looked over the manuscript at a crucial stage. The enthusiasm and intelligence of literally hundreds of students have, I hope, also found a place in this book. Finally, my thanks, as ever, to Ana María Sánchez-Arce who gave me time to finish this book when her own deadline was just as, if not more, pressing. She also suggested the perfect cover image.

"Unfinished Fireplace" from *Exchanging Hats: Paintings* by Elizabeth Bishop edited by William Benton. Copyright © 1996, 1997, 2011 by Alice Methfessel. Collection of Vassar College Library. Reprinted by permission of Farrar, Straus, and Giroux, LLC.

Photo of Elizabeth Bishop on the steps of the Square Roof brothel in Key West. Copyright © James Laughlin. Reprinted by permission of Farrar, Straus, and Giroux, LLC.

Excerpts from unpublished notes by Elizabeth Bishop. Copyright © 2013 by the Alice H. Methfessel Trust. Printed by permission of Farrar, Straus, and Giroux, LLC on behalf of the Elizabeth Bishop Estate.

Quotations from the unpublished writings of Elizabeth Bishop are also used with the permission of Special Collections, Vassar College Libraries.

Thanks to Victoria Fox at Farrar, Straus, and Giroux for generous help in arranging permissions. William Benton and Cynthia Krupat have also provided invaluable assistance in providing digital images.

NOTE ON ABBREVIATIONS

Unless otherwise indicated, poems discussed in this volume are from Elizabeth Bishop, *Poems* (London: Chatto and Windus; New York: Farrar, Straus, and Giroux, 2011).

EAP Elizabeth Bishop, *Edgar Allan Poe & The Juke-Box: Uncollected Poems, Drafts, and Fragments*, ed. Alice Quinn (Manchester: Carcanet; New York: Farrar, Straus, and Giroux, 2006).

EH Elizabeth Bishop, *Exchanging Hats: Elizabeth Bishop Paintings*, ed. William Benton (Manchester: Carcanet; New York: Farrar, Straus, and Giroux, 1996).

NYr Elizabeth Bishop, *Elizabeth Bishop and The New Yorker: The Complete Correspondence*, ed. Joelle Biele (New York: Farrar, Straus, and Giroux, 2011).

OA Elizabeth Bishop, *One Art: Letters*, ed. Robert Giroux (London: Chatto and Windus; New York: Farrar, Straus, and Giroux, 1994).

P Elizabeth Bishop, *Poems* (London: Chatto and Windus; New York: Farrar, Straus, and Giroux, 2011).

PPL Elizabeth Bishop, *Poems, Prose, and Letters*, eds. Robert Giroux and Lloyd Schwartz (New York: Library of America, 2008).

Pr Elizabeth Bishop, *Prose*, ed. Lloyd Schwartz (London: Chatto and Windus; New York: Farrar, Straus, and Giroux, 2011).

VC Elizabeth Bishop Collection, Vassar College Library, Poughkeepsie, New York.

WIA Elizabeth Bishop and Robert Lowell, *Words in Air: The Complete Correspondence between Elizabeth Bishop and Robert Lowell*, ed. Thomas Travisano with Saskia Hamilton (London: Faber and Faber; New York: Farrar, Straus, and Giroux, 2008).

CHRONOLOGY

(*Italics* denote historical events)

1911	February 8: Elizabeth Bishop born in Worcester, Massachusetts, the only child of William Thomas Bishop of Worcester, and Gertrude May Bulmer (or "Boomer") of Great Village, Nova Scotia.
	October 13: Bishop's father dies from Bright's disease.
1914	June 25: The Great Salem Fire destroys more than 1,000 buildings. Bishop watches the fire with her mother from the Bishops' summer home in Marblehead (see the posthumously published poem, "A Drunkard").
1914–1918	*World War I.*
1915	April: Moves from Boston to Great Village, Nova Scotia, with her mother.
1916	June: Bishop's mother admits herself to the Nova Scotia Hospital in Dartmouth. Bishop stays with her maternal grandparents in Great Village where she attends Primer Class.
1917	October: Bishop is taken to live in Worcester by her paternal grandparents. Begins to develop asthma. Decades later, in her story "The Country Mouse," she recalls feeling as if she were being "kidnapped."
	December 6: The Halifax Harbor Explosion. Nearly 2,000 people die following a collision between two ships (one laden with wartime explosives) in Halifax Harbor. The Nova Scotia Hospital, where Bishop's mother is living, is badly damaged.

1918	May: Moves in with her aunt, Maude Bulmer Shepherdson, and uncle, George Shepherdson, in Revere, Massachusetts.
1919	August: Returns to Nova Scotia with her aunt, Grace Bulmer Bowers. Although Bishop never lives permanently in Great Village again, she continues to make yearly summer trips throughout her adolescence.
1926–1927	Attends North Shore Country Day School in Swampscott, Massachusetts, where she publishes her first poems and stories in *The Owl*. For several years, also attends Cape Chequesett on Cape Cod, a summer camp where she learns to sail.
1927–1930	Attends Walnut Hill School in Natick, Massachusetts. Publishes poems and other writings in school magazine, *The Blue Pencil*.
1930	Enters Vassar College. Intends to major in music, but switches to English. Contemporaries at Vassar include Mary McCarthy and Muriel Rukeyser.
1934	March 16: Meets Marianne Moore at the New York Public Library.
	May 29: Bishop's mother dies.
	After graduation, Bishop moves into a small apartment in Greenwich Village, New York, and works briefly at a correspondence school that she later writes about in "The U.S.A. School of Writing." On New Year's Eve, home alone with a cold, she begins "The Map."
1935	Marianne Moore chooses "The Map," "Three Valentines," and "The Reprimand" for the anthology *Trial Balances*. Moore's brief introduction to the poems is the first published criticism of Bishop's work.
	Makes first trip to Europe and North Africa with Louise Crane. Meets Pablo Picasso.
1936–1939	*Spanish Civil War.*
1936	Robert Seaver, who had wanted to marry Bishop, commits suicide.
	First trip to Florida with Louise Crane.

1937 Returns to Europe with Crane. They travel from Ireland to France where they are joined by another Vassar friend, Margaret Miller. In July, while they are traveling in Burgundy, Crane's car is forced off the road. Miller loses her right arm in the accident.

1938 Buys 624 White Street in Key West, Florida, with Louise Crane (White Street is the first of Bishop's "three loved houses" immortalized in "One Art").

1939 *Outbreak of World War II.*

1940 Spends spring and summer in Key West.

October: Disagreement with Marianne Moore over Bishop's poem "Roosters."

1941 Begins six-year-long relationship with Marjorie Stevens.

December 7: Pearl Harbor attack. United States enters World War II.

1942 Travels to Mexico with Stevens. Meets Pablo Neruda.

1943 Bishop works for five days grinding binocular lenses in a U.S. Navy optical shop in Key West. Eyestrain and eczema force her to quit.

1945 June: Wins the Houghton Mifflin Poetry Prize Fellowship.

August: Atomic bombs detonated at Hiroshima and Nagasaki. End of World War II.

1946 July: Returns to Nova Scotia for the first time since 1930. On the bus journey from Great Village to Boston, the bus driver has to stop suddenly for a moose wandering down the road. Bishop takes twenty-six years to complete a poem ("The Moose") about this experience.

August: Publication of Bishop's first book of poems, *North & South*.

1947 January: Meets Robert Lowell at a dinner party hosted by Randall Jarrell. Lowell reviews *North & South* in *Sewanee Review*.

April: Awarded Guggenheim Fellowship.

Begins treatment with Dr. Anny Baumann for depression, asthma, and alcoholism.

Travels to Cape Breton with Marjorie Stevens, a trip remembered in the eponymous poem.

1949 September: Begins year-long appointment as Consultant in Poetry (now Poet Laureate) at the Library of Congress. Meets Robert Frost, Dylan Thomas, and William Carlos Williams. Pays regular visits to Ezra Pound at St. Elizabeths Hospital, where he was confined after a jury decided he was of "unsound mind" and thus unfit to stand trial for treason.

1950–1953 *Korean War.*

1950 Meets May Swenson at Yaddo writers colony.

1951 Receives fellowships from Bryn Mawr College and the American Academy of Arts and Letters. Travels to Sable Island, Nova Scotia, where, according to family tradition, her great-grandfather had been lost at sea.

November 10: Travels to South America on Norwegian freighter *S.S. Bowplate*, intending to stop in Brazil for only a few weeks. While in Brazil, has an allergic reaction to the fruit of a cashew tree and is nursed back to health by her Brazilian friend, Lota de Macedo Soares. The two women fall in love and Bishop accepts Macedo Soares's offer to build her a studio behind Macedo Soares's Modernist house then being constructed at Samambaia in the mountains above Petrópolis.

1952 Wins Shelley Memorial Award.

1953 Publication of stories "Gwendolyn" (June 27) and "In the Village" (December 19) in *The New Yorker*.

1955 July: Publication of *Poems* (a reissue of *North & South* with her new collection, *A Cold Spring*).

Edits and translates Henrique Mindlin's *Modern Architecture in Brazil*.

1956 Receives a *Partisan Review* fellowship and Pulitzer Prize for Poetry for *Poems: North & South – A Cold Spring*.

1957 Receives Amy Lowell Traveling Fellowship.

Publication of her translation of *The Diary of "Helena Morley."*

1958 Aldous and Laura Huxley visit Bishop and Macedo Soares in Petrópolis. Bishop travels with them to Brasília, including a day excursion to see the Uialapiti tribe living on a tributary of the Xingo River.

1959 *First American servicemen die in Vietnam.*

1960 Travels down the Amazon, visiting Manaus, Santarém, Vigia, and Belém. Also visits Ouro Preto.

1961 Macedo Soares begins work on Aterro do Flamengo on the Rio waterfront.

1962 Publication of *Brazil* – written by Bishop, but considerably altered by the book's editors for *Life*'s World Library series.

1964 *April 1: The Brazilian military stages a coup to overthrow President João Goulart. Macedo Soares's friend, Carlos Lacerda, conservative governor of the state of Guanabara (Rio), supports the coup.*

Becomes a Fellow of the Academy of American Poets.

1965 *Beginning of U.S. ground war in Vietnam, which lasted until 1973.*

Purchases and then begins restoring a Colonial house in Ouro Preto. Bishop names it Casa Mariana in honor of Marianne Moore and because of its position on the road from Ouro Preto to Mariana.

November: Publication of *Questions of Travel*, dedicated to Macedo Soares.

1966 Teaches at the University of Washington in Seattle where she begins a relationship with Roxanne Cumming.

November: Travels with Macedo Soares to England and Holland, but cuts trip short when Macedo Soares's health deteriorates. Macedo Soares is hospitalized on her return to Rio.

Anne Stevenson publishes *Elizabeth Bishop* in the Twayne United States Author Series. It is the first critical book on Bishop's poetry.

1967 January: Macedo Soares's doctor recommends a temporary separation. Bishop and Macedo Soares are reunited in the spring, but in June the doctor recommends another break.

July 3: Bishop flies to New York.

September: Against the advice of her doctor, Macedo Soares travels to New York to see Bishop. On September 19, she takes an overdose of Valium and goes into a coma. She dies at St. Vincent's Hospital on September 25. Anny Baumann advises Bishop not to accompany the body back to Rio.

November 15: Returns to Brazil to settle Macedo Soares's estate. Many of Macedo Soares's friends and family blame Bishop for her death. Almost all of Bishop's letters to Macedo Soares are destroyed by Macedo Soares's sister.

1968 Lives for a year in San Francisco with Roxanne Cumming and her son. Meets Thom Gunn and Robert Duncan.

Awarded a grant from the Ingram-Merrill Foundation.

Publication of *The Ballad of the Burglar of Babylon* in a children's edition illustrated by Anne Grifalconi.

1969 April: Publication of *The Complete Poems*.

May: Gives readings at the Library of Congress and the Guggenheim Museum where Robert Lowell introduces her as "the famous eye."

1970 March: Wins National Book Award for *The Complete Poems*.

September: Moves to Cambridge, Massachusetts, to teach at Harvard. Meets Alice Methfessel.

1971 Spends several months in Ouro Preto. Brazilian government awards her the Order of Rio Branco.

August: Meets Alice Methfessel in Quito for a long-planned trip to the Galápagos Islands and Machu Picchu.

Returns to Harvard for the fall term where she teaches a seminar on letter writing "as an art form." Meets Octavio Paz.

1972 February 5: Marianne Moore dies.

March: Bishop and Lowell disagree over the latter's decision to publish versions of Elizabeth Hardwick's letters in *The Dolphin.*

June 13: Reads "The Moose" at Harvard's Phi Beta Kappa ceremony. The poem is dedicated to Grace Bulmer Bowers, Bishop's favorite aunt.

Publication of *An Anthology of Twentieth-Century Brazilian Poetry*, edited with Emanuel Brasil.

1973 Four-year appointment as lecturer at Harvard begins.

1974 August: Purchases a condominium at Lewis Wharf on the Boston waterfront.

1976 February: Awarded Neustadt International Prize for Literature.

Travels to England where she visits Robert Lowell.

December: Publication of *Geography III*; receives National Book Critics Circle Award.

1977 September 12: Robert Lowell dies.

1978 Receives Guggenheim Fellowship.

1979 May: Bishop makes her last visit to Nova Scotia, to receive an honorary degree from Dalhousie University.

October 6: Dies suddenly of a cerebral aneurysm at Lewis Wharf.

1983 Publication of *The Complete Poems: 1927–1979*.

1984 Publication of *Collected Prose*, edited by Robert Giroux.

1991 Elizabeth Bishop Society is formed.

1993 First exhibition of Bishop's paintings is held at the East Martello Tower in Key West.

1994 Publication of *One Art: Letters*, edited by Robert Giroux.

Elizabeth Bishop Society of Nova Scotia is formed.

1996 Publication of *Exchanging Hats: Elizabeth Bishop Paintings*, edited by William Benton.

2006 Publication of *Edgar Allan Poe & The Juke-Box: Uncollected Poems, Drafts, and Fragments*, edited by Alice Quinn.

2008 Publication of the Library of America edition of Bishop's writing, *Poems, Prose, and Letters*, edited by Robert Giroux and Lloyd Schwartz.

Publication of *Words in Air: The Complete Correspondence between Elizabeth Bishop and Robert Lowell*, edited by Thomas Travisano with Saskia Hamilton.

2011 The centennial of Bishop's birth is celebrated by two new editions of her work, *Poems* and *Prose*.

Publication of *Elizabeth Bishop and The New Yorker: The Complete Correspondence*, edited by Joelle Biele.

An exhibition of artworks by Bishop and paintings from her personal collection is held at the Tibor de Nagy Gallery in New York.

ANGUS CLEGHORN AND JONATHAN ELLIS

Introduction: North *and* South

Elizabeth Bishop (1911–1979) published relatively few poems in her lifetime, at least compared to more prolific peers such as John Berryman and Anne Sexton, or her close friend, Robert Lowell. The four main collections published in her lifetime – *North & South* (1946), *A Cold Spring* (1955), *Questions of Travel* (1965), and *Geography III* (1976) – contain just seventy-eight poems (seventy-five if you count "Four Poems" as a single poem), none of them particularly long. Admired for her descriptive powers and the apparent modesty of her poetic persona, Bishop was not quite a Modernist or a confessional poet. At times she appeared an early Postmodernist, but in a completely different register from Language poetry. Indeed, it was not until James Longenbach's *Modern Poetry after Modernism* (1997) that Bishop's centrality within the main shifts and tensions of twentieth-century poetry began to be understood. In historical terms, she is one of the few poets to link the Modern and the Postmodern, Primitive art and Surrealism. A resident in both North and South America, where she owned but lost at least "three loved houses" (*P* 198), she was also an Anglophile who lived in and wrote about her travels in Europe. She explored free verse and traditional verse forms with Marianne Moore and Robert Lowell, Spanish poetry with Pablo Neruda and Octavio Paz, and translated Portuguese literature while living in Brazil, passing on these lessons directly to younger poets such as May Swenson and James Merrill. Her poems speak of life and death in what she calls in one poem an "indrawn breath, / half groan, half acceptance" (*P* 172). At the same time, no detail is ever "too small" for her various peripheral speakers (*P* 131), many of them animals and children. At the beginning of the twenty-first century, her poetry seems, if anything, even more contemporary than during her lifetime, a process facilitated in part by the numerous posthumous publications of her work, but mainly by the sheer originality and variety of her writing.

Bishop was born in Worcester, Massachusetts, in 1911. She lost her father to Bright's disease when she was only eight months old and her mother to mental illness soon afterward. Between April 1915 and October 1917, Bishop lived with her maternal grandparents in Great Village, Nova Scotia, where her mother also lived between breakdowns. The autobiographical story, "In the Village" (1953), recreates two of her most haunting memories from this time: that of her mother's scream and of the "beautiful pure sound" of the blacksmith's anvil that clangs "like a bell-buoy out at sea" (*Pr* 77, 78). Poems such as "Manners," "Sestina," and "First Death in Nova Scotia" also revisit these childhood experiences. Bishop's imaginative preoccupation with the idea of home was arguably one of her main inheritances from childhood. Her poems, as Adrienne Rich once recognized, are full of outsiders for whom the idea of home is precisely that – only an idea. These include the old hermit in "Chemin de Fer," left to fend for himself by the side of his "little pond" (*P* 10); the "specklike" children in "Squatter's Children," waiting for the rain to wash away their "specklike house" (*P* 93); and the gardener in "Manuelzinho," forced to sniff and shiver, "hat in hand" (*P* 95), for a shot of penicillin.

Although Bishop's poems avoid direct political statement, she continually keeps account of the practical consequences of historical events for individual people. She saw "A Miracle for Breakfast" as a "Depression poem" (*Conversations* 25), "Songs for a Colored Singer" as "a prophesy, or prayer, that justice will eventually triumph for the Negro in the USA" (qtd. in Harrison, *Elizabeth Bishop* 168), and "From Trollope's Journal" as "an anti-Eisenhower poem" (*WIA* 594). In "In the Waiting Room," she recalls the experience of being a child during World War I. In "Roosters," she reports from Key West during the buildup to World War II; "12 O'Clock News" is one of the great twentieth-century poems about the reporting of war.

A few months before graduating from Vassar, Bishop met Marianne Moore for the first time on a bench outside the reading room of the New York Public Library (see Bishop's memoir, "Efforts of Affection"). The two poets enjoyed a generous friendship, encouraging each other's writing in spite of the occasional disagreement, most famously over the subject matter of Bishop's "Roosters," a poem Moore and her mother wanted to rename, "The Cock." *North & South*, Bishop's first book of poems, was published in 1946. It took its perfectionist author more than a decade to complete, a pattern repeated with each of her subsequent collections. Bishop was in Nova Scotia on the day *North & South* was published, returning south by bus to Boston, the journey that would later become the setting for one of her greatest poems, "The Moose." The following year, Randall Jarrell introduced Bishop to Robert Lowell, who became a lifelong friend. "I loved him at first sight," she later admitted, "my shyness vanished and we started talking at once" (*WIA* 809). In 1951, Bishop visited South America, where an allergy to the fruit of a cashew tree caused her to fall ill. Bedridden at the home of her hostess, Lota de Macedo Soares, a Brazilian architect and landscape designer whom she had first met in New York ten years earlier, Bishop was overwhelmed by the care she received and, at Macedo Soares's invitation, decided to stay. The two women fell in love. Bishop's asthma and drinking seemed to come under control and she began to write fluently again, after several years of stuttering activity. Her prose masterpiece, "In the Village," was completed in 1953 and her second collection of poems, *A Cold Spring* (1955), soon followed, earning her the Pulitzer Prize. Bishop kept in touch by letter with Moore and Lowell, while at the same time corresponding with new friends such as Ilse Barker and Flannery O'Connor. She translated *The Diary of "Helena Morley"* by Alice Brant in 1957 and was the co-editor and a co-translator of *An Anthology of Brazilian Poetry* with Emanuel Brasil in 1972. *Questions of Travel*, her third collection of poems, appeared in 1965. Bishop's relationship with Macedo Soares grew distant, and in September 1967, Macedo Soares died of an overdose during a trip to see Bishop in New York. In Bishop's papers, she left drafts for an elegiac poem, although she never finished it.

After Macedo Soares's death, Bishop drifted between San Francisco, Ouro Preto (Brazil), and New England. In 1970, she began teaching at Harvard. Bishop's fear of losing her partner at the time, Alice Methfessel, prompted the magnificent villanelle, "One Art." In 1974, Bishop moved into a condominium overlooking Lewis Wharf in Boston. She kept a ship's log beside the window, documenting the vessels that came to port and thinking it "curious" that ships from Nova Scotia must have docked there, perhaps even her great-grandfather's. Her last book of poems, *Geography III* (1976), also revisits Nova Scotia, particularly "Poem" and "The Moose." In the last decade of her life, Bishop became friends with Frank Bidart, Octavio Paz, Lloyd Schwartz, and Helen Vendler, poets and scholars who kept her reputation buoyant in the immediate aftermath of her death in 1979.

"All Those Rich Unfinished Fragments ..."

Bishop authorized the first *Complete Poems* in 1969, adding two new sections, "Translations from the Portuguese" and "New and Uncollected Work," to the three main collections then in print. In an ecstatic review for *The New York Review of Books*, John Ashbery hoped that the title was "an error and that there will be more poems and at least another *Complete Poems*" ("*The Complete Poems*" 201). Four years after her death, Robert Giroux and others supplemented her first selection with the publication of *The Complete Poems, 1927–1979* (1983). The second *Complete Poems* contains Bishop's last collection, *Geography III*, four late poems uncollected at the time of her death ("Santarém," "North Haven," "Pink Dog," and "Sonnet"), and three further sections, "Uncollected Poems," "Poems Written in Youth," and "Translations." The book begins with a "Publisher's Note," the first paragraph of which is worth citing in full:

> This book contains all of the poems of Elizabeth Bishop, from "Behind Stowe" and "To a Tree," written at sixteen, which appeared in the Walnut Hill School magazine in 1927, to "Sonnet," published in *The New Yorker* after her death in 1979. She would not have reprinted the seventeen poems written in her youth; she was too severe a critic of her own work. Yet the variety and range of these early poems are part of her poetic development. Her attitude toward her work was at times unpredictable: she never reprinted "Exchanging Hats," a poem that belongs among her best. First published in *New World Writing* in 1956, it appears here with "Uncollected Poems (1979)." The background of "Pleasure Seas," which appears here for the first time, is odd. Written in 1939, it was accepted by *Harper's Bazaar* but never printed; the sole surviving copy was found among her papers. In the group of occasional poems, there are four which she enclosed in letters to Marianne Moore in the mid-thirties. It was Miss Moore who arranged for her first publication in book form in an anthology, *Trial Balances* (1935). (*The Complete Poems, 1927–1979* xi)

This contradictory narrative suggests that while Bishop had a famously scrupulous eye for revising poetry and "the daily necessity of getting it right," as Wallace Stevens puts it, she could also be haphazard about her material, and was vulnerable to rejection. The brief reference to "her papers" hints at more poems to be found, as did the discovery of four "occasional poems" in letters to Marianne Moore. In addition to bibliographical information about the background to "Pleasure Seas" and the first publication of "Exchanging Hats," the publisher's note also contains implicit criticism of Bishop for being "too severe a critic of her own work." In his essay for this volume (Chapter 9), Lloyd Schwartz notes that she often had second thoughts about her love poems, particularly when *The New Yorker* rejected them. The list of poems rejected or not sent to *The New Yorker* – "Faustina, or Rock Roses" (rejected), "Over 2,000 Illustrations and a Complete Concordance" (rejected), "O Breath" (rejected), "The Shampoo" (rejected), "Exchanging Hats" (rejected), "It is marvellous to wake up together," "Edgar Allan Poe & The Juke-Box," "Apartment in Leme," "A Drunkard," "Vague Poem (*Vaguely love poem*)," "For Grandfather," and "Breakfast Song" (all not sent) – might itself form an astonishing collection of poetry. Indeed, the best of Alice Quinn's 2006 edition of Bishop's uncollected poems, drafts, and fragments consists largely of this material.

As "The Publisher's Note" coyly implies – for all its talk of containing "*all* of the poems of Elizabeth Bishop" (our emphasis) – *The Complete Poems* was very much a provisional volume. Bishop had not just published more poems than the note acknowledged; "her papers" contained more than 3,500 pages of unpublished material, much of it poetry. Robert Lowell, who had only an inkling of what Bishop kept back, once commented enviously on "all those rich unfinished fragments, such a fortune in the bank" (*WIA* 489). Bishop's final "fortune" was left not just in boxes and notebooks deposited at Vassar College, but also in folders and shoe boxes entrusted to close friends such as Linda Nemer in Brazil, not to mention the hundreds of letters she sent to famous and non-famous correspondents and the brittle paintings and shadow boxes she regularly gifted to friends. One poem even turned up in the dedication to a cookbook (*P* 321). Another recently showed up in the end papers of her Modern Library edition of *Jude the Obscure*, found by chance in a flea market in Adamstown, Pennsylvania (Beards "Introducing Elizabeth Bishop"). Might further discoveries be waiting in other friends' attics? Recent additions to the Elizabeth Bishop Collection at Vassar College and a forthcoming edition of Bishop's Notebooks show the flow has not abated. Bishop liked the idea not just of sharing work with others, but also of sharing the responsibility of what to do with that work afterward. When asked by Anne Stevenson about publishing, she replied: "I'm rather against professionalism ... and really often think I would have preferred the days when poems just got handed around among friends" (*NYr* vii–viii). In a similar spirit, her will instructed her literary executors, Alice Methfessel and Frank Bidart, to "determine whether any of my unpublished manuscripts and papers shall be published and, if so, to see them through the press, and with power generally to administer my literary property" (*Elizabeth Bishop in the Twenty-First Century* 2). As Lloyd Schwartz recently observed in answer to Helen Vendler's complaint about the recent appearance of unpublished poems: "Bishop never really 'repudiated' most of her drafts. If anything, she was quite prepared for their posthumous publication" ("Elizabeth Bishop's 'Finished' Unpublished Poems" 54).

In addition to poetry, Bishop also left behind several prose works, including memoirs, short stories, art criticism, book reviews, and blurbs, many of which were published in *The Collected Prose* (1984), edited, like the majority of *The Complete Poems*, by Robert Giroux. The publication of both books certainly kept Bishop's writing in the public eye, leading to important reassessments of her work by Adrienne Rich, Eavan Boland, Thom Gunn, Seamus Heaney, and James Fenton, among others. Lloyd Schwartz and Sybil Estess's edited collection, *Elizabeth Bishop and Her Art* (1983), also played its part. It included a typically strident foreword by Harold Bloom in which he claimed Bishop as a rival to Wallace Stevens, if only "the shorter works" ("Foreword" ix). Brett Millier's 1993 biography, *Elizabeth Bishop: Life and the Memory of It*, and Gary Fountain and Peter Brazeau's collection of oral material brought Bishop's life into focus, as did important book-length studies by Thomas Travisano (1988), David Kalstone (1989), Lorrie Goldensohn (1992), Victoria Harrison (1993), Susan McCabe (1994), and Marilyn May Lombardi (1995). The first edition of her correspondence, *One Art: Letters* (1994), undoubtedly attracted a larger readership, as to a lesser extent did the publication of William Benton's *Exchanging Hats: Elizabeth Bishop Paintings* in 1996.

In the past few years, two further editions of Bishop's letters have appeared, *Words in Air: The Complete Correspondence between Elizabeth Bishop and Robert Lowell* in 2008 and *Elizabeth Bishop and The New Yorker* in 2011. Few twentieth-century poets have as many letters in print. No other twentieth-century poet has received as much praise for his or her correspondence. In one of the most detailed responses to *One Art*, Tom Paulin described its publication as "a historic event, a bit like discovering a new planet or watching a bustling continent emerge, glossy and triumphant from the blank ocean. Here is an immense cultural treasure being suddenly unveiled – and this hefty selection is only the beginning. Before the millennium is out, Bishop will be seen as one of this century's epistolary geniuses" ("Writing to the Moment" 215). Although the majority of critics still privilege Bishop's poetry over her prose because poetry in general is privileged over letter writing, it is important to recognize her unusually original gifts as a correspondent. Bishop saw letter writing both "as an art form" (*OA* 544) and as a way of staying in touch with friends. Its informal formality suited Bishop perfectly, particularly the emphasis on making everyday chatter not just funny, but also significant – what Lowell memorably characterized as her ability for making "the casual perfect" (*WIA* vii). Great poets, it is worth reminding ourselves, are not automatically great letter writers. Indeed, great poet-correspondents such as Keats or Hopkins are very much the exception that proves the rule. Siobhan Phillips devotes an entire chapter to Bishop's epistolary voice in this book, including a fascinating insight into what she terms "correspondent politics," although every contributor has cause to cite from the letters at some point.

Alice Quinn's 2006 edition of Bishop's writing, *Edgar Allan Poe & The Juke-Box: Uncollected Poems, Drafts, and Fragments*, is without doubt the most controversial posthumous publication to date. Its contents include

> wistful and comic poems Bishop wrote in high school; poems begun soon after college, reflecting her passion for Elizabethan verse and surrealist technique; love poems and dream fragments from the 1930s and '40s; poems about her

> Canadian childhood; poems she was working on into the late 1970s, begun decades before; and many other works that have hitherto been quoted almost exclusively in biographical and critical studies." (*EAP*)

While much of this material has been absorbed into the Library of America edition of Bishop's *Poems, Prose, and Letters* (2008) and the centenary editions of Bishop's *Poems* (2011) and *Prose* (2011), critics continue to debate the merits not just of individual drafts and poems, but even of publishing them in the first place. Some of these debates have been aired already, in Helen Vendler's *New Republic* review of *Edgar Allan Poe*, in newspaper reviews of *Poems* and *Prose*, and, more recently, in *Elizabeth Bishop in the Twenty-First Century: Reading the New Editions* (2012). Contributors to this volume help further the debate, most notably in an essay by Lorrie Goldensohn (Chapter 12), which makes the case for keeping any conclusions about the posthumous material tentative: "As the decades begin their slow, volcanic accumulation over this body of poetry, so must our critical reception of it heave and realign." For Charles Simic: "What these uncollected works lay bare for me is how much emotion there was in Bishop's poems to start with, which her endless tinkering tended to obscure in the end. It has made me read her published work differently, discovering intimate elegies and love poems where I previously heard only an anonymous voice" (19).

"Waiting to Be Found"

Bishop was not considered a major poet during her lifetime, even though her poems were read fairly widely and even taught in several universities. She was, in John Ashbery's famous phrase, not even a poet's poet, but "a writer's writer's writer" (Schwartz and Estess xviii). Fellow writers of various schools and traditions have always loved Bishop's writing, probably because she never belonged to any school or tradition herself. Too young to be considered a Modernist, Bishop nevertheless corresponded with Marianne Moore, interviewed T. S. Eliot, and was a regular visitor to Ezra Pound during his confinement at St. Elizabeths Hospital. Too reticent to have anything to do with the confessional movement, she nevertheless influenced the composition of Lowell's seminal collection, *Life Studies* (1959), and was admired by many confessional poets, particularly Plath and Sexton. The latter sent her a fan letter, as did John Ashbery. Other New York School poets, chiefly James Schuyler, similarly loved her work. Thom Gunn and Robert Duncan both enjoyed her company in the late 1960s, as did Seamus Heaney, James Merrill, and Octavio Paz in the 1970s. Anne Stevenson, who wrote the first book-length study of Bishop's poetry in 1966, may not have become a poet without her. May Swenson, Frank Bidart, Jane Shore, and others all benefited from her personal encouragement and practical advice. If poets agreed on anything during Bishop's lifetime, which they seldom did, they agreed on rating Bishop's poetry highly. And so, although Bishop traveled a great deal during her lifetime and lived outside of North America for at least twenty years, the literary establishment never forgot her. She was appointed poetry consultant in Washington in 1949 when just thirty-eight years old. She did not miss out on any fellowships or prizes, either. Her many awards included a Guggenheim Fellowship, a Pulitzer Prize, a National Book Award, and the Neustadt International Prize for Literature. And yet at the time of her death, of a cerebral aneurysm in October 1979, Bishop's poetry was very much in the shadow of Lowell and Plath and most of her poetic peers. James Merrill called her "our greatest national treasure" (Schwartz and Estess 243), but he did not speak for everyone, and certainly not for most contemporary poetry readers.

"I envy the mind hiding in her words," wrote Mary McCarthy four years after Bishop's death in 1983, "like an 'I' counting up to a hundred waiting to be found" ("Symposium" 267). For McCarthy, as for many readers, Bishop's mind, equivalent to but not identical to an autobiographical voice, is somehow there and not there in her poems, the act of reading them akin to a game of hide-and-seek. Objects, people, even places, often get lost, or are on the way to being lost, in Bishop's work. One of her most famous poems, "One Art," is about the art of losing. Is this Bishop's one art? The thing she does best? Perhaps it is *the* rhetorical gesture, *the* poem, for which she is best known. And yet, as contributors in this book point out, Bishop is also an astonishing poet of touch and sensation, interested in the detailed, intimate connections between people and in the ways in which people struggle to connect as well. Her love poems, often written in the aftermath of an argument or separation, always cling to the possibility of forgiveness and reconciliation. "Love should be put into action," screams an old hermit in a very early poem, even if it rarely is (*P* 10). "Insomnia," one of a series of poems from *A Cold Spring* on the false dream of a happy relationship, similarly ends on the hope that "you love me" (*P* 68). This desperate poem, rejected by *The New Yorker* for being "small" and "personal" (*NYr* 112), reflects in a cryptic form Bishop's lifelong struggle to express lesbian desire poetically. Whereas the poems published in Bishop's lifetime cage such desire, many of the posthumous writings set it free. Bishop's queer politics are a key concern of at least a third of the essays in this volume. According to Susan Rosenbaum (Chapter 4), Bishop naturalizes female and lesbian desire in a manner comparable to other women artists interested in surrealism, such as Leonor Fini and Lee Miller. Bonnie Costello, in a wide-ranging assessment of Bishop's engagement with the poetic tradition (Chapter 5), links many of the love poems to her close reading of first Herbert and Hopkins, and later Baudelaire. Bethany Hicok (Chapter 7) credits a change in Bishop's lyric voice to her specific experience of living in Key West in the 1930s–1940s, while Barbara Page (Chapter 8) moves the story on to Brazil in the 1950s–1960s, in particular Bishop's love for Lota de Macedo Soares, arguably her most significant romantic relationship.

Bishop's cautious engagement with politics can be connected to her love lyrics, as essays in this volume by Steven Axelrod (Chapter 2), Bethany Hicok (Chapter 7), and Kirstin Hotelling Zona (Chapter 3), among others, point out. From a personal position of privilege, she consistently attempted to negotiate between rich and poor, master and servant, colonizer and colonized, while aware that the very position of being a negotiator was itself compromising. This unease is foregrounded in Bishop's Key West poems, including "Jerónimo's House," "Cootchie," "Songs for a Colored Singer," and particularly "Faustina, or Rock Roses." To what extent are the awkward encounters depicted in these poems deliberate? Did Bishop, as Renée Curry suggests in her book *White Women Writing White* (2000), always fail to see past her own origins as a white middle-class woman? Did she ever poetically cross the color divide? Axelrod thinks not, or at least not until the late poem, "In the Waiting Room": "Perhaps this one moment represents the culmination of Bishop's racial politics – the achievement of the desired empathy that had so long eluded her" (quotation from Chapter 2). Kirstin Hotelling Zona is equally cautious about crediting Bishop with too much insight into the experiences of being an outsider in modern society. Like Axelrod, she sees "In the Waiting Room" as the summation of Bishop's repeated attempts to face up to the "part she plays in constructing the other's ideality or 'strangeness.'" Comparing the constantly shifting perspective of the poem to a film, she praises Bishop's honesty in reminding us of "the particular, and limited perspective – 'Elizabeth's' – through which we are viewing her world" (quotation from Chapter 3).

Bishop is on safer ground when approaching a subject from the position of being an outsider herself. This was clearly the case during her long residence in Brazil. Her poems about the meaning and purpose of travel, in particular the sequence of poems that opens *Questions of Travel* ("Arrival at Santos," "Brazil, January 1, 1502," and "Questions of Travel"), are justly-celebrated for their investigation of the relationship between home and elsewhere. In "Manuelzinho," adopting the voice of "a friend of the writer" (almost certainly Macedo Soares) allows her to translate class tension from Brazilian into English. For Steven Axelrod, the poem ends up siding with "its satirized title character," the gardener of Macedo Soares and Bishop's house at Samambaia. Barbara Page agrees: "Manuelzinho *deserves* to inherit, if not the earth, certainly a good piece of it." "The Riverman" is another Brazilian poem that modifies Bishop's perspective through a different voice; in this case, Charles Wagley's book, *Amazon Town*. In "Going to the Bakery" and "Under the Window: Ouro Prêto," she listens in on the conversations nearby. Barbara Page's essay on Bishop's Brazilian writing demonstrates how "from the buffering distance of South America, Bishop's long mediation on home and homelessness branched into new considerations of what it means to be a lifelong traveler."

As Bishop moved literally from north to south, crossing the equator, she arguably became less cautious about taking a political stance in her poetry. In the Key West poem, "Roosters," for example, "unwanted love, conceit and war" are as much a feature of the human world as the avian one, but the poem lets the reader join the dots. If "Roosters" is a poem that emphasizes "the essential baseness of militarism" (*OA* 96), as she asserts in a famous 1940 letter to Marianne Moore, it does so obliquely. The poems from Bishop's second collection, *A Cold Spring*, are just as elusive. According to Bethany Hicok, in poems such as "Over 2,000 Illustrations and a Complete Concordance," we find Bishop "playing, Nabokov-like, with the reader's desire to find meaning." In "The Armadillo," a Brazilian poem from *Questions of Travel*, however, the speaker makes her feelings about human carelessness, in this case toward the natural world, much clearer. The illegal fire balloons cause devastation to the animals that live downwind – from the owls that flee their burnt-out nests to a glistening armadillo that leaves the scene "head down, tail down" (*P* 102). The poem's final image is a "baby rabbit" jumping out at the poet: "So soft! – a handful of intangible ash / with fixed, ignited eyes" (*P* 102). Perhaps Bishop reserves her most empathetic moments for animals? Do they do the work of mediating between man and nature better than the poet? In addition to Bishop's much-anthologized poem, "The Fish," we might add "At the Fishhouses," "In the Village," "Sandpiper," "The Hanging of the Mouse," "Crusoe in England," "The Moose," and "Pink Dog" to a list of memorable animal writings, not to mention her fondness for hybrid creatures such as "The Man-Moth" and "The Riverman." Animal studies and eco-critical approaches to Bishop's poetry may, as Susan Rosenbaum observes, "reorient our understanding of modernist experiments by women poets and artists in particular." Like the moose's sudden appearance at the end of the eponymous poem, there is something both "homely" and "otherworldly" about all of Bishop's animal poems (*P* 193). Tempted to see likeness in the activity of a sandpiper on the shoreline or the appearance of a dog in the street, Bishop also reminds us that seeing likeness may, like many acts of comparison, also be illusory.

Although Brazil was in many ways Bishop's second home, it was never home in the same way that Canada was. An American by birth who was half-Canadian by parentage and upbringing, Bishop grew up in New England and Nova Scotia, frequently moving between the two. As Sandra Barry makes clear in Chapter 6 in this volume, although Bishop spent much of her childhood and certainly most of her adolescence in New England, she felt most at home in Great Village, Nova Scotia, the home of her maternal relatives. Nova Scotia is, more than any other place in her writing, the one place she kept writing about – her "true north" as it were: "Dear, my compass / still points north," she wrote in an unpublished poem of the mid-1960s (*P* 313). In fact, Barry makes a compelling case for a relatively unknown influence on Bishop's writing: her mother, Gertrude May Bulmer. As Barry points out: "While Gertrude's physical absence and its impact were real in Bishop's life, her emotional presence and its impact were equally real." Gertrude has been more or less absent from Bishop's artistic story not because Bishop did not write about her, but because she wrote about her in non-canonical places – letters, stories, fragments, unpublished poems and prose. Did writing about her in some way make such writing unpublishable? Barry fascinatingly links Bishop's physical experiences with her mother to a key trope in the published writing: mobility. "This way of being and creating came about in part because Bishop held onto and let go of her mother, over and over again."

Lloyd Schwartz, who was a close friend of Bishop in the 1970s, provides the most personal contribution to this book in Chapter 9. In addition to its evocation of Bishop's Boston, it also bears eloquent testimony to Bishop's gifts as a friend and teacher. Much has rightly been made of Marianne Moore's role as mentor in Bishop's development as a writer. Bishop herself makes much of it in letters and other places, including the poem, "Invitation to Miss Marianne Moore," and the memoir, "Efforts of Affection." Perhaps more needs to be written about Bishop's own gifts as a friend? All of Bishop's letters demonstrate this capacity for friendship, as Siobhan Phillips's essay shows (Chapter 10). James Merrill, in his obituary for Bishop, wrote of her "instinctive, modest, lifelong impersonations of an ordinary woman, someone who during the day did errands, went to the beach, would perhaps that evening jot a phrase or two inside the nightclub matchbook before returning to the dance floor" (259). Merrill implies but does not mention Bishop's ability to maintain lifelong friendships (another one of her "impersonations of an ordinary woman"?). Vassar friends such as Louise Crane, Margaret Miller, and Frani Blough Muser kept in touch with Bishop her entire life, as did her Walnut Hill and Vassar classmate, Rhoda Wheeler Sheehan. An extensive correspondence with Anne Stevenson, the first real Elizabeth Bishop scholar and a considerable poet in her own right, was published in the 2011 *Prose* edition (see Ellis, "'Between us': Letters and Poems of Stevenson and Bishop"). Bishop never lost touch with her Nova Scotian relatives either. Bishop's favorite aunt – Grace Bulmer Bowers, the dedicatee of one of her most ambitious poems, "The Moose" – was a regular correspondent, as was her cousin Phyllis Sutherland. The absence of Bishop's correspondence to them is one of the more glaring omissions from *One Art* and suggests a more generous *Selected Letters* will be required soon.

Bonnie Costello's essay on Bishop's relationship to the poetic tradition (Chapter 5) focuses on Bishop's literary "friendships," many of which are just as neglected as her relationships with real people. In an unpublished prose piece included in *Edgar Allan Poe*, Bishop had this to say about her poetic influences: "The three qualities I admire in the poetry I like best are: *Accuracy, Spontaneity, Mystery*. My three 'favorite' poets – not the best poets whom we all admire, but favorite in the sense of one's 'best friends,' are Herbert, Hopkins, and Baudelaire" (*EAP* 208). Costello's essay highlights less obvious influences too, including Milton, Coleridge, Keats, Stevens, and Auden. Siobhan Phillips (Chapter 10) assesses the importance of letter writers such as Charles Darwin and Henry James to Bishop's development, whereas Peggy Samuels (Chapter 11) demonstrates the significance to her of mid-century visual artists such as Joseph Cornell, Paul Klee, and Kurt Schwitters. We are still awaiting a full assessment of Bishop's translations, not just in Portuguese, but also in French, Spanish, and even ancient Greek.

Finished/Unfinished

The slow-then-sudden publication of Bishop's posthumous writing has led some critics to compare the nature of her scholarly reception, if not the nature of her writing itself, to that of Emily Dickinson. For Christina Pugh, the impact of *Edgar Allan Poe* on Bishop's reputation might be similar to the impact of R. W. Franklin's manuscript edition of Dickinson's poems on Dickinson studies "wherein critics' concerns have become arguably less 'poetic' and more graphic or archival in their orientation" (275). Bishop studies has not yet experienced anything akin to the so-called Emily Dickinson wars (Erkkila), where rival biographers and critics squared up to each other not just about different interpretations of Dickinson's biography, but also about the correct edition in which to read her work. It is difficult to tell whether Bishop studies is on the threshold of a similar upheaval. Do Bishop critics privately prefer one edition to another with the vehemence that Dickinson critics demonstrate more publicly? Is there a danger, as Pugh points out, of the criticism of poetry losing out to archival questions of where and in what form those poems were published? English poet Frances

Leviston asks "whether this expanded canon is actually representative of Bishop, or whether it does, in some fundamental and disconcerting way, 'exceed' her" (44). Likewise, Jeffrey Gray highlights the problem of "excess" in Bishop's drafts ("Postcards" 35).

However we evaluate the inconsistent quality of the material in *Edgar Allan Poe* or the reasons behind Alice Quinn's original choices, we undoubtedly find "striking moments of self-clarity," as Charles Berger observes (49). But what kind of artistic voice do we hear? On the one hand, Bishop nearly always sounds like Bishop. On the other hand, is Bishop's "unfinished" voice sufficiently poetic? What kind of finish actually exists? Sometimes the polish is not applied, or worn out, as in "A Drunkard," which ends with the potentially frustrating line, "And all I'm telling you may be a lie ..." (*P* 319). This ending undercuts the confessional prize sought by the reader – a poetic narrative about a traumatic source of Bishop's alcoholism. Many critics see the poem as a failure, perhaps because of its self-questioning conclusion. But isn't it apt in the context of the speaker's excessive drinking that she admits to in the poem's title? The speaker's questioning of truth is typical of Bishop's published poetry. Think of the variable interpretations of "The Monument," or the first line of "Santarém": "Of course I may be remembering it all wrong / after, after – how many years?" (*P* 207). Pugh highlights Bishop's concern with finishes by citing one of her earliest poems as a case in point: "A lovely finish I have seen ..." (*EAP* 11). Those six words sum up Bishop's artistry; its polish as already achieved but now being re-seen, the past not so much "recollected in tranquillity" like Wordsworth, but reconstructed with what she calls in "Crusoe in England" the "blanks" left in (*P* 184). Such acts of seeing occur on the page but are susceptible to flux, too. "Watch it closely" as her monument evolves into another form, another genre: "It is the beginning of a painting, / a piece of sculpture, or poem, or monument, / and all of wood" (*P* 27).

For readers who prefer the treasures of Bishop's established canon, the previously unpublished work allows a deeper look into the artist's evolution – "that sense of constant re-adjustment" (*P* 12) that Lorrie Goldensohn shows is glacial. With slow time and long drift, often flowing between various drafts and prose writings, Bishop's images crystallize into the lines and rhythms of her best poems. Goldensohn traces some of these glacial shifts intricately in Chapter 12 in this volume. Bishop drew a clear line – sometimes a very literal one, as drafts show – between finished and unfinished poems, even though there are several finished poems that she either only submitted once for publication (normally *The New Yorker*) or never submitted at all. Then there are the unfinished poems of magnitude: "Edgar Allan Poe & The Juke-Box" and "Apartment in Leme," for example. Goldensohn notes that "Apartment in Leme," written from Bishop's flat overlooking Copacabana Beach, "went through approximately thirty pages of draft revisions and could have been as arresting a poem about Brazil as any of the dozen that Bishop left completed" ("Elizabeth Bishop's Drafts" 104). The poem looks out at "the open mouth" of the sea, and "those islands, named and renamed / so many times now everyone's forgotten / their names" (*P* 307). We hear an echo of "Crusoe in England," but "Apartment in Leme" embodies Brazilian culture specifically through the physical manifestation of nature as it affects life and myth. This "fairy tale," with its festive bottles of "white alcohol" on the beach, has the sea's moist breath tarnishing the silverware in the apartment and corroding mirrors. Bishop took great delight in the Brazilian seasons, particularly the rainy season. Her published poem, "Song for the Rainy Season," also celebrates the "warm touch" of fog, dew, rain, and waterfall (*P* 100). Yet in this poem, something does not quite cohere. The first section looks finished, the second and third sections nearly there. But in the fourth and final section, as the speaker greets the morning sun as so often in Bishop's poetry, something goes awry:

> But for now the sun. Slowly, reluctantly,
> you let go of it; it as slowly rises;   [you're letting go
> metallic; two-dimensional   of it; it slowly rises:]
>
> You sigh, and sigh again. We live at your open mouth,
> with your cold breath blowing warm, your warm breath cold
> like in the fairy tale
> —no, ~~as in the~~ legend.   [no—the legend.]
>   [I mean]
>
> (*P* 311)

The repetition of "it" – "you're letting go of it; it slowly rises" – is bold, almost clumsy. Interestingly, Bishop already employed this effect in her earlier poem, "At the Fishhouses": "If you tasted it, it would taste bitter." "At the Fishhouses" is a poem, such as this one, in which the speaker addresses the sea as something "cold dark deep and absolutely clear" that might be akin to "what we imagine knowledge to be" (*P* 64). In "Apartment in Leme," it is almost as if she is attempting to go back to and perhaps rewrite this earlier poem in a different register – the "cold dark deep" ocean of knowledge becoming a warm breath of sea mist lifted by the Rio dawn, much as Wordsworth rewrites an earlier poem in "Yarrow Revisited." "Letting go of it" also evokes the last line of one of her most famous poems, "The Fish": "And I let the fish go" (*P* 44). But here, unlike in "Poem" in which "Large Bad Picture" is successfully recast and remembered, this attempt remains unfinished.

"Imagined Places"

The Cambridge Companion to Elizabeth Bishop looks backward and forward. While summarizing contemporary Bishop studies, it also suggests new approaches, points of comparison, and questions. The issue of biography, for example, continues to loom large among Bishop critics as Thomas Travisano's Chapter 1 in this volume proves, in part because of the concealed autobiographical nature of much of Bishop's writing. "It is," Travisano observes, "a central paradox of Elizabeth Bishop studies that while many – including Bishop herself, when it suited her – have described the poet's style as 'impersonal,' her work has proven, after all, to be pervasively autobiographical." Thomas Travisano links the rise in Bishop's reputation to "our awareness of the poet's life and worlds." "Life and the memory of it' (*P* 197) are clearly central to her achievements; in particular, her ability to commemorate without sentimentality what she herself felt was a "prize 'unhappy childhood'" (*Pr* 431). In the case of most twentieth-century poets, the critical task has been to extricate the work intact from a messy, unruly life. Eliot, Pound, and Larkin are all notable examples of this trend. But with Bishop, one is constantly struck by the apparent equanimity of the poetry in comparison with the life. Reading biography back into the work helps us to disturb the poetry's smooth surfaces, making the work more confessional and honest than it seemed initially, but perhaps we have to be careful of making the work say too much? As Travisano points out, Bishop's "art of displacement" is "one of her most pervasive and persistent artistic strategies." Octavio Paz comments in a similar vein in an essay on Bishop's poetry first published in 1975:

> We have forgotten that poetry is not in what words say but in what is said between them, that which appears fleetingly in pauses and silences ... The enormous power of reticence – that is the great lesson of Elizabeth Bishop. But I am wrong to speak of lessons. Her poetry teaches us nothing. To hear it is not to hear a lesson; it is a pleasure, verbal and mental, as great as a spiritual experience. (213)

The verdict is still out on whether posthumous publication of drafts, fragments, juvenilia, letters, prose works, and other writings has proved Bishop's initial refusal to publish correct. Has enlarging the canon of published material aided or hampered attempts to boost her reputation? Certainly, the "old" poems published in Bishop's lifetime and the "new" poems published posthumously exist in uneasy tension. Robert Giroux and Lloyd Schwartz's Library of America edition offers the most generous selection from *Edgar Allan Poe* in "Uncollected" and "Unpublished" sections placed after the main collections of poetry. The 2011 *Poems*, however, scoops up just twenty-seven poems, some already published in the 1983 *Complete Poems*, exiling them to an Appendix titled "Unpublished Manuscript Poems." The latter title is at best misleading. Some poems labelled "unpublished" have been published at least three times. At what point will these poems be seen as "published" and allowed entry into the Bishop canon? *The Cambridge Companion to Elizabeth Bishop* does not answer this question explicitly, although perhaps the contributors' choice of similar "unpublished" poems does offer a provisional response. "To Be Written on the Mirror in Whitewash," "It is marvellous to wake up together," "Edgar Allan Poe & The Juke-Box," "The Soldier and the Slot-Machine," "For M.B.S., buried in Nova Scotia," "Apartment in Leme," "A Drunkard," "Breakfast Song," and "For Grandfather," all receive repeated consideration here. Might this be the beginning of a critical consensus?

Thomas Travisano and Lloyd Schwartz, for example, both celebrate the appearance of previously unpublished love poems such as "It is marvellous to wake up together" and "Breakfast Song" for opening up the established Bishop canon to new readings. Less controversially, most Bishop critics, like most contributors to this book, still privilege Bishop's poetry over her prose. Even though the majority of Bishop's stories will never eclipse the achievements of her poems, they certainly deserve more critical scrutiny than has hitherto been the case. This is true even of "In the Village," the Nova Scotian story that Bishop placed at the very heart of her third book of poems, *Questions of Travel*; a decision ignored by almost every subsequent editor of Bishop's poetry. Is "In the Village" actually a prose-poem? It is often described as such. Certainly, it is both a memoir *and* a story, a kind of half-remembered reverie like nearly all of Bishop's best work. Other Nova Scotian stories are almost as good; so, too, the very elegant stories about the acts of reading and writing that she published in the late 1930s, "The Sea and Its Shore" in 1937 and "In Prison" in 1938. Bishop was always interested in blurring genre boundaries as her lifelong interest in the prose poem shows. In addition to "In the Village," she published at least a half dozen other prose poems in her lifetime, including one of her most original poems, "12 O'Clock News" – a poem that Paul Muldoon felt significant enough to merit an entire chapter of his book, *The End of the Poem*. "Bishop's Prose Poetry" is arguably an original article or book still-to-be-written. As a Vassar undergraduate, Bishop was a marvellous literary critic too, particularly on the difficult subjects of meter and timing. In terms of her prose, she was most proud of a 1969 "Gallery Note for Wesley Wehr" (*Pr* 352–353), one of her many formal and informal forays into the area of art criticism. Essays by Susan Rosenbaum (Chapter 4) and Peggy Samuels (Chapter 11) show how much Bishop's love of visual art contributed to her writing, and how much her writing was itself a form of visual art.

Whatever new directions Bishop critics take, Bishop's place in the canon is now certain. She is in every anthology, and certainly every reading list. Few have been as ecstatic as David Orr, reviewing *Edgar Allan Poe* for *The New York Times* in 2006: "Nothing matches the impact of a great artist, and in the second half of the 20th century, no American artist in any medium was greater than Bishop" (1). April Bernard, reviewing the centenary editions of *Poems* and *Prose* in *The New York Review of Books*, was almost as praiseworthy: "Bishop was one of the great artists of the twentieth century; her poems now tower over the landscape alongside those of Eliot and Stevens" (16). One should be careful of ranking poets like this. Bishop herself urged caution: "I'm not a critic. Critics can't rest easy until they have put poets in descending order of merit; they change their lists every night before they go to bed. A poet doesn't have to be consistent" (*EAP* 210). A generation ago, Lowell rather than Bishop would have probably taken most of the plaudits. In Britain and Ireland, Seamus Heaney, Ted Hughes or Philip Larkin would probably win the order of merit, at least when talking about the second half of the twentieth century. Where Bishop is unique among twentieth-century poets is in her continuing influence on contemporary poetry; that is to say, contemporary poetry in every English-speaking country. Michael Hoffman, in an ambivalent review of *Poems*, wonders when and why Bishop became so popular among poets:

> It was mainly her contemporaries' straightforward and never fathomed fascination with her difference that set her up and kept her there. In the 1960s and 1970s younger American poets – James Merrill, Frank Bidart – sat at her feet; later, others, younger still, filled her classes when she taught, protestingly, at Harvard and MIT. Nor is hers at all a transatlantic reputation: she is ours as much as theirs, or even theirs as much as ours. I can think of dozens of British and Irish poets, men and women, younger and older, who have written about her, thought about her, commended her, invoked her example, sworn by her. Nowhere such unanimity. (14)

Hoffman sounds baffled, almost put out by "such unanimity." Indeed, he begins the review feeling "a wholly impersonal desire to pan her." "Is Bishop really as good as everyone says?" he appears to wonder aloud. One source of "such unanimity" might be the fact that Bishop's poetry *is* as good as everyone says it is; another might be that her poetry rejects strict adherence to any poetic school or tradition, and thus can be accepted by all. A further mark of Bishop's originality is the sheer number of Bishop poems that other poets select as their favorites. No single poem stands out. Thomas Travisano's seminal essay, "The Elizabeth Bishop Phenomenon," gives further compelling reasons for the sudden popularity of Bishop's writing.

In Chapter 5 in this book, Bonnie Costello lists several major poets who have cited Bishop's influence on their own work, including (among Bishop's generation) John Ashbery, Robert Lowell, Sylvia Plath, and Adrienne Rich, and, in the generation that came after her, Amy Clampitt, Seamus Heaney, and Paul Muldoon. In Erik Martiny's recent *Companion to Poetic Genre* (2012), only Auden is cited more. Certainly, the contemporary popularity of at least two poetic forms, the sestina and villanelle, can be directly attributed to the influence of Bishop's poems, "Sestina" and "One Art." In the same book, Jo Gill praises her animal poems and Meg Tyler her "idiosyncratic" use of the sonnet form (226). English poet Lavinia Greenlaw has just published two Bishop-related books: a collection of poetry called *The Casual Perfect* (2011), after Lowell's description of Bishop's voice; and *Questions of Travel* (2011), a selection of prose extracts from William Morris's *Icelandic Journal*, interposed with her own comments and questions in the margin. Bishop asks different questions of different poets, just as they ask different questions of her. Seamus Heaney, who knew Bishop in the 1970s and wrote several times on her poetry, has one of the most eloquent answers to the question of what makes Bishop sound both contemporary and traditional:

> By her sense of proportion and awareness of tradition, she makes what is an entirely personal and contemporary style seem continuous with the canonical poetry of the past. She writes the kind of poem that makes us want to exclaim with admiration at its professional thoroughness, its technical and formal perfections, and yet at the same time she tempts us to regard technical and formal matters as something of a distraction, since the poem is so candidly *about* something, engaged with its own business of observing the world and discovering meaning. (249–250)

The many ways in which Bishop's poetry and other writings, in many forms and in many states of finish, are "*about* something" is the subject of this book. We hope it encourages old and new readers of Bishop to see through her eyes again.

PART I

Contexts and Issues

I

THOMAS TRAVISANO

Bishop and Biography

It is a central paradox of Elizabeth Bishop studies that although many – including Bishop herself, when it suited her – have described the poet's style as "impersonal," her work has proven, after all, to be pervasively autobiographical. As Mutlu Konuk Blasing phrased it, Bishop "is an autobiographical poet with an impersonal touch" (341). Bishop never attempted a full-scale memoir or autobiographical narrative, but in her poetry, prose, and letters she continually alludes to, retells, or reexamines not just her quotidian observations, but her life's recurring obsessions and preoccupations, particularly its experiences of childhood, exploration, love, dislocation, and loss. Many of Bishop's best-known poems, memoirs, and stories deal more or less directly with important aspects of her life experience, including such poems as "First Death in Nova Scotia," "In the Waiting Room," and "One Art," and such prose pieces as "In the Village," "Gwendolyn," and "The U.S.A. School of Writing." Even in such comparatively direct examples of self-exploration, ambiguities of identity and voice are often heard, mingled with Bishop's characteristic blend of spot-on, verifiable facts and subtly interwoven leavenings of fancy. Both "In the Village" and "Gwendolyn" were labeled short stories when they first appeared in *The New Yorker*, a designation maintained in various subsequent book collections, yet each contains numerous biographically accurate details, especially important names, events, and places. In works labeled stories, Bishop's most common strategy is simply to change an actual person's name. In "Gwendolyn," for example, the surname of her childhood friend Gwendolyn Patriquin is changed to "Appletree," but many details of her friend's early death from diabetes in 1922 correlate closely with the facts of the case. Curiously, a study of Bishop's high school yearbook reveals that one of her classmates at Walnut Hill School was named Gwendolyn Appleyard, so Bishop's substitution of the fictional surname may involve a conscious or subconscious memory of this other Gwendolyn. In any case, the gravestone of Gwendolyn L. Patriquin, inscribed with the birth and death dates "1913–1922," and with the names and dates of her parents and a brother lost in the Great War, still stands in Mahon Cemetery near her Nova Scotian home in Great Village, where many of Bishop's own maternal (Bulmer) relatives are also buried.

On the other hand, pieces published as factual reporting, such as "A Trip to Vigia," contain a significant measure of outright invention. Even in one of her most avowedly autobiographical poems such as "In the Waiting Room," in which the speaker self-identifies as "an *I*, / [...] an *Elizabeth*," the poet herself acknowledged, both to her *New Yorker* editors and twice to interviewers (Monteiro 73, 87), that she had combined the February and March 1918 issues of *The National Geographic* – remembering these, or so she told Howard Moss at *The New Yorker*, "for 52 years" (*NYr* 319) – to provide crucial elements of the poem. Moreover, the account in "In the Waiting Room" itself parallels a briefer version of the same events that concludes her posthumously published memoir, "The Country Mouse" (*Pr* 99). So we have versions of this particular event in both prose and verse, each adding elements that are not in the other. For readers approaching Bishop's precisely observed and often deviously self-exploratory art, the line between memoir and fiction, fact and imagination, can be very hard to draw. And this matters not because there is so little fact in her writing, but because there is so much. Lloyd Schwartz, editor of Bishop's *Prose*, found at least a partial resolution to this conundrum by including each of the aforementioned prose writings, and several others, under the heading "Stories and Memoirs."

Bishop once insisted that "I hate interviews" (Bernlef 63), yet she gave more than twenty during her lifetime. When, in 1978, the year before her death, *The Paris Review* at last proposed to interview her for their distinguished series, Bishop lamented to editor Jonathan Galassi that "they should have interviewed me at the same time they interviewed everyone else" (Fountain 342). The interviews Bishop consented to give make an entire volume: the consistently engrossing and revealing *Conversations with Elizabeth Bishop* (1996), edited by George Monteiro. Bishop's conversations with U.S. poets, journalists, students, and devotees provide many insights into her literary opinions and artistic methods, but the interviews Bishop gave to foreign journalists tend to be more forthcoming about her emotional life and its relation to her poetry.

Of particular interest is an interview Bishop gave to Beatriz Schiller in 1977 during her last years in Boston; an interview that did not appear in the United States during her lifetime. Rather, it was published in Portuguese in *Journal do Brasil*, a fact that may have encouraged Bishop to feel more comfortable when it came to offering intriguing self-disclosures, or near disclosures. Schiller sets the stage for her Brazilian readers by characterizing Bishop not simply as a "poetess of the poets" and "the most refined talent in North-American literature" but also – accurately – as a writer "famous for her elusiveness" (Schiller 74). Bishop then engages her interlocutor in a kind of dance of hints and misdirections, of discretion and poignant self-revelation.

For example, when Schiller suggests that Bishop's poetry is "indisputably buoyant, hopeful," the poet replies that "I am really optimistic. At least on the surface." Bishop then adds, rather implausibly, "Once a year I get depressed" and suggests that by contrast, Brazilians "are much more given to depression" (Schiller 75). However, Bishop then abruptly volunteers: "Just this week I became greatly depressed. My physician visited me and brought over my whole medical history, my entire life since I was a little girl. It was too much for me." Still, she concedes, "I did not want to let my sadness show, and we did have a good time" (76). Then comes the final and decisive disclosure: "See, the Americans from New England are great hypocrites. It's part of tradition not to show one's feelings. But sometimes I show mine" (76). The suggestive dance of discretion and revelation, of showing and hiding, which Bishop engaged in with her Brazilian interlocutor in 1977 closely parallels the subtle interplay of impersonality and sudden intimacy, the elusive hiding and showing of emotion and personal experience that Bonnie Costello terms Bishop's "Impersonal Personal" (334) and that Bishop's poetry realizes with such consummate art. Significantly, even though Schiller began her dialogue with Bishop by suggesting that her poetry was "buoyant" and "hopeful," she ultimately chose to name her piece: "Poetry Born Out of Suffering." Moreover, she appears to have been guided toward this title, as we've seen, by hints from the poet herself. That Bishop's poetry remains witty, persevering, and curiously buoyant even as it grows out of and confronts suffering is one of the great enigmas and achievements of her art.

In that same Brazilian interview with Schiller in which Bishop admits that "sometimes" she shows her feelings, Bishop describes her style as "impersonal" (76). Yet the more we have learned about her life and work, the clearer it has become that as a writer, Bishop was persistently drawn, however obliquely, to exploring the stories of her own life. Randall Jarrell famously remarked in his prescient review of Bishop's first book *North & South* (1946) that "all of Bishop's poems have written under them, '*I have seen it*'" (235). This is, of course, true. But by now it should be clear that nearly all of Bishop's poems, prose pieces, and letters might just as well have written under them, "*I have lived it*," even if the way she lived it might be rendered obliquely or with what she called "just the right changes" (*Pr* 31).

Still, the crucial facts of Bishop's adult life remained elusive to all but her most private circle while she lived. In the decades that followed her death in 1979, Bishop's reputation has risen – at first steadily and then meteorically – elevating her well beyond the coterie status of "poetess of the poets." She is now recognized as one of the most admired, studied, and influential poetic voices of the twentieth century, and this elevation in her reputation may in part be linked to our increasing awareness of the poet's life and worlds – knowledge that provides many points of entry into what once seemed such an elusive or even, to certain readers, such an impenetrable style. For as Bishop's reputation has risen, Bishop studies have evolved along four parallel and mutually supportive lines of development: 1) a deepening insight into her biography, 2) an ever-closer study of her intricate artistic methods, 3) a steadily expanding bibliography of her work in publication, and 4) a deepening knowledge of her remarkably extensive network of friendships and cultural engagements in literature, the visual arts, music, architecture, geography, and politics. Bishop's life has been revealed in considerable detail, not only through the investigations of critical studies and biographies – particularly, among the latter, Brett Millier's *Elizabeth Bishop: Life and the Memory of It* (1993) and Gary Fountain and Peter Brazeau's *Elizabeth Bishop: An Oral Biography* (1994) – but also through the posthumous publication of an extensive body of poems, prose, and correspondence that has vastly expanded her published oeuvre and established Bishop not only as a surprisingly wide-ranging and prolific poet, and as a deft and original prose writer, but also as one of the most brilliant and entertaining letter writers in the Language.

Bishop's sadly humorous and profoundly human body of self-exploratory writing complexly links the outward observer with the inward eye, a gaze that Adrienne Rich characterized as "The Eye of the Outsider" (16). During her lifetime, the linkage between Bishop's outward and inward gaze may not have been readily apparent to her more casual readers. Yet in the years since her death, as knowledge of her life has deepened, and as volume upon volume of posthumously published writing has appeared, Bishop's personal struggles can now be read back into her previously published canon, including such "abstract self-portraits" (Travisano, "Geography IV" 227) as "The Man-Moth" and "The Gentleman of Shalott." These readings reveal a great deal about Bishop's creative process. Moreover, they demonstrate convincingly that marks of her personal struggles, anxieties, and yearnings had always been present, lurking beneath the brilliant surfaces of nearly every poem and prose piece in her public oeuvre. Bishop herself may have been ready to encourage readings of her ever-expanding posthumous legacy because in her will she granted her executors, her partner Alice Methfessel and the poet Frank Bidart, the "power to determine whether any of my unpublished manuscripts and papers shall be published and, if so, to see them through the press, and with power generally to administer my literary property" (Cleghorn, Hicok, and Travisano, "Introduction" 2). Therefore, it was Bishop herself who knew better than anyone the extent, value, and the self-exploratory and self-revelatory content of her vast trove of unpublished work in manuscript; who established terms that enabled the extraordinary sequence of posthumous publications previously cited. The bibliographical and biographical impulse that has guided Bishop studies since the late 1980s has revolutionized our understanding of her previously published canon; the carte blanche Bishop gave her executors regarding the posthumous publication of her extensive body of work in poetry, prose, and letters has extended and enriched the body of her writing now available to readers. Bishop wrote to Robert Lowell in 1957, "But it is hell to realize that one has wasted half one's talent through timidity" (*WIA* 247), and she may have felt ready to welcome, and she in any case did nothing to discourage, a posthumous understanding of her life and world, and of the breadth and depth of her literary achievement, that she would have found uncomfortable or even threatening to reveal during her lifetime.

Despite the teasingly self-revelatory element in her writing, Bishop did not set out to live an emblematic life or to create a personal myth in the manner of Whitman, Yeats, Pound, Hemingway, Millay, or such contemporaries as Berryman, Rich, Plath, or her close friend Lowell. Instead, the extensive body of biographical and autobiographical knowledge that has emerged since her death invites a reading of her life (and by extension, a reading of her work) as representing a private and personal struggle against chronic challenges, a struggle with which many readers appear to identify. Bishop undertook this struggle with the twin goals of finding a rich, diverse, and quietly adventurous life experience and of achieving a vividly realized, unique, and immutable art. The challenges against which Bishop struggled have now been characterized in some detail through the work of several generations of scholars. But while biographical readings of Bishop have for the most part been guided by sympathy and insight, one could argue that they have perhaps too often represented this author as a passive victim of her frailties (particularly her periodic abuse of alcohol) rather than as the agent of a personal destiny. An alternative reading of Bishop's life might see her as a quietly determined individualist whose actions and choices were marked by a pervasive tenacity, curiosity, and originality – flavored by a dry and distinctly wicked sense of humor. Bishop was a woman who struggled persistently against physical and emotional liabilities to achieve a life that, with all its imperfections, was marked by wit, energy, courage, artistic dedication, and lasting accomplishment.

Writing to her friend Lowell, who was six years Bishop's junior and who had not yet turned sixty, Bishop replied to one of the increasingly fretful letters of his later years:

> I am now going to be very impertinent and aggressive. Please, please don't talk about old age so much, my dear old friend! You are giving me the creeps ... The thing Lota admired so much about us North Americans was our determined youthfulness and energy, our 'never-say-die'ness – and I think she was right! ... I just *won't* feel ancient – I wish Auden hadn't gone on about it in his last years, and I hope you won't. (*WIA* 778)

Bishop's Brazilian lover and companion Lota de Macedo Soares, who shared Bishop's life from 1951–1967, would no doubt have included Bishop herself in this characterization of "us North Americans." And despite Bishop's frequent battles with depression, despite her periodic episodes of alcohol abuse, and despite ongoing attacks of asthma and eczema that might have limited or even disabled a less tenacious personality, Bishop's commitment to her vocation as a writer, observer, and world traveler did not cease until her sudden death from a cerebral aneurysm when she was sixty-eight and at the height of her artistic powers. Indeed, she had recently traveled to the Galápagos Islands, and she was contemplating a journey to Alaska in the months before her death. During her years in Brazil, Bishop made trips deep into the nation's remote interior, traveling on the Amazon and other major rivers and exploring the tropical rainforest, where she studied – and was studied by – the Uialapiti Indians. Indeed, as she told Lowell, one member of the community, "a widower, asked me to stay and marry him – this was a slightly dubious compliment" (*WIA* 264).

In Lowell's prescient review of Bishop's first book, *North & South,* which he published in *Sewanee Review* in the summer of 1947, a few months after he had met Bishop, he identified as a key factor in her poetry: "something in motion, weary but persisting, almost always failing and on the point of disintegrating, and yet, for the most part, stoically maintained. This is morality, memory, the weed that grows to divide, and the dawn that advances, illuminates and calls to work" (*Collected Prose* 76–77). Arguably, Lowell was offering a reading not only of Bishop's work, but also of her personality, which he had recently come to know and admire. In 1964, Bishop herself posthumously praised Flannery O'Connor – a writer who persisted in her art despite a chronically debilitating and ultimately fatal case of lupus – for having lived her life with a "Christian stoicism and wonderful wit and humor that put most of us to shame" (*Pr* 340–341). Yet perhaps, despite her own implied self-deprecation, Bishop herself achieved in her life and writing some measure of the qualities she celebrated in the late O'Connor. In "One Art," the trademark villanelle Bishop published almost three decades after Lowell's prophetic review, she offers – in a poem laced with memory, morality, and something "weary but persisting" – a poignant and masterfully performative self-critique of the aspirations to and limitations of a more secular kind of stoicism. Moreover, throughout Bishop's correspondence, a "wonderful wit and humor" illuminates letters written during even some of her darkest hours.

Bishop drew a self-protective, if "semi-translucent" (*P* 13), veil over significant aspects of life, particularly her lesbian sexuality and her frequent struggles with alcohol. And understandably so; had these predilections been exposed in her lifetime, particularly with regard to her sexuality, the personal repercussions might have been severe. Still, by the 1950s, when she resided in Brazil, her friends knew through her letters, sometimes in considerable detail, about her life with her lover Lota de Macedo Soares. And by the time of her death, her sexuality was very much an open secret in the literary community. Yet in her published poetry and prose, although she represented love, loss, and personal turmoil pervasively, she also represented it for the most part obliquely, not only as a form of self-protection or even (in the case of her unpublished poems) self-censorship, but in order to avoid projecting a sentimentalism about suffering that she particularly abhorred. Yet in daily intercourse with others, Bishop was, by nature, wittily and sometimes even aggressively plainspoken. Nor did she suffer fools gladly. Bishop often seemed to chafe at the decorous image she had allowed to grow up around her, and, without divulging any potentially embarrassing details, she appeared at times in her interviews to relish pointing out the cracks and fissures dividing her demure and constrained public persona – which in fact may have somewhat limited the public appeal of a poet referred to in her own lifetime as "Miss Bishop" – from her distinctly bohemian lifestyle and from her frequently troubled inner self.

As she stated in a conversation recorded in 1966 by Wesley Wehr, her student at the University of Washington, "Because I write the kind of poetry I do, people seem to assume that I'm a *calm* person. Sometimes they even tell me how *sane* I am. But I'm not a calm person at all .... There are times when I really start to wonder what holds me together – awful times" (Wehr 43). Still, as she acknowledged to Wehr, she felt a need to present that composed persona in her public role as a faculty member during her first-ever stint of teaching in 1966–1967: "I feel a responsibility, while I'm here at least, to *appear* calm and collected." This memoir of Bishop was published posthumously, yet Bishop made a similar statement in a 1978 interview in the *Christian Science Monitor*, for when Alexandra Johnson praised her interviewee for what she heard as "the calm, consistent voice of Elizabeth Bishop" in "almost every one" of her poems, Bishop shot back, "Well, I'm not calm, but it's nice to hear!" (103).

The apparent self-contradiction between the sanity and calm of Bishop's public persona and her often troubled inner life draws us toward an examination of Bishop's complex relationship with what has become perhaps the most notorious poetic movement of her day. Bishop famously stated in 1966 that "I *hate* confessional poetry" (Wehr 45), but her favorite contemporary poet and closest literary friend was, of course, Robert Lowell, then widely acknowledged as the leader of the so-called confessional school. I have argued elsewhere (*Midcentury Quartet* 32–70) that the term "confessional poetry" is deeply problematic on a number of levels, and that the label "confessional poet" that critics long applied to Lowell and Berryman and "impersonal poet" that critics long applied to Bishop were artificial constructions that served only to obscure the real similarities in their self-exploratory art. Moreover, these labels obscure the obvious bonds of friendship and mutual support that were revealed in their reviews and interviews, in the manuscript record, and, most importantly, in their letters to one another. For Bishop, the courage, honesty, self-irony, and artistic control of Lowell's best work trumped critically constructed labels every time. And in fact, in her mind, these qualities separated him from the confessional poetry that she disparaged, largely because she considered it mawkish, self-indulgent, and egocentric in its self-representation.

Bishop praised Lowell's breakthrough volume *Life Studies* glowingly as she read the poems in manuscript in 1957 – confessing she was "green with envy" (*WIA* 247). And she contributed an enthusiastic and insightful blurb on the book's first publication in 1959. She observed that "a poem like 'My Last Afternoon with Uncle Devereaux Winslow,' or 'Skunk Hour,' can tell us as much about the state of society as a volume of Henry James" (*WIA* 289–290), and this comparison to Henry James suggests her appreciation of a subtlety, discretion, and formal mastery, as well as a breadth of social reference, that she found lacking in the work she disparaged as confessional.

A year before the publication of *Life Studies*, she wrote to Lowell that "your poetry is as different from the rest of our contemporaries as, say, ice from slush" (*WIA* 278). In 1961, writing to reassure Lowell of her continuing admiration, she insisted on the difference between Lowell's "better imitators" and Lowell himself: "You tell things – but never wind up with your own darling gestures, the way [W. D. Snodgrass] does (he'd be giving Lepke home-made cookies or something). I went straight through *Life Studies* again and there is not a trace of it, and that is really 'masculine' writing – courageous and honest" (*WIA* 360). As Richard Flynn has recently argued, Bishop was not only the first reader, but also the decisive influence on the form and content of *Life Studies*. Flynn admits that Bishop struggled with "the ethical dimension of self-presentation" in her letters to Lowell, a struggle that came to a head in 1972 over "the ethics of using Elizabeth Hardwick's letters in [Lowell's] *The Dolphin*" (Flynn 208). Yet this disagreement came fifteen years after *Life Studies*, which Bishop had so enthusiastically praised, and her 1972 disagreement with Lowell related not to an aesthetic of self-exploration, but to the ethics of publishing excerpts of private letters from an estranged spouse. Flynn argues further that Lowell's artistically successful use of self-representation in *Life Studies* encouraged Bishop toward the more open self-referentiality that one encounters in her later poetry, and particularly in her last and most widely lauded book, *Geography III*.

Thus, ultimately for Flynn, despite their differences, "Bishop and Lowell are allies in their joint exploration of the aesthetics of autobiography" (213). In another letter to Lowell, Bishop drew a line between Lowell and Anne Sexton with the observation that "She is good, in spots, – but there is all the difference in the world, I'm afraid, between her kind of simplicity and that of *Life Studies*, her kind of egocentricity that is simply that, and yours that has been – what would be the reverse of sublimated, I wonder – anyway, made intensely interesting, and painfully applicable to every reader" (*WIA* 327). What Bishop found in Lowell's work was an artistic integrity and scope that took it well beyond a mere expression of his own personal disquiets. And perhaps it is something like these same qualities that draws contemporary readers to Bishop's poetry, prose, and letters. Her writing, even at its most autobiographical, rarely if ever seems egocentric and when she represents painful experience, whether her own or that of others, these struggles are presented with restraint and seem "applicable to every reader." Bishop observed to Lowell about Sexton: "I feel I know too much about her, whereas, although I know much more about you, I'd like to know a great deal more, etc." (*WIA* 327). Bishop's own readers have clearly demonstrated a desire to know "a great deal more" about Bishop, a desire that helps to explain that cavalcade of new editions of her work and the avalanche of critical studies that have appeared in the decades since her death.

By far the most extensive body of Bishop's posthumous autobiographical writing has been her correspondence. Bishop had a gift for friendship. Moreover, as the three published volumes of her correspondence appearing to date have demonstrated, she was also one of the great letter writers in the Language. She carried on lifelong epistolary exchanges with an enormous range of friends and artistic colleagues. And to each of these correspondents, many of them famous and others less well known, she presented vivid portraits of her daily life and revealed intimate aspects of her emotional experience that she would have shared with no one else. Given the nature of Bishop's letter-writing style, which is laden with quotidian facts, keen observation, literary and artistic judgments, sly gossip, and personal anecdote, her correspondence provides a trove of biographically significant information as well as insight into her artistic processes. Her 168 letters and postcards to her high school and college friend Frani Blough Muser reach back to 1928 when Bishop was seventeen and continue into her final year, and these provide a different kind of record of her experience than her letters to Marianne Moore or to Lowell.

Meanwhile, her letters to Lowell reveal not only a great deal about her emotional life and her artistic methods, but also point to sources in her experience of poems such as "Faustina," "The Bight," and "Cape Breton." The sources of other poems are revealed in her letters to Moore and other correspondents, including the editors of *The New Yorker*, and we now have these letters, too, in their complete forms. The autobiographical sources Bishop reveals for her poems can sometimes lead to startling reconsiderations. To cite a single example, I for one had always assumed, perhaps along with others, that Bishop's poem "Filling Station" was describing a Nova Scotian filling station. In my own mind, this view was supported by the fact that this poem is placed in the "Elsewhere" section of *Questions of Travel*, which is largely concerned with Nova Scotia, rather than in the "Brazil" section, and in part because an Esso station – with or without a "row of cans" that "softly say: / ESSO – SO – SO – SO" (*P* 126) – stood opposite her maternal family's home in Great Village, Nova Scotia for many years. In my own mind, the absent mother in "Filling Station" who left many (to the poem's speaker) mildly comic feminine domestic touches in this apparently male-dominated "family filling station" – touches that include an oil-soaked doily and wicker-work taboret, and a "big, hirsute of begonia" (*P* 125) – seemed in part a subtle and poignantly gentle allusion to Bishop's absent mother Gertrude Bulmer Bishop, who had departed that Nova Scotian house and village under such painful circumstances in 1916 when the poet was five, leaving behind only "the echo of a scream" (*Pr* 62). Yet as her correspondence with Moss at *The New Yorker* makes clear, Bishop's initial description was of a Brazilian filling station, not a Nova Scotian one, and Moss even relayed Katherine White's suggestion that "it might possibly help if the title read something like 'Station No. 2 – Rio de Janerio to …' (you fill in the name)" (*NYr* 158). The poems would certainly have inspired a different kind of reading in my own mind with such a title. It was Bishop, as the correspondence makes clear, who argued for the more generic title "Filling Station," suggesting that "I hadn't thought of it as being an especially Brazilian poem – couldn't it be equally true of an out-of-the-way filling station anywhere?" (*NYr* 158–159). This new information has caused me to revise somewhat my own understanding of the poem without causing me to completely abandon the view that a subtle allusion to her own absent mother remains an important dimension, a view that seems perhaps encouraged by Bishop's suggestion that the poem might be "true of an out-of-the-way filling station anywhere" and also by the fact that in *Questions of Travel*, "Filling Station" follows "In the Village," where the echo of her mother's scream may yet be heard, by only a handful of pages.

Indeed, one of the strongest artistic bonds linking Bishop and Lowell was their shared preoccupation with the experience of a troubled and dislocated childhood. At the core of Bishop's own private challenges lay the succession of early losses and dislocations that she suffered as a child. Bishop might well have felt daunted when, as she told Schiller in 1977, her physician and close friend Dr. Anny Baumann "brought over my whole medical history, my entire life since I was a little girl." Bishop's challenges began before the end of her first year when the father she never knew, William Thomas Bishop, died of Bright's disease when she was eight months old. Moreover, as "In the Village" suggests, her mother, Gertrude Bulmer Bishop, never fully recovered from the loss, and after a series of psychological disturbances, she suffered a permanent mental breakdown while residing with her parents in the company of her only child when Bishop was five years old. Another trauma was Bishop's unwilling separation from her maternal (Bulmer) grandparents in Nova Scotia, a separation engineered by her paternal (Bishop) grandparents in Worcester, Massachusetts. Her response to this relocation to Worcester included dangerous outbreaks of asthma and eczema that left her debilitated and (her grandparents feared) on the brink of death. Early deaths figure heavily in her writings about her Great Village years, including the poem "First Death in Nova Scotia" about the death of a young cousin and, as we have seen, in the story "Gwendolyn." Other published Nova Scotian writings that represent an ongoing connection to a lost world include such poems as "The Prodigal," "Manners," "At the Fishhouses," "The Moose," "Poem," "Sestina," and the story or memoir, "Memories of Uncle Neddy" – each of which was based, although often with significant alterations, on personal experience. This is the aspect of her private experience that, although painful, Bishop seemed most willing to examine while she lived.

Yet along with Bishop's published poems, memoirs, and stories about her childhood, there are many poems and stories exploring this period that appeared only posthumously. These include prose pieces such as "The Country Mouse," "Primer Class" (first published in *Collected Prose* in 1984), and "Mrs. Sullivan Downstairs" (first published in *Edgar Allan Poe & The Juke-Box* in 2006). Each of these memoirs (or, if you prefer, stories) is of significant literary merit, each is certainly of great biographical interest, and each provides background that could inform our reading of Bishop's previously published oeuvre. Along with these posthumous prose pieces, which have been more or less universally appreciated, *Edgar Allan Poe & The Juke-Box* collected a cluster of elegiac poems about childhood and family elegies: "For Grandfather," "Where are the dolls who loved me so," "A Short, Slow Life," and "For M. B. S., buried in Nova Scotia." While the biographical interest of these poems is obviously considerable, some readers have expressed doubts about their aesthetic value. Personally, however, I find myself persuaded by the argument for their merits made in Charles Berger's essay, "Bishop's Buried Elegies." Berger reads this group of elegiac poems as "less aesthetically annealed against the display of affect, less enameled in defense against what the poet was enamored of" (43) than was typical of Bishop's published poetry of loss. Yet Berger argues for the significant aesthetic value of these poems, observing for example of "For M. B. S., buried in Nova Scotia," that "I can hardly think of a more quietly moving twentieth-century elegy, one that so masterfully backgathers so many elements of the elegiac tradition, but then refuses to bequeath itself to the reader as a present, by remaining unpublished" (45). Whatever one's opinion of the artistic worth of Bishop's brief elegy to her Aunt Maude Bulmer Shepherson, who served as Bishop's surrogate mother for many years after Bishop lost both of her parents, it is clear that when this poem is added to Bishop's posthumously published story, "Mrs. Sullivan Downstairs" – which charts her early life with Aunt Maude in a working-class neighborhood in Revere, Massachusetts – and to the posthumously published poem, "Salem Willows" – which explores the same period – the reader derives an insight into a vital period of her life that is not represented in her published oeuvre. Indeed, if one arranges in chronological order Bishop's published and posthumous writings in prose and verse about her childhood experience, one is confronted by an extensive autobiographical sequence exploring crucial events of Bishop's early life – from her earliest memories of mother, family, and home through her exploration in later adolescence of her unfolding artistic gifts, her emerging sexuality, and her lifelong preoccupations with childhood experience and with loss. These writings begin with the unfinished poem "A Drunkard" (which records Bishop's experience of the Great Salem Fire when she was just three years old) and move through "First Death in Nova Scotia," "In the Village," "Primer Class," "Memories of Uncle Neddy," "The Country Mouse," "Mrs. Sullivan Downstairs," "Gwendolyn," and "Salem Willows." They continue with the precocious series of poems, stories, memoirs, and reflective essays Bishop published in her high school literary magazines, North Shore Country Day's *The Owl* and Walnut Hill School's *The Blue Pencil* (many of them centered on her Nova Scotian years), and the perhaps less-personal but no less haunting Nova Scotian stories "The Baptism" and "The Farmer's Children," and they conclude with the elegiac family poems discussed by Berger.

The very fact that this fragmentary self-portrait of the artist as a young girl emerging into womanhood is such a varicolored mosaic of the published and the unpublished – blending fact, fiction, and extrapolation in differing proportions from piece to piece – adds to its potential fascination as a never quite deliberate, or fully deliberated, but nonetheless deep and important autobiographical narrative.

Of course, Bishop's posthumously published poems include not only those that add to the sequence previously characterized, but also such elegantly crafted poems of lesbian sexuality as "It is marvellous to wake up together," "Close close all night," "Dear, my compass," and "Breakfast Song," many of which give the sense of being finished but deliberately suppressed. They also include a group of closely observed and often rather edgy poems centered on Key West including "Edgar Allan Poe & The Juke-Box," "The Soldier and the Slot-Machine," and "Full Moon, Key West," and poems exploring her life in Brazil including "Suicide of a Moderate Dictator," "Gypsophilia," "All afternoon the freighters," and "Apartment in Leme." Several of these Key West and Brazilian poems exist as drafts, many in several versions and in varying states of completion. Although these Key West and Brazilian poems are worthy of extensive examination, I want to close with a brief consideration of perhaps the most artistically intriguing of these groups: her often apparently finished, but self-censored, poems of lesbian sexuality.

Lloyd Schwartz, in his examination of "Elizabeth Bishop's 'Finished' Unpublished Poems," argues that the posthumously discovered poem of lesbian sexuality, "It is marvellous to wake up together," appears to be "an earlier (and far more explicitly narrative) version of what became 'Rain Towards Morning' ... Yet many Bishop readers today seem to be more touched by 'It is marvellous' and prefer its colloquial, almost prosy openness" (55). Schwartz concludes that "'Rain Towards Morning' is a refined, prismatic gem, but seems emotionally evasive in comparison. Its absence from the anthologies should surprise no one" (55). Given the period in which she lived, Bishop understandably avoided publishing poems that directly represented her lesbian sexuality, although it may now seem clear that hints of a series of lesbian love relationships flash out of many poems in her established canon, including examples such as "Roosters," "Insomnia," "Argument," "Letter to N.Y.," "The Shampoo," "Song for the Rainy Season," and "Sonnet," although the identity of the speaker and the beloved are in general artfully concealed behind such genderless pronouns without antecedents as "you" or "we." The comparative openness of the best of her posthumous poems that explore this theme offer significant insights not only into the buried content of sexuality, longing, love, and loss in many poems in Bishop's published canon, but also into significant aspects of their form. In particular, these poems invite us to consider the obliquities of self-reference so frequent in her published canon, even in poems not directly or obviously referencing sexuality.

The prevalence of such "impersonally personal" pronouns as the "we" in "We'd rather have the iceberg than the ship" that opens "The Imaginary Iceberg" (*P* 6) or the curiously cool yet sensuous observation in "The Map" that "We can stroke these lovely bays / under a glass as if they were expected to blossom" (*P* 5) both express and distance an expression of a degree of feeling that Bishop was often willing at least partially to show, even in her earliest and apparently most hermetic work. Moreover, if we remember Bishop's displacement in "The Map" of an "emotion that too far exceeds its cause" onto the otherwise apparently innocent "names of seashore towns" running out to sea or the equally innocent "names of cities" that "cross the neighboring mountains," we may come to better understand her art of displacement, which remained throughout her life one of her most pervasive and persistent artistic strategies. It is at such moments as these, even in her earliest and apparently most impersonal work, that Bishop hints that she was not as calm or decorous as she sometimes might have seemed – even if she felt a pressure to appear calm and collected, at least "while I'm here."

2

STEVEN GOULD AXELROD

Bishop, History, and Politics

Although often understood as a poet of observation, introspection, or formal design, and therefore as largely ahistorical and apolitical, Elizabeth Bishop was deeply enmeshed in historical and political discourses. Her texts provide understated explorations of such charged zones of inquiry as colonialism, war, class, race, and sexual politics. In the present essay, I attempt to shed light on Bishop's complex negotiations with the cultural influences and interior drives that informed her textual engagements with the public sphere.

Despite employing the phrase "one art," Elizabeth Bishop was in reality a "creature divided" in multiple ways (*P* 198, 214). Her writing had both progressive and conservative elements. It was chronologically bifurcated, manifesting a Modernist aestheticism at first while reflecting a growing interest in "social problems and politics" later on (Brown 294). It was reticent in the poems published in her lifetime and more open in the poems published after her death in Alice Quinn's collection. Finally, Bishop was internally divided. As a person with an emotionally wounded childhood and an economically privileged adulthood, she had unsorted feelings that she wished both to conceal and reveal. She had ancestral libertarian affinities and felt isolated from others, yet she could also at times identify powerfully with others, and she believed in social equality. Bishop was a "Radical" who felt "uncomfortable in the presence of political commitment" (Millier 138, 200). She was a "socialist" who disliked "'social conscious' writing" (Brown 293). Paradoxically, her skittishness about public poetry may have suggested not so much a desire to pursue privacy as to avoid it. Her poetic engagement with history and politics inevitably opened the door to queer history and politics, just those aspects of her personal identity that she famously wished to confine in "closets, closets, and more closets" even as she also longed to expose them (Fountain 327).

Like anyone else, Bishop altered her views from time to time. At Vassar she struck most friends as apolitical, but Mary McCarthy said her private views tended toward "the socialist" camp (Fountain 48). In her adult life, she was thrilled by Roosevelt, felt superior to Truman, mocked Joseph McCarthy, considered Adlai Stevenson "someone nice & neurotic," criticized Eisenhower, felt "cheered up" by Kennedy, disparaged Barry Goldwater, disdained both Nixon and Hubert Humphrey, and vowed that "every time I see Reagan on TV I plan to leave it immediately" (*OA* 247, 392, 505). She regularly read *Partisan Review*, *The New Statesman*, *The New Yorker*, and *Time*. She read and quoted Reinhold Niebuhr, a theologian and political philosopher who also influenced John F. Kennedy, Martin Luther King, and Barack Obama (*OA* 78, 245; Bishop, "On *Life Studies*"). In Brazil, sharing her life with the aristocratic Lota de Macedo Soares, she backed moderate conservative Governor Carlos Lacerda and opposed leftist President João Goulart, although her most telling commentaries on economic injustice emanate from the Brazilian experience. Back in the United States, she migrated seamlessly back into American center-left politics, participating in a student-faculty strike and opposing the draft, but resisting the entreaties of friends to march in a gay rights parade (*OA* 504; Fountain 328).

Despite her shifts and nuances, Bishop belonged within the broad borders of what midcentury intellectuals variously termed "the vital center" (Arthur Schlesinger), "the liberal imagination" (Lionel Trilling), "our modern liberal culture" (Reinhold Niebuhr), and "the liberal tradition" (Louis Hartz). Niebuhr was representative in that he criticized "the cruelty of Communism," but worried equally about the place of "justice" within an American creed "too individualistic to measure the social dimension of human existence" (Niebuhr 3, 10). He wondered if, "in the relation of power to justice and virtue," the United States did not sometimes verge "on that curious combination of cynicism and idealism which characterizes communism" – the final Cold War irony (5). Robert von Hallberg has attributed an anti-Communist, pro-social justice stance to the mainstream culture of the time. Bishop adhered to that liberal consensus, but with one exception. The exception, as this chapter will discuss, was her textual anticipation of a queer politics, which was not yet part of any widespread understanding. Bishop's historical and political awareness has often remained hidden from view. Perhaps she was too absorbed by her personal struggles to exhibit her politics or feared that her politics would reveal too much about those struggles; perhaps she was confrontation-avoidant; or perhaps she adhered to an Arnoldian ideal of disinterestedness. Whatever the case, her texts do have public resonances, and as her career progressed, those resonances became more notable. Although not overtly political, the poems are indirectly so. Even if one does not know fully what to make of the political implications, one feels their presence and wrestles with them.

As a poet of movement across spaces, Bishop inevitably encountered issues of colonialism, which for her were conflated with psychological issues. Her early life had been punctuated by transits across the U.S.-Canadian border that corresponded to a sequence of devastating losses: her American father's death when she was only eight months old, her Canadian mother's removal to a mental institution when she was five, and her own removal from the loving care of her maternal grandparents to the inimical household of her paternal grandparents when she was six. In her adult life, the poet became an inveterate traveler, and this wandering compulsion may signal the severity of her childhood disturbance; in effect, marking her ceaseless need to seek her lost parents. Although Caren Kaplan has critiqued Bishop's travel poems for implicitly "celebrating" the colonial impulse, Jeffrey Gray has compellingly portrayed Bishop's poems as encounters with "absence or loss" rather than with "colonial mastery" (Kaplan 7; Gray 17). If Bishop's poems primarily evoke the anxiety of travel, they subvert notions of colonial control and foster imaginative identification with the colonized and displaced.

In her travels, Bishop was usually ready to take the side of the colonized. For example, in Morocco in 1936, she wrote to Marianne Moore that "Morocco was so nice – in spite of ... the rather unfriendly atmosphere which has been caused by the French occupation (one immediately sympathizes with the Moors)" (*OA* 40). But Bishop's anti-colonial sympathy coexisted with a privacy-protecting armor that at times radiated neocolonial condescension. Although she liked living in Brazil and worried about its "poor *poor* people," in times of personal crisis she could also call such people "backward and irrational" (*OA* 284–285, 491–492). It is between those poles of identification and distance that her poetry vibrates. In Bishop's poems, history, like human awareness itself, is not one fixed thing, but a dynamic multiformity that perpetually resists the "complete comprehension" that her speaker in "Arrival at Santos" claims to seek (*P* 87). As Bishop's lyric "I" acknowledges in "At the Fishhouses": "our knowledge is historical, flowing, and flown" (*P* 64). In this verbally brilliant account, history not only moves like a water current ("flowing"), but also flies off like a bird ("flown"). We can see Bishop meditating on the lability of historical understanding throughout her career.

"Brazil, January 1, 1502" recalls the arrival of the colonial Portuguese in Rio de Janeiro. The poem begins by placing "our" eyes in the imagined position of "theirs," thus aligning "our" gaze with that of the European colonizers (*P* 89–90). Yet the gazes divide almost from the beginning. Whereas the speaker composes the landscape as colorful, like a Postimpressionist painting just "taken off the frame," she imagines the Portuguese conceptualizing the landscape according to their own early modern culture, with "Sin" dominating and the hummed tune of a Latin mass in the background. The "Christian predators," as Jeffrey Gray calls them, rip into the landscape and the indigenous culture, each colonist seeking to "catch" an Indian, but the "maddening little women" call to each other and escape (Gray 39). Although it is tempting to read the poem as simply anticolonial, the text reveals its involvement with, as well as its critique of, the colonial moment. For one thing, the speaker's equation of women to landscape perpetuates the world view of the colonists themselves, who saw both land and women as objects to be controlled. For another, we know that, despite the resistant moments Jan Roselle describes in "Corporeal Sovereignty," the continent's first peoples were indeed subordinated by the newcomers. The very term "little women" may in fact echo (however ironically) a colonial sense of cultural superiority. Finally, the speaker's exoticization of the landscape, her focus on native flora instead of human beings, and her figurative transformation of people into "symbolic birds" and "a few palms, swarthy, squat, but delicate" seem to repeat the invaders' representational strategies. Nevertheless, Bishop ultimately opposes what Niebuhr called "hegemony" (Niebuhr 110). Her portrayal of an oppositional indigenous presence establishes the agency of first peoples and the persistence of their culture. Furthermore, the poem, which began by identifying the poet's "famous eye" with that of the Europeans, ends by identifying her voice with those of the Indians (*PPL* 915). The poem thus engages with history in a sophisticated way, foregrounding the inevitably partial magic of its attempt to recreate both the colonists' domineering gaze and the native peoples' resistance.

Bishop's "12 O'Clock News" portrays a U.S. military venture during the Cold War as a neocolonial enterprise. Camille Roman has shown that this poem, originally called "Desk at Night," was begun in 1950 in response to the Korean War and was then developed over many years "into the Vietnam-era published poem" (Roman 20–21). Thus, "12 O'Clock News" began life several years earlier than "Brazil, January 1, 1502," but appeared in print fourteen years later. The impulse behind it derives less from a specific war than from U.S. interventionism more generally. Again, Bishop portrays the imperial power's expansion into a new country as basically disastrous. The poem's long gestation period demonstrates the cultural shift during those years toward what Mark Poster has called "the mode of information," in which electronic devices increasingly mediate human awareness. Whereas the 1950 draft focused entirely on the objects on the poet's desk, "viewed as a war zone" (Roman 143), the reconceived "12 O'Clock News" positions that trope within the conventions of a television newscast. Rather than reproduce literal newscasts, in the manner of Allen Ginsberg's "Wichita Vortex Sutra" and Paul Simon's song "6 O'Clock News," Bishop's poem constructs a parody newscast – one broadcasting from a particularly dark midnight of the writer's soul. Reporting its imaginary war story in the style of network news or documentary, "12 O'Clock News" brings to light an eerie confluence of military, corporate, anthropological, travel, and neocolonial discourses (*P* 194–195). The television journalist's prose narration (on the right side of the page) turns desktop objects (indicated in italics on the left) into scenes from a televised war zone (see Muldoon 87–88). Trying to give his viewers "some idea of the lay of the land and the present situation," the broadcaster describes the "*typewriter keys*" as agricultural "terraces" in an implicitly Asian "principality." As revealed by aerial reconnaissance and mediated through imperialist condescension, the desktop nation is a "backward" Third-World country – a description uncannily echoing Bishop's own reference to Brazil as "backward" (*OA* 491). The "indigenes" are "small," "proud," "elusive," and with "black hair," much like the elusive Vietcong as portrayed in U.S. news coverage – but also like the elusive "little" women who flee the arriving colonists in "Brazil, January 1, 1502." Employing ethnocentric terminology, the narrator of "12 O'Clock News" ascribes "childishness" and "corruption" to these "inscrutable people" and thereby exposes the political biases concealed within the electronic media's seemingly objective, authoritative voice. The poem reveals the mixture of "desire and derision" inherent in colonial discourse (Bhabha 67) and it satirizes the "superior vantage point" claimed by such discourse. But the poem also uses Third-World landscapes and peoples as figures for the poet's writing block, a gesture contiguous with the news media's own self-involvement. The poet with the famous eye satirizes televisual imperialism from an ironically analogous or complicit position.

"One Art," published in the same volume as "12 O'Clock News," invokes the neocolonial impulse in a different way (*P* 198). Most scholars have justifiably considered the poem one of Bishop's most moving personal texts. According to Thomas Travisano, it reflects the "threatened departure" of Bishop's intimate partner, Alice Methfessel, as well as her prior losses of her mother and Lota de Macedo Soares. But the poem enfolds this private matter within a strikingly public vocabulary. Both of the key words – "master" and "disaster" – have historical resonances. "Master" appears in discourse about colonialism, white supremacy, male dominance, and genocide in such dyads as "master-slave" and "master-lady" and in the Nazi idea of a "master race" ("die Herrenrasse"). "Disaster" is also freighted with associations to war, genocide, and famine. Bishop presumably had events of this magnitude in mind when she referred to the twentieth century as "our worst century so far" ("On *Life Studies*"). Therefore, the poem conflates Bishop's personal experience of "losing" with a global history of mastery and disaster and with the fear of defeat that haunts every colonial and military project. Indeed, the personal locus at times merges with the global. The speaker loses "places, and names," "two cities, lovely ones. And vaster, / some realms I owned, two rivers, a continent" (*P* 178). The cities might be Rio de Janeiro and Ouro Preto; the rivers might be the Amazon and the Tapajós (the "two great rivers" featured in "Santarém"); and the continent might be South America. The language of conquest and proprietization ("realms I owned") seems to make the same self-mocking link between the poet's personal behaviors and an imperial desire for control that we noted in Bishop's other poems implicating neocolonialism.

Moreover, "One Art" echoes a Cold War discourse of mastery and loss that came to the fore in relation to the Vietnam War. In 1965, when President Lyndon Johnson committed the United States to war in a televised address, he said: "We must have the courage to resist or we will see it all – all that we have built, all that we hope to build, all of our dreams for freedom – all – all – will be swept away" (Johnson). Before the escalation, he had insisted that "I am not going to lose Vietnam," and afterward, with defeat threatening, he told a television interviewer, "I'm not going to be the first American president to lose a war" (Dallek; Herbert). Bishop's poem echoes this rhetoric partly to shed an ironic light on the speaker's personal defeats but also to reflect on American foreign policy itself. Johnson and his supporters also dreaded the loss of "places, and names," "realms," and a "continent." "One Art" conflates its speaker's private life with public policy not so much to mourn such losses as to comprehend them and to help readers do so as well. As so often occurs in a Bishop text, the poem ends ambiguously: the speaker's loss of "you," placed in a future tense inflected with a conditional-subjunctive mood, remains in doubt – a more judicious stance than Johnson's inaccurate prediction that mastery's absence will cause "all – all" to be "swept away." Indeed, Bishop's poem associates the very desire to master with loss, a sardonic commentary not only on the personal life but on what Tom Engelhardt has called American "victory culture." Whereas Hannah Arendt lamented that "in the modern world, the social and the political realms are much less distinct" (Arendt 33), Bishop accepted the collapse of the public-private binary as a necessary condition of postmodernity. She said that "we live in a horrible and terrifying world, and the worst moments of horrible and terrifying lives are an allegory of the world" (*PPL* 914).

One core belief related to the texts' anticolonialism is, as Roman has shown, Bishop's opposition to war. "Roosters" – written as World War II raged, but before the United States entered it – figures the horror of armed conflict (*P* 36–40). Writing to Marianne Moore, Bishop explained that the poem's "'violence' of tone" emphasizes "the essential baseness of militarism" (*OA* 96). She wrote that she was thinking not only of Key West (where she lived when she wrote the poem), but also of those "dismal little towns in Finland and Norway, when the Germans took over" and of the "violent roosters" appearing in Pablo Picasso's *Guernica*. Early in the poem, sensory descriptors link the animal fable specifically to the discourses of war: "gun-metal blue," "cries galore," and "green-gold medals." The roosters' crowing suggests the sounds of gunfire and bombs, registered as a phallic activity. The word "cock" performs a dual-semantic function, one that Moore, who innocently wanted to rename the poem "The Cock," never understood (*PPL* 909). The "virile" roosters glare at each other "with stupid eyes / while from their beaks there rise / the uncontrolled, traditional cries" (*P* 36). If "Roosters" genders war as male, it also marks it as aristocratic and racially hierarchical: the warriors wear a red "crown" and are admired for their color. This combination of social rank and masculinist aggression produces mass death: a "fallen" rooster lies in dung "with his dead wives." The poem ends with Bishop's characteristic ambiguity: the sun rises, "faithful as enemy, or friend" (*P* 40). One potential objection to the poem is that the speaker seems to be a neutral observer, commenting from above about violence in which he or she is not complicit. Susan Schweik helpfully suggests that the depicted mayhem may indeed hint at conflicts in the narrator's domestic life, suggested by the "we" of the first stanza and the "faithful as enemy" of the final line (Schweik 231–234). Yet the poem does not tease out these complicating factors.

Later poems move toward more complex antiwar poetics. They articulate war as a human activity that must be abolished not because it is "senseless," but because it adheres to a destructive logic. In "View of the Capitol from the Library of Congress," the speaker wishes both to hear and not to hear the "*boom – boom*" of warrior culture (*P* 67). She thus places herself ambiguously inside and outside of containment culture, employing "the language of the Cold War against itself" (Axelrod 843). The speaker's sense of war is inward as well as outward, while the antipathy toward war itself remains powerfully articulated. In "The Armadillo," fire balloons – which at first appear to be as "frail" as human hearts – suddenly turn "dangerous," splattering fire on innocents and causing "*piercing cry / and panic*" (*P* 101–102). This poem associates war imagery with initial acts of faith gone awry; "12 O'Clock News" similarly ends with a harrowing vision of soldiers "heaped together" in "hideously contorted positions, all dead" (*P* 195). "In the Waiting Room" is set against the backdrop of the Great War (*P* 179–181), and the atmospherics of war inflect the entire poem. The text features "rivulets of fire," "pith helmets," a central "*oh!* of pain," and an aspirational vision of a world where all of us are "just one" – an echo of both Woodrow Wilson's First Inaugural Address ("this new age ... where justice and mercy are reconciled and the judge and the brother are one") and Wendell Willkie's *One World*. In various ways, Bishop's poetry continued to reflect the pain of the World Wars, the Korean War, and the Vietnam War – and an enduring wish for a time beyond war.

Bishop had a particularly compounded relation to issues of class. Although her childhood was marked by abrupt withdrawals of security and love, her economic well being was never in question after her removal to Worcester, Massachusetts. She attended fine schools (Walnut Hill, Vassar), and although she worked hard at writing, she never had to work for long at a job she found unfulfilling. She lived frugally but comfortably. She confessed to Lowell that in Brazil, she became "awfully used to being waited on" (*WIA* 702). At times she took her class advantages for granted. Her letters are filled with commentary – usually sympathetic – about her ever-changing cast of servants, all identified by their first names: Lottie, Flossie, Lilian, Blanche. She separated herself from them while at the same time identifying herself with them, recurrently fantasizing herself as a servant: "Maybe I should move out to the Casa Marina as a scullery maid. The Polish girl of course writes poetry, too" (*OA* 181). Maids and poets at times seemed to become overlapping concepts in her mind. Bishop also cared, in an ambivalent fashion, for the impoverished people she encountered on the streets and in shops. Writing to her Aunt Grace from Rio, she commented: "Now I know why poor children cry more than rich ones: their parents are so dumb" (*OA* xv). This apparently callous critique of poor parents was derived from her empathic, even anguished concern for the poor children who cry. In her letters, Bishop worried about "poor dirty dying Rio" and its inhabitants who were also poor and dying (*OA* xvii). In "The Burglar of Babylon," she mourned, "the poor who come to Rio / And can't go home again" (*P* 110). In "Pink Dog," she tells a pink dog, who figures Rio's homeless and hungry masses, to "Dress up and dance at Carnival!" This is at once an obviously impossible strategy and an anguished call for social outcasts to survive through any possible deception.

Bishop's awareness of class difference comes to the fore in her poems written in Brazil, where a vibrant multiculturalism did nothing to ameliorate a stark economic divide that usually correlated with race. Although Brett Millier correctly asserts that Bishop had an "esthetic appreciation of poor people" (Millier 273), I want to suggest that her texts often go beyond aesthetic appreciation to identification and protest. As Octavio Paz reportedly said, "Elizabeth was concerned with economic justice" (Fountain 326). "Squatter's Children" poignantly depicts an impoverished, presumably indigenous or mixed-race girl and boy playing in the dirt – and then in the mud, as the rain begins to pour (*P* 93). As in the letter previously quoted that contrasts poor children with their parents, this poem also makes a distinction between the children's appealing "laughter" and their "Mother's voice, ugly as sin." The kids' playful ingenuity marks them as objects of identification and as creative individuals essentially similar to the observing poet, who addresses them directly at the end as "Children"; implying that they are her own children, if only in the imagination and for a moment. In a similar way, "Manuelzinho" seems to side with its satirized title character, a tenant who creates "Dream Books" and elaborate gardens that teeter between ravishing beauty and ruin (*P* 94–97).

In "A Baby Found in the Garbage," composed in the mid-1950s but never quite finished, the poet evokes the death of a baby who "must have been a servant's" (*PPL* 239). The poem focuses on the anguish of the newborn's demise, which the text frames in several alternative ways: as "quiet" and lonely, as punctuated by her crying out, and finally as accompanied by strangers trying to help: "In spite of everything they tried / she died, and scarcely having cried" (*PPL* 240). This is the cathected moment that the poem repetitively returns to, echoing Bishop's epistolary concern for "poor children" who "cry" and her poetic recollection of her own interrupted childhood as a "*time to plant tears*" (*OA* xv; *P* 122). Beyond its characteristic concern for a child's suffering, this poem also turns our gaze to a scene usually concealed from view: the dump at the city limits being scavenged by "the buzzards and the poor." The dispossessed pick through "varicolored muck" for their daily sustenance while flapping their arms to keep the birds at bay. Contrasting the comfortable "apartment house built for the rich" with the social devastation of "the dump," the poem laments and wishes to alleviate what Niebuhr called "the hopelessness and desperation of the poor" (Niebuhr 110). In such poems, Bishop performs as a Latin American political poet, protesting the prevailing socioeconomic norms.

Bishop had a particularly complex relationship to race, as did many European-American liberals of her generation. She sympathized and identified with ethnic others, but often on a basis of ignorance. She saw black people, but did not know them well. In an early unfinished poem, "Key West," she poignantly and pointedly concludes a description of a white-only carnival by acknowledging those who have been excluded: "While Negro children, who are not allowed, / Look on solemnly from among the crowd" (*PPL* 222). Her only "deep friendship" with an African American was a brief one at Yaddo with the painter and singer Beauford Delaney (Fountain 122). She was interested in her black and Latina/o servants, but her relations with them remained on a hierarchical basis. A great admirer of "beautiful

Negro singing" (*OA* 19), she venerated Bessie Smith, Robert Johnson, Billie Holiday, Mabel Mercer, and Odetta, but she did not meet any of them. Her interest in black individuals and cultures appears in such early poems as "Cootchie" and "Songs for a Colored Singer" (*P* 46–51), yet the poems reveal naïve and anxious feelings. She was also interested enough in black politics to have interviewed Kathleen Cleaver for a never-completed article. But she had no enduring friendships with people of color.

In 1950, Bishop wrote an anonymous, positive review of Gwendolyn Brooks's *Annie Allen*, suggesting an interest in the great African-American poet that most other European-American poets lacked (*Pr* 260). In it, she praised Brooks's "experimentation in language" and her "wildly colored images," so she definitely knew Brooks's work, although the reference to "wildly colored images" makes one wonder how well. At the time, neither poet made an effort to establish personal contact. When they finally did meet at Harvard twenty-three years later, Bishop's lack of familiarity with persons of color appeared in a particularly painful form. Brooks had been invited to read, and Bishop was to introduce her. According to Jane Shore, who was there at the dinner before the reading, Bishop "said that as children, she and friends used to dress up in costumes and smear burnt cork or coal on their faces" (Fountain 315). Having just described a version of white minstrelsy, she abruptly cut herself off in embarrassment. Shore comments that "I'm sure this remark was unintended," but the point of this episode is not in Bishop's conscious intention. She must have been so struck by Brooks's racial difference that she searched her mind for some personal story involving Africanness, and this was the story she came up with. Perhaps the only alternative would have been a story about a maid or about a musical performance or recording. At the reading itself, the awkwardness continued. Bishop introduced Brooks by calling her "the 'American Robert Burns'" (*PPL* 917). Bishop transparently believed that she could only fit Brooks into her audience's cognitive framework by comparing her to a respected white poet. That she chose a Scottish poet – one who, however honored in his homeland, is known in the United States primarily as a dialect poet almost, but not quite, of the first rank – was something of an unintended insult. It echoed the earlier blackface story, although this time it was Brooks who was insinuated as a white figure in blackface. After the reading, according to Shore, Brooks surrounded herself with other audience members while Bishop, perhaps understandably, stood off by herself.

Bishop's racial naïveté and anxiety become central to her story, "Memories of Uncle Neddy" (*Pr* 146–161), begun in 1958 but only published in 1977, four years after her meeting with Brooks. The story returns to the scene of blackface that embarrassed Bishop at that meeting. This time it is the narrator's Uncle Neddy, costumed as Santa Claus, who appears in black face:

> And then Santa Claus came in, an ordinary brown potato sack over his shoulder, with the other presents sagging in it. He was terrifying. He couldn't have been dressed in black, but that was my impression, and I did start to cry .... The face that showed above the rope beard looked, to me, like a Negro's. I shrieked. Then this Santa from the depths of a coal mine put down his sack that could have been filled with coal, and hugged and kissed me. Through my sobs, I recognized, by touch and smell and his suddenly everyday voice, that it was only Uncle Neddy. (*Pr* 157)

Again, normativity returns only when black fades into white. The association of a black man with the "boogey man" reveals a white supremacist perspective that may make sense for a young girl growing up in rural Nova Scotia and exposed to a racist discourse in books and illustrations, but it makes less sense for the narrator who is retelling the story decades later. Observing that "I realize only now that he represented 'the devil' for me, not a violent, active Devil, but a gentle black one," she reveals that her childhood understandings have hardly changed (*Pr* 147). The dual image of terrifying threat and pleasing subservience still organizes the narrator's notions of racial otherness.

Bishop's great poem of 1970, "In the Waiting Room," attempts to transcend her sense of racial imprisonment (*P* 179–181). As the protagonist waits for her (fictionalized) Latin American aunt named "Consuelo," she looks at images of Africans seen in a (similarly fabricated) issue of *National Geographic*. She sees "a dead man slung on a pole," "babies with pointed heads," and "black, naked women with necks / wound round and round with wire" and with "awful hanging breasts." We observe here, again, the shock of customs and skin tones perceived to be non-normative. Stranger anxiety seems to be a persistent theme in all of Bishop's racialized texts. Yet we also observe Bishop's characteristic sympathy for people of color, mixed for perhaps the first time with empathy. The speaker's Aunt Consuelo may be of indigenous or mixed-race background, so it is possible that her niece, the speaker, is also not entirely white. The little girl loses a sense of boundary separating herself and her aunt, and then she loses even the distinction between herself and the African women with "those awful hanging breasts." She is shocked now not by otherness but by similarity – the human contiguity that "made us all just one." Perhaps this moment represents the culmination of Bishop's racial politics – the achievement of the desired empathy that had so long eluded her.

Bishop's queer politics consistently informed and distinguished her social writing. It was the most radical side of her public awareness, the one area in which she moved far beyond her era's liberal consensus. Frank Bidart remembers her as "passionately feminist," and Jane Shore says she called herself "a feminist since *way* back" (Fountain 327, 329). Lloyd Schwartz observes that the poet's "sexual life was inevitably more surprising and complicated than most people assume," implying that it may have included straight as well as gay encounters (Fountain 328). In a similar vein, Michael Davidson places Bishop among those women poets "whose sexuality cannot be named, ... the lines between whose homosexual and heterosexual lives are blurred out" and who therefore are positioned "*between* rather than *at* one or another pole of a dyadic gender structure" (Davidson 169). Bishop often dressed in desexualized clothing. She consented to being published only in gender-neutral anthologies, because, as she said, "I felt it was a lot of nonsense, separating the sexes. I suppose this feeling came from feminist principles" (Starbuck 322). Bishop was an out lesbian among her friends, but because of what Bidart calls "her distrust of the straight world," she avoided the ghettoization that she believed came with a public lesbian identity (Fountain 327). Although she may have believed in "closets," she also pried the closet door open in her writing and sometimes simply stepped out.

As Catherine Cucinella has written, Bishop's "poems often undo the ties among gender, sexuality, and body" (Cucinella 57). In "Cape Breton," it is a man, not a woman, who is "carrying a baby" home (*P* 66). In "First Death in Nova Scotia," a male loon has a "caressable" breast, and a doll-like little Arthur clutches a lily (*P* 123–124). "Keaton" celebrates comic actor Buster Keaton – who cross-dressed in such films as *His Wedding Night*, *Our Hospitality*, and *Sidewalks of New York* – as a figure "made at right angles to the world" (*P* 303). The gender-dysphoric young girl of "In the Waiting Room" finds the sight of female breasts "horrifying" and fears "to see what it was I was" (*P* 179–180). In "Memories of Uncle Neddy," Neddy's portrait shows him with cheeks like "a girl's," whereas a portrait of his sister makes her look "almost more like a boy than he does" (*Pr* 148, 150). The speaker of "Pink Dog" advises the pooch to dress in a "*fantasía*" so as to make her gender identity invisible within a crowd of similarly disguised celebrants (*P* 213).

Bishop's critique of the gender binary culminates in "Exchanging Hats" (*P* 230–231). In this poem, "unfunny uncles" try on a lady's hat. The quoted term plays on the cliché of the "funny uncle," the family member who cracks jokes and/or is somehow outside of gender norms. But these particular uncles are "unfunny," implying both that their joke does not amuse and that their ostensible gender peculiarity is really not unusual. Indeed, the poem insists that we all "share" their "transvestite twist." Cucinella observes that the uncles' joke fails because "no joke exists. In one sense, all gendered identities depend on parody and performance" (68). Like the dancers at the end of "Pink Dog," we experience gender as an impersonation, a "signifier" (as Carole Anne Tyler says) through which we are all "only *passing*" (Tyler 221). The poem posits that because "costume and custom are complex," we quite happily "experiment" with gender assignment. In a similar way, "anandrous aunts" try on yachtmen's caps. The adjective "anandrous" reminds us that the aunts remain technically female, despite a masculine appearance, and it also suggests that they find males unnecessary. The poem's frequent indulgence in verbal play ("custom," "costume," "drag," "perversities") implicates gender as subject to playfulness as well. Although Bonnie Costello argues that the poem exhibits "sexual anxiety" (Costello 83), the tone (until the elegiac ending) seems to suggest instead a boisterous pleasure that, as in the film *Paris Is Burning*, subverts the gravity of gender distinction.

Beyond troubling gender, Bishop challenged her era's heteronormativity by writing about lesbian desire. The poems of *A Cold Spring* approach the topic obliquely, frequently focusing on a conjugal "we," with carefully unspecified genders (inevitably a code for homosexuality). "Insomnia," for instance, invokes a "world inverted" (another gay code) in which "you love me" – a world opposite to the current one in which the "you" either does not or is not permitted to love the speaker (*P* 68). In "Rain Towards Morning," an "unexpected kiss" leads to the lifting of a cage (*P* 75). In "The Shampoo," the speaker asks to wash the bright, black hair of her "dear friend," a character based on Lota de Macedo Soares (*P* 82). Some of the posthumously published poems are more explicit. "It is marvellous to wake up together" erotically evokes "the light falling of kisses" and the way the kisses change as desire increases (*P* 283). Interestingly, the same association of sexual orgasm with a cage that occurs in "Rain Towards Morning" appears in this poem, which may be an earlier, more graphic version of the same poem. Here the lovers imagine themselves inhabiting a "bird-cage of lightning," which they think would be "delightful rather than frightening" (*P 283*). The autobiographical "A Drunkard" recalls an early manifestation of the poet's homosexual interest (*P* 317–319). "Vague Poem (*Vaguely love poem*)" evokes a moment when the speaker sees her beloved naked and feels transfixed by the vaginal "rose of sex" (*P* 323–325). Unlike the "awful" breasts lamented in "In the Waiting Room," the "clear pink breasts and darker, crystalline nipples" in this poem evoke the joys of the female body and lesbian sexuality.

The very last "new" poem in Bishop's 1983 *Complete Poems* – in fact, the very last poem she published before her death – also makes her lesbian identity explicit. "Sonnet" describes a divided creature much like Bishop herself, partially "caught," but partially "freed" (*P* 214). The freed self triumphs in the poem, flying wherever it feels like, "gay!" That is the last word of the poem and, in effect, the intended last word in Bishop's published oeuvre. It is an old word for Bishop, one she used so many times before, but it is new here, with its multiple valences of happiness and homosexuality clearer than ever before. Some of Bishop's friends, aware of her reticence, may have difficulty accepting this final word as a self-outing. But readers who know Bishop only through the texts – who contemplate her radical play with gender and her subtle attempts to open her closet door wider – may have less difficulty in believing that her textual immanence made her escape at last.

The "dream of an apolitical poetry" is a vivid and enduring one (Scully 47). It has helped shape the reception of Elizabeth Bishop. Some readers have hoped to find in Bishop's writing a self-referential world elsewhere – an island of beautiful words. I am suggesting, however, that in the light of day, her work appears neither ahistorical nor apolitical, but deeply implicated in the public discourses swirling around and through her. Indeed, her writing is especially striking for the degree of self-awareness it brings to its involvement with the history and politics of her time.

3

KIRSTIN HOTELLING ZONA

Bishop: Race, Class, and Gender

For Elizabeth Bishop, writing poetry had less to do with self-expression than it did with probing the complex and often discomforting nature of self as it is shaped through interaction with the world. From the gendered inversions in "The Gentleman of Shalott" to Bishop's racially and economically marked characters, we find a commitment to subverting – and sometimes securing – the idea of an autonomous self and its attending markers of difference that persists through "Santarém" and "Pink Dog" in 1979, the year of Bishop's death. As the majority of Bishop's poems suggest, the parameters that delimit one's sensation of individual being are defined by one's unconsciously internalized images of "the other" – images that often coalesce around perceptions of race, class, and gender. The proximity of early poems such as "The Gentleman of Shalott" and "The Map" to poems like "Cootchie" and "Songs for a Colored Singer" in *North & South* should not, then, be overlooked as coincidence; the transformation of black faces into a "conspiring root" in part IV of "Songs for a Colored Singer" (*P* 50) carry over the tropes of division, unconscious processes, perspective, and reconstruction that populate more overtly surreal poems such as "The Weed," "The Man-Moth," and "Sleeping Standing Up."

This does not mean that Bishop's interrogations of difference are innocent of her own prejudices as a white, middle-class woman of (for the most part) mid-twentieth century America; I agree with Adrienne Rich's claim that Bishop's portraits of people of color are a "risky undertaking" (Rich 16) and also with Renée Curry's more recent (and more pointed) assertion that "Bishop was not a racial outsider; she was, in fact, implicated in the continuance of racial outsiderness, a situation that she does come to suspect and fear" (Curry 83). And yet, it is precisely Bishop's determination to expose the tension between her attempts to identify with those marked as radically different from herself *and* her own investment in maintaining those very distinctions that creates the opportunity for us to reexamine our own habits of identification while reading her poems. Characters such as the Man-Moth, the Gentleman of Shalott, and certainly seven-year-old "Elizabeth" long for the promise of plenitude that identification with the normative ideal confers just as they expose the impossible and ultimately coercive nature of such representations. Consequently, what may appear in Bishop's work to be a gradually liberated expression of herself is more suitably described as an increasingly sophisticated understanding of her contingency – and of her complicity – and the ways in which her own observations are embroiled in the dual project of confronting this awareness and covering it up.

Thus, while I am grateful to Curry for calling attention to the unchecked racism now evident to us in Bishop's letters, I question her interpretation of Bishop's motives: that Bishop "toned down the 'savage' attributes of the letter discourse in order to write a more polite whiteness into her poetry" (Curry 77). As Curry herself notes, Bishop "recognized the power of language to betray any attempts at sheltering attitudes, politics, or emotions. Bishop not only knew that the 'unconscious spots' would be left in the work, she argued that it is impossible to erase or negate them" (Curry 77). How, and to what end, Bishop situated and explored the simultaneously resistant and transformative potential of these "unconscious spots" is the focus of this chapter.

Recognizing the interdependence in Bishop's work between the unstable "I" and her portraits of exoticized and disenfranchised others enables us to place the latter poems within the logic of her oeuvre as a whole and not, as they have often been read, as "something other than ... Elizabeth Bishop['s] poem[s]" (Doreski 122). As I have argued elsewhere (Zona 2002), Bishop reminds us repeatedly that maintaining the illusion of wholeness depends on one's refusal to identify with anything alien from one's own sensational ego, as well as a concurrent clinging to those images that reflect one's ego; for this reason, destabilizing the coherent self is indispensible to dismantling staid conceptions of difference. Hence, our frequent encounters, especially in the early poems of *North & South*, with mirror images, distorted and exaggerated corporeal parameters, askance perspectives, dream worlds, and fragile identities. Indeed, the title character of "The Gentleman of Shalott," a poem written at the start of Bishop's career in 1936, embodies precisely this meeting between perspective and (literal) self-consciousness: "Which eye's his eye? / Which limb lies next the mirror? / For neither is clearer / nor a different color than the other, / nor meets a stranger / in this arrangement / of leg and leg and / arm and so on" (*P* 11). In these opening lines we are introduced to the issue at the heart of the poem: the paradoxical interplay between singular perspective and the sensation of coherent selfhood. The Gentleman's "I" (importantly never named as such) is punningly contingent on the "eye" through which the poem's imagery is framed. Unlike Tennyson's Lady of Shalott, who "in her web she still delights / To weave the mirror's magic sights," or even the posthumously published "Keaton," whose title character "was made at right angles to the world" and "can only see it so" (*P* 303), Bishop's Gentleman cannot distinguish between "reality" and the mirrored reflection. "Which eye's his eye?" asks the speaker, a question that, typically, is posed only to expose the impossibility of an answer. The Gentleman does not assume that one's mirrored reflection frames his body once-removed; on the contrary, as in "The Map," reflection (or representation) and "real" are fused to generate his sense of being.

At the same time, the Gentleman maintains that he is *part* mirrored reflection, "Half," to be precise (*P* 12), so that his perception of self assimilates that which is, according to Lacan, normally always exterior: the visual image of one's "self" which, by its very distance from the viewing subject, will always generate in him or her a sense of lack, and thus desire – hence, one's sensation of individuality as always dependent on one's sense of the other. The Gentleman *is* the mirror, *and* the reflection, *and* that which exists before the mirror altogether. But just as the poem names these distinct elements of the Gentleman's being, it renders each element, for all intents and purposes, neither "clearer / nor a different color / than the other." The distance between representation of self and self is collapsed in this poem, so that "he's in doubt / as to which side's in or out / of the mirror." The Gentleman knows that "There's little margin for error, / but there's no proof, either," as Bishop's poems in general suggest (*P* 11). Hovering between one's eye and "I," Bishop's Gentleman exposes the dialectic of seeing and being that scripts the human experience of "self." He insists that subjectivity is an unfinished process, or in his words, "that sense of constant re-adjustment" (*P* 12).

Like any number of Bishop's early poems, "The Gentleman of Shalott" reminds us that one's perspective is mapped by one's physical location that, in turn, is apprehended only through one's bodily sensations – a condition of being that Bishop returns to in poems such as "At the Fishhouses," "Questions of Travel," and "The Moose." Caught in the precarious balance between his sensual ego and his visual image, the Gentleman at first searches for *his* eye, *his* limbs, longing for a feeling of wholeness. Living at the literal juncture of his sensual self ("this arrangement / of leg and leg and / arm and so on") and his visual imago ("the indication / of a mirrored reflection"), the Gentleman's search for his "real" half is overwhelmed by his deepening inability to distinguish the real from the reflected. Eventually, the Gentleman accepts this: "he's resigned / to such economical design" (*P* 11), and in doing so, admits of the impossibility of finding an a priori self beyond or before the mirror. At the same time, however, the Gentleman feels the split in his being: although he cannot distinguish between these different aspects of his subjectivity, neither can he escape the awareness that they exist as such. In this way, the Gentleman, like so many of Bishop's characters, longs for normativity while exposing the impossibility of satisfying his desire.

Parallel to the tension between life in the symbolic register and a longing for the real in "The Gentleman of Shalott" is Bishop's general refusal to delineate clean lines between the abject and the ideal in her poems about race and class; this is in part what makes these poems a "risky undertaking." In "Cootchie," for instance, we are introduced to the title character, "Miss Lula's servant," whose "life was spent / in caring for Miss Lula, who is deaf, / eating her dinner off the kitchen sink / while Lula ate hers off the kitchen table" (*P* 46). Clearly, this description begs our sympathies for Cootchie, whose suicide provides the impetus for the poem: "black into white she went / below the surface of the coral-reef." The opening stanza layers opposition upon opposition: servant versus master, life versus death, freedom versus servitude, black versus white. The "sable" faces at Cootchie's funeral stand in stark contrast to the "egg-white" skies that, as the canopy above the funeral, align the heavenly and sublime with whiteness and Miss Lula, whereas death and blackness seem to signal the domain of Cootchie and her mourners (*P* 46). The binary of black versus white weighs heavily on the first stanza of this poem, framing it and concluding it with images wherein whiteness occupies the register of immortality and nature, whereas blackness, along with Cootchie herself, continually slides "into [the] white" (*P* 46).

Yet, as Margaret Dickie notes, "the poem is titled 'Cootchie' not 'Miss Lula,'" and the exaggerated emphasis on dark versus light within the first half of the poem suggests the speaker's mockery; it is the absent maid whose presence is immortalized through this poem, and as we move from the first to the second and last stanza, the moonlight disbands the stark contrasts of black versus white that came before it: "Tonight the moonlight will alleviate / the melting of the pink wax roses" while the lighthouse "will discover Cootchie's grave / and dismiss all as trivial" (*P* 46). Foreshadowing the "conflux of two great rivers" and their impact on "literary interpretations" in "Santarém" (*P* 207), the moon here "alleviates" more than the melting of wax flowers. In the silvery light of night, the lighthouse's beam crosshatches the moon's, and in place of sharp binaries we are left with a shifting, shadowy landscape in which such contrasts are literally unsustainable. At the same time, the speaker's purpose becomes more nebulous, a point that Dickie associates with Bishop's own ambivalence in the face of the other: while Bishop's "interests in people that are distanced from her by class or race ... suggest that she was much more receptive to others, more openly involved with them, than she has appeared to be," it also seems that "writing so often about people foreign" to Bishop made her "afraid of losing her own identity in theirs, a fear that she both courted and held off" (Dickie 57–58).

No longer charting loyalties and injustices along a deepening division of black versus white, "Cootchie" concludes with philosophical uncertainty: does the lighthouse "dismiss all as trivial" because, within the shadow of endless tides and infinite lives, Cootchie's death and Miss Lula's "deafness" are mere undulations in the greater scheme of things? Or is the lighthouse's dismissal an echo of Miss Lula's uncomprehending ear, yet another gesture of the world's injustice that will always triumph over the sea's silent urgings? The answer is, of course, a matter of perspective, and one possibility does not exclude the other. Having carefully teased our habits of seeing with familiar oppositions, Bishop abruptly asks that we look again; this time at our own patterns of identification and the need to make sense of things in the absence of established resolve.

In the later "Faustina, or Rock Roses," Bishop picks up where "Cootchie" leaves off. Having posed the laden opposition of black versus white in the earlier poem, Bishop relentlessly deconstructs the traditional alignment of whiteness and ideality in "Faustina." Like "Cootchie," this poem is named after a black female servant who tends an aging white woman. But unlike the earlier poem, "Faustina" is structured on an exaggerated, disquieting field of white-on-white into which blackness – Faustina's "sinister kind" face – emerges disproportionately in the last third of the poem. Furthermore, the whiteness that at least postured as a sign of immortality and natural superiority in "Cootchie" is rendered frail and illusory in "Faustina" from the start. In the first two-thirds of the poem, we are introduced to the "white woman [who] whispers / to herself," propped up in her "chipped enamel" bed, surrounded by "white disordered sheets / like wilted roses." The table near her holds a can of talcum and five boxes of "little pills" in addition to a "white bowl of farina." The woman's thin "white hair" blends associatively into her nightgown with the "undershirt / showing at the neck" and the palm leaf fan "she holds but cannot wield." Meanwhile, a "visitor sits and watches" dew shimmer on the screen while an "eighty-watt bulb / betrays us all, / discovering the concern / within our stupefaction; / lighting as well on heads / of tacks in the wallpaper" (*P* 70–72). The brightness of the eighty-watt bulb leaves nothing untouched by its glare, and it does not discriminate: tack-heads are no less structurally important in this description than is "our stupefaction." Twelve short stanzas link image after image of whiteness into a cohesive scene, like a series of props, while the repetition of their small identical structures functions much like acts in a play, drawing attention to the manipulation of discrete parts into an illusory whole. It is as if we are being led behind the scenes, to the barefaced world without makeup or soft lighting where imperfections stand out and rolling hills are revealed as two-dimensional cardboard paintings. Consequently, tired efforts (the older woman's, Faustina's, the speaker's, the visitor's) to maintain the triumphant status of the white lady's world are exposed, becoming sources of embarrassment through their failures to do so.

Hardly a trope of natural superiority in this poem, whiteness is the mark of vulnerability, failed illusions, and tenuous, decayed control. The "shade[s] of white" that might, through a different perspective, represent a "clutter of trophies," have been reduced to a disheartening "chamber of bleached flags." What was presumably once the white woman's winning mastery (of herself, her surroundings, and Faustina) is exposed as no more or less than the haphazard combination of scattered images through which the woman is sketched in this poem. Because the images of whiteness that construct this woman are, like the various garments hung up around her on "chairs and hooks," both distinct from one another and always slightly unaligned (i.e., the juxtaposition of "white disordered sheets/ like wilted roses" and the "Clutter of trophies / chamber of bleached flags!" [*P* 71]), we are urged to see the space between the trope of whiteness and the subject who embodies it. The nameless woman is made visible to us almost entirely by way of her surroundings; a descriptive strategy that underlines both her particularity and her artifice: the scene inside the woman's disordered house is littered with her personal touches – her pills, her farina, her hair, her "pallid" palm-leaf fan – so that the exaggerated whiteness that she clearly represents stands at an awkward distance from the frail individual she is "betray[ed]" to be. At the same time, this distance is measured by "our stupefaction," by the embarrassment we feel right along with the visitor in the face of such disillusionment. Indeed, as Bonnie Costello suggests, Bishop may have identified herself with the visitor in this poem; in notes from this period, Bishop wrote, "Lying on my bed in the dark. I can look across into the bedroom of the people whose back-yard [sic] adjoins ours. The blinds are up and the light bulb hanging over the double bed must be an *80 watt*, the room is so bright" (Costello 71). Costello's observation underscores my point that in a poem such as "Faustina," making sense of our feelings means confronting our own "confusing" discomfort with the old woman's pathetic attempts – or more precisely, her *failures* – to represent the stereotypical ideal that whiteness traditionally signifies.

The reduction of the trope of whiteness to its disparate, "undazzling" shades is what ushers confusion into this poem, as we are refused the image of an ostensibly unmediated ideal around which to organize our identifications. Furthermore, we must remember that the puzzling discomfort that this poem establishes within the first eight stanzas is the context into which Faustina is introduced, "complaining of, explaining, / the terms of her employment" while her "sinister kind face / presents a cruel black / coincident conundrum" (*P* 71). Read against the backdrop of carefully crafted disorder established in the first two-thirds of the poem, Faustina's looming dark face will inevitably puzzle as it no longer signifies the abject side to her mistress's white ideal. Thus, Faustina requests "a little coñac" and openly discusses the terms of her employment while her mistress eats farina and whispers to herself. To deconstruct the conventional hierarchy between white and black without establishing a clear replacement of any sort – indeed, to blend the perspectives of Faustina and her mistress into a climactic series of questions that could emanate from either woman – is, as the opening stanza asserts, to yield a "crazy house" replete with a "crooked" table and floorboards that "sag / this way and that" (*P* 70). As in Bishop's poems about fantastical others, the slightly surreal or "crooked" perspective through which the poem unfolds is a manifestation of her refusal to accommodate normative, oppositional processes of ideality and identification.

Like "Cootchie," "Faustina" ends with deliberate ambiguity: "The acuteness of the question / forks instantly and starts / a snake-tongue flickering ... There is no way of telling. / The eyes say only either" (*P* 72). The question sparked by Faustina's entrance could be either woman's, or even the simultaneous musings of each. More important than deciphering the origins of the "eyes" that "say only either," however, is the tension generated by the question itself – a tension that deepens exponentially as its "acuteness" is increasingly felt. The mutual dependence the two women share with one another cannot be extricated from the limits such dependencies impart, and in turn, the mechanisms of exchange between Faustina and her mistress become inextricable from our own efforts to understand them, so that the opposition of self and other "blurs further, blunts, softens, / separates, [and] falls." Under Bishop's eighty-watt eye, "difference" thus becomes "our" problem, and a "helplessly / proliferative" one at that. It is the visitor, after all, whose mounting discomfort draws an end to the poem, as she "awkwardly" offers a bouquet of "rust-perforated roses" (a gesture that forecasts, provocatively, the exchange of overtly sexualized "Rose Rocks" in the posthumously published "Vague Poem (*Vaguely love poem*)" [*P* 323]) and clumsily leaves the scene (*P* 72).

Bishop's lack of resolution, or clear moral assertion, is surely partly responsible for the sketchy approval her poems about race in particular have garnered from her readers. And it is just as likely that Bishop's own racism, however unconscious it may have been, explains in part the moments of marked ambivalence that structure these poems. What is so provocative about these pieces, however, is Bishop's willingness to interrogate her own discomfort in the face of otherness, a willingness necessitated by her restless desire to transcend the mundane exchanges of self versus other, or a one-way perspective. Even though Bishop's passion for accurate observation does not yield firm political conclusions within her poetry, it does demonstrate what David Kalstone described as "a language, open-eyed, that is unembarrassed by anomaly" (Kalstone 199). Such endurance is necessary for confronting one's own limited perspective, and for accepting the predicate of lack upon which one's relations to others is based. Although visibly uncomfortable for a variety of reasons – the impending death of the white woman; the disruptive rearrangement of power relations between mistress and servant, white woman and woman of color; the recognition of her own implication in the "helplessly proliferative" "problems" of difference – the visitor in "Faustina" perseveres through twelve stanzas, rising "At last" to go. But her awkward departure is, typically, foiled by her offering of rock-roses – a tenacious flower that grows in rocky soil and is, as Costello points out, "viable and mutable, defying the barren whiteness of the scene" (Costello 72).

The "problems" of difference that start "a snake-tongue flickering" at the end of "Faustina" show up repeatedly in Bishop's work, with an increasingly explicit proximity to Bishop's own life as the years go on. In the first three *Brazil* poems of *Questions of Travel*, for instance, Bishop interrogates the relationship between self and other and its impact on notions of difference through the lens of travel in South America, where she lived for nearly fifteen years with her lover Lota de Macedo Soares, to whom the collection is dedicated. Whereas dismantling the trope of whiteness in "Faustina, or Rock Roses" de-essentialized the normative ideal, Bishop's poems about travel confront explicitly the viewing subject's effort to inhabit bodily otherness. Tellingly, "Questions of Travel" went through many versions under the heading "Problems of Travelers" before Bishop finally settled on the published choice (VC 57.8 and 73.2). This early title suggests that the voyeuristic eye of the visitor in "Faustina" becomes Bishop's locus of inquiry while writing *Questions of Travel*; think of the "Rich people in apartments" who "Watched through binoculars" in the "Burglar of Babylon" (*P* 113), or even the speaker in the posthumously published "Apartment in Leme" (written during Bishop's Brazil years) who describes the homeless men she watches sleeping on a beach (*P* 306–311).

Nowhere, however, is this gaze confronted more explicitly than in *Questions of Travel*'s title poem wherein the speaker asks, "Should we have stayed at home and thought of here? / Where should we be today? / Is it right to be watching strangers in a play / in this strangest of theatres?" (*P* 91). Obviously the speaker thrives, even depends on "watching strangers in a play / in this strangest of theatres," as the gorgeous series of descriptions that follow these lines attest. But at the same time, the speaker is aware of the limits of her own perspective; she can only "ponder" "blurr'dly and inconclusively" on the observations she collects. Although the "inexplicable old stonework" the speaker admires is "inexplicable and impenetrable, / at any view," it is, to the eye of this observer, "instantly seen and always, always delightful" (*P* 91). These lines, coming as they do on the heels of "Brazil, January 1, 1502," must be read in conjunction with the concluding lines of the latter poem wherein Bishop condemns the colonizer's gaze and attendant, gleeful pursuit of "an Indian for himself" (*P* 90). While Bishop's disgust toward the "Christians, hard as nails" is scarcely concealed in this poem, her description of "those maddening little [Indian] women" who "kept calling, / calling ... and retreating, always retreating" suggests a discomforting likeness between the colonizing hand in "Brazil, January 1, 1502" and the speaker of "Questions of Travel" for whom the foreign remains "inexplicable and impenetrable, / at any view" (*P* 90).

Aware of her own complicity as a white, well-fed tourist of European descent making her home, and her art, in Brazil, Bishop is cognizant of the liminal position she occupies between native and tourist, self and stranger, and ultimately, as the liaison between us, the readers, and the subjects of her observations. Consequently, while she idealizes the customs and objects in her view ("always, always delightful"), the speaker in "Questions of Travel" recognizes that such idealization is mediated by her own eye/"I": "*the choice is never wide and never free*" (*P* 92). Moreover, even though the speaker calls the land and its inhabitants "strange" in the second stanza, this sentiment is complicated in the opening lines of the poem by the familiarity with which the speaker describes the "crowded streams," the "waterfalls," and the "many clouds" like "mile-long, shiny, tearstains" that, "in a quick age or so as ages go here," "probably will" turn to waterfalls as well (*P* 91). Just as Bishop does not maintain neat lines of demarcation between the symbolic and the "real" and the abject and the ideal, she frustrates the fine line between romanticizing and identifying with the other in this poem. As such, "Questions of Travel," along with "Arrival at Santos" and especially "Brazil, January 1, 1502," dramatizes what Costello describes as the "double impulse of nostalgia and novelty": "Bishop's travelers are driven by contradictory impulses. They want change, renewal, originality, but also mastery ... over the world they approach, in terms of the world they left behind. Bishop sees this double impulse of nostalgia and novelty as inescapable; she also sees both aims as illusory" (Costello 128).

Bishop's romanticizing of this "strangest of theatres" is checked by the continual questioning of her motives: the trees' "exaggerated beauty," the breathless determination to see "the sun the other way around," the "always, always delightful," are subject to scrutiny within the interrogative, self-questioning tenor of the poem as a whole. Just as we are enticed by the exotic otherness of these images, we are asked to "ponder," however "blurr'dly and inconclusively," if such idealizations are, after all, "right." The mastery of this poem is the way in which it maintains a productive tension between these two gestures. While romanticizing the other, the speaker consistently makes us aware of the part she plays in constructing the other's ideality or "strangeness." Even though the land and its inhabitants are described as "strangers," they are also positioned as actors "in a play / in this strangest of theatres," a play for which the poem itself functions as script.

The contingency between travel and home – or other and self – that runs through "Questions of Travel" becomes a crucial backdrop to the overtly personal poems of *Geography III*. This last published collection of Bishop's lifetime includes some of her most well-known pieces, such as "In the Waiting Room," "Crusoe in England," "The Moose," and "One Art" – poems generally heralded as final proof of Bishop's autobiographical bent. As we have seen, however, Bishop's poetry probes the processes of ego-formation from the start; the emphatic "I" of "In the Waiting Room" is named "Elizabeth" precisely because the poet is, at this later stage of life, so conscious of her lack as a prerequisite to self-formation as well as the details of her relations to the abject. It is fitting, then, that at the end of Bishop's life we meet the seven-year old "Elizabeth" who, although horrified by the images of "black, naked women with necks / wound round and round with wire" in the *National Geographic*, reads it "right straight through" because, she says, she is "too shy to stop" (*P* 179). While sitting in the dentist's waiting room among adult strangers waiting for her "foolish, timid" Aunt Consuelo, the young Elizabeth is seized by the understanding that she is "an *I*," "an *Elizabeth*," "one of *them*." "*Why*," she asks herself, "should you be one, too? / I scarcely dared to look / to see what it was I was" (*P* 180). Elizabeth's understanding of being an "I" is wholly dependent in this poem on her articulation of what she despises in the images of those around her: the foolish timidity of her aunt and the black, naked, "awful hanging breasts" of the women in the *National Geographic*. Not only is Elizabeth's "I" expressed, typically, through its association with what she is not, but what makes those others *other* is revealed in this poem more clearly than in any piece that Bishop ever wrote.

Looking at the original drafts of this poem, it becomes apparent just how central the struggle to see the otherness of the ideal self *and* the familiarity of the despised other was for Bishop while writing "In the Waiting Room." More worked over than any other portion of the poem, the description of the black women's breasts went through six versions before Bishop settled on the final one. What was initially "Their breasts filled me with awe" becomes "Their breasts filled me with awe and terrified me," and then "their black breasts horrified me" ("frightened" is written in the margin). Working through variations of these phrases Bishop eventually decided on the somewhat less explicit "Their breasts horrified me" of the published version (VC 58.14). What these drafts reveal is the degree to which the image of these black breasts both attracted *and* revulsed Bishop, and the interlacing of blackness and femaleness at the core of this tension. This image clearly fascinated Bishop; like the young "Elizabeth," she cannot stop looking at, or rewriting them, and according to the sequence of drafts, what the poet is initially cognizant of is the "awe" she feels in their presence. "Awe" is an especially revealing word in this context, meaning a "fearful or profound respect or wonder inspired by the greatness, superiority, grandeur, etc. of a person or thing" (*Webster's New World Dictionary*, 1979). Echoing Bishop's notorious conclusion to "The Bight" ("All the untidy activity continues, / awful but cheerful"), "Elizabeth's" awe suggests at the outset that allure and aversion are bound inextricably, a suggestion that is certainly borne out by the poem as a whole. These drafts also underline the link that exists for Bishop between race and gender and, given the focus on "I" in this poem, the central role this link occupies in the articulation of identity for the poet. With this understanding, it becomes all the more clear why earlier poems like "Cootchie" and "Faustina" are key in comprehending the pulse of Bishop's poetry at large.

The small "Elizabeth" struggles with the apprehension of herself, and it is this struggle that charts the flow of the poem. While "suddenly" realizing the "similarities" that link her to Aunt Consuelo and "those awful hanging breasts," "Elizabeth" simultaneously sees such kinship as "'unlikely'"; it is just when she comprehends the overlap between her "self" and others that she grasps the lack that, paradoxically, fosters her subjectivity, an insight literalized by the "sensation of falling / off the round, turning world / into cold, blue-black space" that permeates the poem (*P* 180). Realizing that the utterance of her "I" is enabled by her relationship to what she deems most horrific, "Elizabeth" describes the oneness of being as, indeed, "unlikely." This understanding is what allows her to recognize herself within those others to whom she would otherwise react with revulsion and avoidance. Both attracted and revulsed by the black women's breasts and the foolishness of her aunt, "Elizabeth's" "I" is simultaneously crystallized and destabilized through her interactions with them, and in turn, their images become inextricable; it is after the moments when "Elizabeth" most keenly articulates her proximity to those she is repelled by that her "self" is most anchored

("I said to myself: three days / and you'll be seven years old" *and* most uprooted ("I was saying it to stop / the sensation of falling off / the round, turning world" [*P* 180]). Maintaining this tension throughout the poem, "Elizabeth" resists the appeasement of self-sameness in favor of "constant re-adjustment," never once losing sight of what it is "Outside" (*P* 181) that keeps her safe, in the waiting room, while the wintry night and war-torn world spins ceaselessly around her.

The horror that "Elizabeth" feels when gazing at the black women's breasts does not preempt her desire to keep looking – indeed, it seems to fuel her desire to do so. What began, then, for Bishop as "awe" becomes, for "Elizabeth," a never-ending journey along the slippery path from ideality to abjection and back again. Just as Bishop's speakers routinely tread the threshold between "you versus me," frustrating the possibility of subsuming one in the other in the dialectic of self-sameness, "Elizabeth's" look remains slightly ajar from the greater gaze constructed by those around her in the poem. Her "sidelong glance" emanates at an angle against the horizontal plane of "shadowy gray knees, / trousers and skirts and boots," so that just as it reveals the "similarities" between her "self" and the others, her look insures the distance between them as well. It is no coincidence that this kind of crooked vision brings us back to Bishop's earliest pieces, in which perspectives are skewed and subjects seem fantastic. Like her ancestor the Gentleman, "Elizabeth" steers her course through revelation by way of her eyes. While Aunt Consuelo is "inside / what seemed like a long time," the young girl picks up the *National Geographic* and "carefully / studied the photographs" (*P* 179). It is this act that leads her to the images of black breasts, and then, to her next look, "at the cover: / the yellow margins, the date" (*P* 179), in an effort, as Lee Edelman explains, "to contextualize the text so as to prevent her suffocation, her strangulation within it" (Edelman 104). Throughout the poem "Elizabeth" maneuvers her look to stop herself from "falling off / the round, turning world" or sliding into the seductions of easy oppositions. It is her "sidelong glance," for instance, that enables her to see "what it was I was" without looking "any higher" – allowing her, that is, to be both one of "them" and something quite separate from the "trousers and skirts and boots / and different pairs of hands / lying under the lamps" (*P* 180). The camera-like lens of "In the Waiting Room," with its abrupt turns and twists, its sudden zooms and cuts, constantly reminds us of the particular, and limited, perspective – "Elizabeth's" – through which we are viewing her world.

Consciously reviewing our habits of identification while admitting the necessity of the act is what allows us to identify with others without either repudiating their otherness or thoroughly assimilating it within our own sense of self. The "problems" of "difference" within Bishop's poetry are thus always "helplessly proliferative," affirming neither the abject nor the ideal but rather, the degree to which one's sensation of autonomy depends on the play between the two. As such, her poems are inflected with a tenor that is often read as reticence – the confusion of intermediary shades in place of stark, familiar contrasts. In a letter from Brazil to her friend and doctor Anny Baumann, Bishop once wrote that it "seems to be mid-winter, and yet it is time to plant things – but my Anglo-Saxon blood is gradually relinquishing its seasonal cycle and I'm quite content to live in complete confusion, about seasons, fruits, languages, geography, everything" (*OA* 243). The beauty of Bishop's art resides, in part, in her ability to translate this "confusion" into questions that challenge us all to relinquish our "seasonal cycles." The brilliance of Bishop's poems lies in her knowledge that "home" is where such efforts lead us, "wherever that may be" (*P* 92).

4

SUSAN ROSENBAUM

Bishop and the Natural World

Nature Through a Glass Eye

In a talk that Bishop apparently drafted but never delivered in Brazil in the 1960s (*EAP* xi), she wrote: "writing poetry is an unnatural act. It takes great skill to make it seem natural. Most of the poet's energies are really directed towards this goal: to convince himself (perhaps, with luck, eventually some readers) that what he's up to and what he's saying is really an inevitable, *only* natural way of behaving under the circumstances" (*Pr* 327). The talk concludes with a telling figure for the artifice involved in making poetry seem natural:

> My maternal grandmother had a glass eye. It fascinated me as a child, and the idea of it has fascinated me all my life. She was religious, in the Puritanical Protestant sense and didn't believe in looking into mirrors very much. Quite often the glass eye looked heavenward, or off at an angle, while the real eye looked at you.... Off and on I have written out a poem called 'Grandmother's Glass Eye' which should be about the problem of writing poetry. The situation of my grandmother strikes me as rather like the situation of the poet: the difficulty of combining the real with the decidedly un-real; the natural with the unnatural; the curious effect a poem produces of being as normal as *sight* and yet as synthetic, as artificial, as a *glass eye*. (*Pr* 331)

Bishop associates the "natural" with "being as normal as *sight*," yet emphasizes that the natural can only come into view through the mediation of artificial instruments, such as her grandmother's glass eye, or poetic language. Bishop read Newton's *Optics* and worked briefly at the Optical Shop in the Key West Submarine Base during World War Two (*Pr* 416); her work is rife with optical instruments including spectacles, microscopes, binoculars, telescopes, cameras, and magnifying glasses (Riggs). These instruments connote the scientific effort to visually discover the physical patterns and laws of the natural world by enhancing the power of the human eye, and the related aim of conveying the visible world through the accuracy and precision of realist detail. Although Bishop was inspired by the scientific understanding of nature, and particularly by natural history, she was equally inspired by "the decidedly un-real": her grandmother's glass eye is not only synthetic, but blind, a placeholder for an eye that paradoxically emphasizes its absence. The "blind" glass eye looks to the side, or heavenward, suggesting vision beyond the mechanics of the eye as it encounters the material world.

Inseparable from Bishop's realist emphasis on bringing nature into focus through visual imagery, detail, and tropes is her surrealist-inspired effort to blur or obfuscate nature as visually knowable through shifts in and distortions of scale and perspective; turns from external, physical vision to the internal eye (of imagination, memory, dream, desire) or to the eye of an animal; and self-reflexive attention to the rhetorical stages, images, and figures that materialize nature. Thus, alongside Bishop's accurate description of the natural world inspired by science and natural history, emerges a nature that she figures as dreamed, imagined, embroidered, painted, staged, mapped, fingered, written upon, photographed, traveled, gardened, fished, domesticated, catalogued, measured, colonized, caged, discarded, polluted. In short, nature comes into view in Bishop's work as it is mediated by technology, art, and human history. For Bishop, nature serves as the essential medium for considering the particular extensions of and limits of the human, as nature is transformed into culture, or conversely, as it resists such transformation. Put differently, culture is the central term – or artificial optical lens – through which nature comes into or out of focus in Bishop's work.

A key problem in defining "the natural world" is deciding whether humans are part of nature or whether nature is the realm of the nonhuman, and this choice in turn reflects beliefs about how humans should engage nature (Boschmann 9, Keller 603–605). Kate Soper usefully summarizes the complex, even contradictory, overlaps between nature and culture at work in common uses of the word "nature": "The natural is both distinguished from the human and the cultural, but also the concept through which we pose questions about the more or less natural or artificial quality of our own behaviour and cultural formations; about the existence and quality of human nature; and about the respective roles of nature and culture in the formation of individuals and their social milieu" (2). Although Bishop's work draws attention to and at times imagines the ways in which the natural world may oppose or subvert human efforts to know, represent, or possess it, she does not present an idealized nature untouched by forms of human mediation.

In engaging nature, Bishop arrives at the bedrock of language as an inevitable human transformation of nature into culture, even when an attempt is made in language to resist appropriative and anthropomorphic extensions of the human (e.g., Stevens's "Nothing that is not there and the nothing that is"). Nonhuman nature can only be fathomed, pointed to, or intuited through an understanding of human capacities and limits. Bishop follows Marianne Moore in focusing on the contact between and complex mixtures of nature and culture – a mix that can be fluid but also contested, even at times becoming a violent "border war" (Haraway 150). And, like Moore, Bishop develops an "environmental ethic" (Schulze 15) based on a respect for the integrity and otherness of the natural world, and critical of the human exploitation of nature. Yet Bishop did not see nature as a mirror of human morality; like John Ashbery and other late Modernists, Bishop reveals her debts to Surrealism and the French tradition through her exploration of the otherness, unknowability, and moral ambiguity of nature, pursuing Rimbaud's "Je est un autre" (I is an other) to find inhuman nature not simply outside the self, but often at its center. The Bishop that emerges here – gazing through her grandmother's glass eye at the natural world both inner and outer – is stranger and more experimental than readers may have recognized: through her mixtures of the real and the "decidedly unreal," she investigates our cultural lens on nature in its various dimensions.

"A minor female Wordsworth": Nature in the Romantic and Post-Romantic Tradition

In considering her own uses of nature, Bishop explicitly identified herself as an inheritor of the Romantic tradition, writing to Anne Stevenson in 1963 that "I also feel that Cal (Lowell) and I in our very different ways are both descendants from the Transcendentalists" (*Pr* 396). Similarly, Bishop wrote to Lowell in 1951 about the poems for *A Cold Spring* that "on reading over what I've got on hand I find I'm really a minor female Wordsworth – at least, I don't know anyone else who seems to be such a Nature Lover" (*OA* 221–222). What does it mean to be a "minor female Wordsworth," and how did Bishop's identification as "minor" and "female" inform her uses of the Romantic tradition? Given the gendering of nature in the Romantic tradition, Bishop's status as a female, lesbian poet profoundly influenced her negotiation of that tradition. "Minor" connotes a diminution in scale and value, suggesting Bishop's awareness of the kind of belittling reception she would meet as a female "Nature Lover" dedicated to miniaturist description (Rosenbaum 61–64). But "minor" also refers to a diminished musical key, suggesting that Bishop, who was as indebted to Modernism as to Romanticism, was playing a Modernist variation on the Romantic nature poem. In this sense, the modifier "minor female" does not simply indicate Bishop's anxiety about the values of the critical establishment, but poses a challenge to and departure from Wordsworth's (major, male, Romantic) poetics.

Many critics have argued that "nature" emerges as a distinct concept in poetry only when the natural landscape and the human capacity for "natural" experience is threatened by industrialization, urbanization, and new technologies, and begins to be seen as something finite and in need of preservation (Gilcrest 2–3, Boschmann 11–13, Bate 145). Romantic poetry in the English and American traditions explores man's rift from nature due to the forces of modernization, and attempts to renew man's connection to the natural environment, to provide what Emerson called an original relation to the universe. This aim is particularly clear in the tradition of the greater Romantic lyric; as described by M. H. Abrams, such lyrics present:

> a determinate speaker in a particularized, and usually a localized, outdoor setting ... The speaker begins with a description of the landscape; an aspect or change of aspect in the landscape evokes a varied but integral process of memory, thought, anticipation, and feeling which remains closely intervolved with the outer scene ... the lyric speaker achieves an insight, faces up to a tragic loss, comes to a moral decision, or resolves an emotional problem. Often the poem rounds upon itself to end where it began, at the outer scene, but with an altered mood and deepened understanding. (201)

Abrams's definition can easily be applied to Bishop's "At the Fishhouses," which in theme and style alludes to Wordsworth's leech gatherer in "Resolution and Independence" (Rotella 221). Bishop's speaker describes the fishhouses, where "an old man sits netting" "at the water's edge," a location where land and sea, the human and the natural, meet and mix (*P* 62–63). The speaker's conversation with the old man occasions a "process of memory, thought, anticipation, and feeling" that deepens and transforms the speaker's connection to the landscape: the speaker reveals that "He was a friend of my grandfather. / We talk of the decline in the population / and of codfish and herring / while he waits for a herring boat to come in" (*P* 62). The old man has made his living from nature, with his knife embodying this way of life: "He has scraped the scales, the principal beauty, / from unnumbered fish with that black old knife, / the blade of which is almost worn away" (*P* 63). Bishop's speaker draws attention to the aesthetic properties of the fish scales, allowing the old man to be seen as a humble, "home-made" artist figure who transforms nature into culture out of necessity, wearing "sequins on his vest and on his thumb." Like Wordsworth's leech gatherer, who finds that leeches have "dwindled long by slow decay" (line 125), the fisherman signifies a relation to nature that is disappearing – one of local use for sustenance, rather than large-scale commercial production. Although Bishop's speaker does not state specifically the "tragic loss" or "emotional problem" that occasions the poem, we can infer that it involves the speaker's attenuated relation to this place and its embodiment of a vanishing relationship to nature. Yet the poem is not simply nostalgic for old habits; as Rotella points out, "the old man's netting and scaling ... imply harmonious, although not innocent, intersections of the human and natural" (221). The fisherman's worn knife, the scales like "creamy iridescent coats of mail," and the "ancient wooden capstan / cracked, with two long bleached handles / and some melancholy stains, like dried blood, / where the ironwork has rusted" bear the signs of the literal mixing of saltwater and air, sea and humanity, but figuratively connote weaponry, armor, and wounds, indicating a more violent encounter (*P* 62). The beauty of the scales as a coat or cover depends on their violent separation from the fish.

Conventionally, the greater Romantic lyric finds a means of reconciling man's alienation from nature. Geoffrey Hartman argues that the Romantic poet's self-consciousness cuts him off from nature, but also provides the means of resolving this rift: "The traditional scheme of Eden, fall, and redemption merges with the new triad of nature, self-consciousness, imagination; while the last term in both involves a kind of return to the first" (185). The return to nature through imagination is the source of romance: "Depicting these trials by horror and by enchantment, Romanticism is genuinely a rebirth of Romance" (186). Hartman, Bate, and others note that nature takes on a religious function in Romantic poetry (Bate 145; Hartman 184–185). As Emerson argues, nature is not "the frail and weary weed in which God dresses the soul," but rather the source of "truth, and goodness, and beauty" and "ever the ally of religion": "the moral law lies at the centre of nature and radiates to the circumference" ("Nature").

Bishop resists a spiritual resolution to man's alienation from the natural world and does not depict a nature that "radiates" moral law: "At the Fishhouses" renders nature increasingly alien to humanity, moving from the old man to a boat ramp made of tree trunks descending into water, and finally into the sea itself, that "element bearable to no mortal, / to fish and to seals" (P 63). Just as a swimmer entering the cold sea must slowly acclimate the body to the frigid temperature, so Bishop gradually moves from the human into the nonhuman, signaling, as Rotella argues, features of the landscape that potentially serve as moral, Christian emblems – from the seal who seems to listen to the speaker singing Baptist hymns, to the "million Christmas trees" that "stand / waiting for Christmas" (*P* 63). Rotella emphasizes that although Bishop maintains the structure of Transcendentalist lyrics and was inspired by religious poets including Herbert and Hopkins, she subjects this tradition to skeptical questioning: "she might be called a religious poet without religious faith" (189). Thus, Bishop alerts us to the imposition of Christian meanings on the seal and trees, our desire to anthropomorphize and to find a moral reflection in what is essentially an indifferent nature (Boschmann 145, Rotella 223). Stylistically, critics have connected Bishop's preference for simile over metaphor to her reluctance to posit an analogy between the physical and "metaphysical" realms (Rotella 197, Bate 65, 233).

Although the structure of "At the Fishhouses" recalls the greater Romantic lyrics that find reconciling and mediating truths in nature, the conclusion of the poem refuses such truths (Rotella 221–223). Bishop describes a kind of baptism, but a baptism into an experience of nature informed not by religion, but by natural history (Costello 114). "The cold hard mouth / of the world" is a self-reflexive metaphor about the desire to make nature "speak" through metaphor. Showing the world's "mouth" to be hard and its "breasts" to be rocky, Bishop exposes humanizing metaphors as fragile impositions on an entity more powerful and permanent than the human. In this poem and others, such as "The Mountain," Bishop employs what Paton has usefully termed a "critical anthropomorphism" ("Beppo"). Like Stevens's Snowman, Bishop's speaker makes an effort to undo human projections onto an indifferent nature by imaginatively taking the sea inside the mouth and "burn[ing] [the] tongue," in a notable reversal of a fish breathing in air, a violent experience described in "The Fish" and implied through the scales that coat the Fishhouse landscape. More than a "taste" of the sea could kill the speaker. Although Bishop implicates herself in man's violent, if necessary, use of nature through fishing and the transformation of scraped fish scales into aesthetic details, the effort to taste and imaginatively enter the medium "bearable to no mortal" implies a desire to resist asserting the human through the scraping of the blade. Bishop subsumes the human to a nature that remains powerfully alien, that opposes transformation into culture, and permits fish and poems to be "drawn" with difficulty from its "cold hard mouth."

In its vision of knowledge and poems that are "historical, flowing, and flown" – whose claims are temporal, impermanent, and subject to nature (Costello 115) – "At the Fishhouses" builds on an alternative strain of Romanticism opposed to what Keats called the "Wordsworthian or egotistical sublime" visible in the poetry of Keats, John Clare, Charlotte Smith, and others (Curran, *Poems* xxviii, "I altered" 20; Bate 170–172; Morton 186). One legacy of this alternative Romanticism can be seen in "deep ecology" and in poets like Robinson Jeffers who idealize a nonhuman wilderness (Keller "Green Reading" 603, 610; Boschmann 9–12, Bate 148). In contrast, Bishop emphasizes mixtures of and potential conflicts between nature and culture, as in "The Moose," which emerges from the woods and "sniffs at /

the bus's hot hood," leaving behind "a dim / smell of moose, an acrid / smell of gasoline" (*P* 192–193; Cleghorn 70–71). Bishop's poems tend to denaturalize "nature" understood as a Romantic ideal or ideology used to resolve conflicts at the level of language, nature, and imagination (McGann).

How does gender influence Bishop's denaturalization of Romantic nature? Keats's criticism of Wordsworth's egotism has been fleshed out by feminist critics who argue that a feminized nature served as a preconscious ideal, the material body to be transformed and subsumed into Wordsworth's self-conscious attempts to unify the human with the natural world (Homans 13, Mellor 145–151). Wordsworth is less interested in nature's "irreducible alterity" than in art as "nature passed through the alembic of man" (Emerson). Nature created through poetic art has become culture, but this transformation depends on a gendered hierarchy, one that conflates woman with nature and naturalizes, through moral codes, women's reproductive and maternal roles (Ortner 73). Bishop was not only entering the Romantic tradition as a "minor female Wordsworth," but also as a lesbian poet, one deemed "unnatural" according to Christian morality. Thus, her poetic treatments of nature often comment, implicitly or explicitly, on gendered and sexual norms.

A satirical essay on Pope's gardens written while she was a student at Vassar in 1933 indicates that Bishop was both well-versed in the treatment of nature as feminine, and interested in revealing that "somehow [nature] is scarcely what [Pope] has led us to believe. She's not nearly so agreeable, her sensibilities do not seem to be in harmony with his" (*PPL* 547). Mutlu Konuk Blasing points out that two key poems in which Bishop explicitly feminizes nature – "The Moose" and "Brazil, January 1, 1502" – challenge the poetic tradition in which nature is feminized and colonized (269–270, 273–274). Indeed, numerous critics have emphasized that as Bishop critically interrogates nature's historical definition and representation, she connects it to a longer history of imperialism, conquest, and patriarchy, drawing attention to the Christian conquest of the New World as involving a figurative "rape" of a feminized nature (Bate 65–67, Rotella 225, Paton 138). Blasing connects Bishop's self-conscious attention to her own "rhetorical processes" as a "subversive" reflection on "the given discursive framework – with its polarities of civilization versus nature, male versus female, historical and narrative sequence versus the visionary moment" (282).

When Bishop imagines knowledge as "drawn from the cold hard mouth / of the world, derived from the rocky breasts," she challenges such polarities. This metaphor not only indicates the problems with anthropomorphizing an alien, indifferent nature, but specifically points to the limits of the trope of nature as a "nurturing" mother. In addition, Costello argues that the imagery of the "cold hard mouth" and "rocky breasts" "denies the gendered ascendancy of Mind as source over Nature" (115; Paton, "Landscape" 139). Paton (139), Costello (115), and Merrin (168) see the flow and flux of the sea as indicating Bishop's preference for knowledge understood as subject to the changes of nature, rather than nature enabling permanent truths "to him who looks / in steadiness" (Wordsworth). Bishop's description of the sea as "bitter," "briny," and "dark, salt, clear" alludes to Elizabeth Barrett Browning's curse ("A curse from the depths of womanhood, / Is very salt, and bitter, and good" (*Poems* 280; Lootens) and suggests the complicated gendered inheritance "derived from the rocky breasts." In their mixture of human and inhuman, bodily and geological imagery, Merrin reads these lines as "a compressed and hauntingly odd story of origin in which father and mother, male and female, are peculiarly conflated" (166). She connects this "questioning or blurring of gender boundaries" to Bishop's interest in "thirdness" and "gender in-betweenness ... her sense that in indefinition resides possibility, the chance for almost alchemical change into some other reality, some third thing or tertium quid" (167). Similarly, Feit Diehl sees Bishop's work diverging from the "inherently dualistic" tradition of the American sublime (104) in that "Bishop's poems inscribe a map of language where the limitations of sexuality yield before a disengendered, highly eroticized imagination" (109).

If we trace Bishop's treatments of the natural landscape, we find an interest in not only criticizing its historical exploitation as feminized other, but in expanding and shifting a view of the natural landscape so as to *naturalize* female and lesbian erotic desire. Bishop chose not to publish many of her erotic poems, and critics have speculated that this choice was shaped by Modernist aesthetics, the intolerance of the times, an inherent sense of privacy, and perhaps the nature of the erotic itself. Scholarship inspired by the recent publication of this material has demonstrated the importance of the erotic to Bishop's understanding of nature. Paton sees Bishop's treatment of landscape as recoding an image of lesbian desire, "the desire to find, cherish, and love the 'feminine'" ("Landscape" 134). She argues that poems such as "Song for the Rainy Season" enable women to create a home that is "erotic and sublime" ("Landscape" 148), at once protected by and open to nature (Ellis, "Aubade" 173). Similarly, Cleghorn connects Bishop's "erotic awakening" in the unpublished Bone Key poems to "a new approach to nature in the modern world"; instead of the mechanization of erotic desire that Bishop explores in "Edgar Allan Poe & The Juke-Box" (80), technology – and the trope as a "technological extension of reality" (86) – works in concert with "natural growth" to "express sexual awakening" (79). The erotic also emerges through the juxtaposition of "intimate, low-voiced, and delicate things" (*Pr* 352), such as giving a lover a shampoo, with the vast, inhuman scope of "planetary time" (Ellis 176). Unsettling human scale and perspective expands the scope and meaning of the erotic: in the unfinished "Vague Poem (*Vaguely love poem*)," Bishop envisions the crystal formations called "rock roses" as akin to "exacting roses from the body / and the even darker, accurate rose of sex" (*P* 325; Goldensohn 82–84). Through "rocky breasts" and "crystallography and its laws," Bishop redraws the lines of the human and the natural as a means of reimagining "natural" sex and gender roles and of crystallizing new possibilities for eros.

Natural History: Bishop and the Surrealism of Everyday Life

Bishop spent time in Paris in the 1930s and her interest in Surrealism is well known. Surrealism would prove central to Bishop's expansion of the "natural," influencing not only her early fantastical poems, but providing an essential grounding for her career-long exploration of the unconscious, irrational, and perverse; the experience of sleep, dream, and imagination; and the ubiquity of mixed feelings and moral ambiguity. Even a late, apparently realist narrative poem such as "The Moose" can be read as "a dreamy divagation ... a gentle, auditory, / slow hallucination" (*P* 191): as Craig Dworkin has argued, the imagery of dentition in this poem connotes the inside of the mouth, as if the narrator of "In the Waiting Room" had fallen through her aunt's mouth into the "cold hard mouth" of the world, a landscape at once internal and external, human and nonhuman, familial and strange.

In the "First Surrealist Manifesto," André Breton stated: "I believe in the future resolution of these two states, dream and reality, which are seemingly so contradictory, into a kind of absolute reality, a surreality, if one may so speak" (*Manifestoes* 14). Bishop alludes to this simultaneity of the real and unreal in her discussion of her grandmother's eyes: "Quite often the glass eye looked heavenward, or off at an angle, while the real eye looked at you." Susan McCabe and Lynn Keller emphasize that Bishop's rejection of inherited dualisms was inspired by Breton's statement "Everything tends to make us believe that there exists a certain point of the mind at which life and death, the real and the imagined, past and the future, the communicable and the incommunicable, high and low, cease to be perceived as contradictions" (McCabe, *Poetics* 90; Keller, *Re-Making* 135; Breton, *Manifestoes* 123). Bishop adapted and transformed surrealist ideas and methods in ways that were quite consistent with the responses of other U.S. poets, from Eugene Jolas and Charles Henri Ford to Wallace Stevens,

W. C. Williams, John Ashbery, and Barbara Guest (Rosenbaum "Exquisite Corpse"; Mullen 63).

As a late phase of the Romantic movement, Surrealism located the source of natural experience in the unconscious, and employed idealizations of women as "closer" to these irrational states (Chadwick 13, 16). In her departures from Surrealism, Bishop has much in common with other female and queer poets and artists who were inspired by Surrealism, but objected to Breton's homophobia and to the movement's circumscribed understandings of women (Rosemont; DuPlessis; Chadwick; Caws). Thus, it is significant that Bishop addresses Surrealism in the context of natural history, and specifically, Darwin, in what has come to be known as her 1964 "Darwin Letter" to Anne Stevenson. Bishop was a particular admirer of Darwin; she called him her favorite English writer, read *The Origin of Species* and *Voyage of the Beagle*, visited his home in England, and traced his journey to the Galápagos (*OA* 255, Millier 346, 357, 367, 445–446). Like the Surrealists, Bishop emphasized that there is "no 'split'" between conscious and unconscious experience, fact and dream. Reading Darwin against his rational aims, Bishop expands an understanding of his task and in turn of natural history, to encompass "the strangeness of his undertaking ... the lonely young man, his eyes fixed on facts and minute details, sinking or sliding giddily off into the unknown" (*Pr* 414). Bishop's reading of Darwin enables "a peripheral vision of whatever it is one can never really see full-face" (*Pr* 414): the unknowability of the natural world.

Just as Bishop filters Darwin through the surreal, she redefines the surreal through Darwin. As Robin Schulze points out in a discussion of Moore's uses of Darwin, Darwin signified "a scientific tradition that saw no need to ascribe moral impetus to natural forms or processes – a tradition ... that took God's spirit out of nature altogether" (6). Thus, natural historians implicitly challenged conventional readings of a feminized nature and of "natural" feminine roles. Susan McCabe argues that Darwin's theories of natural history appealed to both Moore's and Bishop's "sense of sexual and aesthetic deviation": "Darwin's vivid presentation of slow transitions over extended geological time, peculiar forms, gradual adaptations, and transitional states held out a less binary model than either sexology's invert or Freud's female homosexual" ("Queerly Fit" 548). Darwin's emphasis on "nonreproductive sexuality" (549) and his downplaying of "the maternal" (550) made natural history a particularly attractive alternative to "Freud's human-centered oedipal structure and the sexual drama it dictates" (548). As "outsiders" to the "collective mythology of Surrealism," Bishop joined other women artists interested in Surrealism – such as Eileen Agar, Lee Miller, and Leonor Fini – in looking beyond Freud to natural history, indicating a common desire for an expanded view of nature that included the queer and the complexity of the feminine (Chadwick 126, 129, 142, 161). Like Darwin and the late nineteenth-century French poets, the Surrealists offered an unsentimental view of the natural world, including its perverse, gothic, and grotesque elements. For instance, in his explicit rejection of a Romantic view of nature as morally good, and in his embrace of urban artifice and of sexuality untethered to reproduction, Baudelaire (one of Bishop's favorite poets *Pr* 328) opened up nature to include artifice and sexual possibilities not dictated by "natural" biological roles (31–33).

In "The Man-Moth," Bishop explores a nature defined by mixtures of the real and the fantastical, the rational and irrational, the human and animal, the urban and pastoral, the masculine and feminine. The title connotes Freudian case studies such as "The Wolfman." Bishop may have had Oscar Wilde in mind (Wilde died in Paris in a "small, obscure hotel ... under the name of Manmoth" [NYT 12/1/1900, pg. 1]), while both Lombardi (115) and Ellis (98–99) see the influence of Baudelaire's urban poetry. The Man-Moth also resembles the human-animal hybrids common in the work of female Surrealist painters, and the fantastical creatures that emerge in the "Natural History" frottages of Max Ernst, which interested Bishop at this time (*Pr* 393, 413, 430, *OA* 478; Millier 89; Mullen 65, 67–71; Page 202–203). Chadwick comments of these hybrids: "symbolic intermediaries between the unconscious and the natural world, they replace ... the image of woman as the mediating link between man and the 'marvelous'" (79).

Bishop, like Stevens and Williams, preferred a Surrealism latent in the real, revealed through a shift in or distortion of perspective, as opposed to a Surrealism conveyed through the surrealist image, involving the juxtaposition of discordant elements (Breton *Manifestoes* 20). The newspaper as a key purveyor of "the real" occasioned these distortions for both Williams and Bishop. In reply to a 1942 *View* questionnaire ("what is the disappearing point of the unconscious?"), Williams answered, "the *NY Evening Star*" that gives us "all sorts of fascinating detail, the most accurate and expensive that the imagination can buy." He added, "In this congeries of factual events is caught the sublime and the irrational." Perhaps Williams had Bishop's poem in mind, for "The Man-Moth," published in 1936, was inspired by a *New York Times* misprint for "mammoth," as Bishop mentions in a note to the poem. The misprint is the accident in the machine, the irrational eruption of nature that emerges from the center of rational, urban culture, and resembles the puns that occasioned the work of Roussel and Duchamp. Not coincidentally, the "man-moth" is the mechanically induced offspring of a "mammoth," an extinct prehistoric mammal, with one theory of its extinction involving overhunting by man.

Paton argues that for Bishop, "to rethink the animal is to rethink the human": "the animal defines the human by antithesis, as 'other,' the beast to be conquered by enlightened civilization. Rethinking the potential of the animal thus means rethinking mindedness and physicality, domination and ethics, otherness and identity" ("Beppo," 197). In that the Man-Moth is part animal, he enables a glimpse of what Rimbaud termed "Je est un autre," or "I is an other." By describing this human-animal hybrid, Bishop brings to light the hidden or repressed aspects of human nature, those often associated with the animal: critics have read the Man-Moth as a figure of the unconscious; as a meditation on homosexuality, sexual deviance, sexual indeterminacy, and "thirdness"; as a vampire or embodiment of the gothic, monstrous, and grotesque; and as a figure for the struggle with bodily susceptibility or addiction (Costello 51, 55; McCabe 563–564; Merrin 169; Lombardi 115; Ellis 99). In the latter vein, we might read the Man-Moth as a reflection on the mechanical nature of bodily desire and compulsion: in "Edgar Allan Poe & The Juke-Box," the speaker comments "All pleasures are mechanical" (*P* 285), and the Man-Moth avoids looking out the subway window at "the third rail, the unbroken draught of poison ... a disease / he has inherited the susceptibility to" (*P* 17).

In describing the Man-Moth as what defies rational human culture, Bishop seeks to blur or obfuscate nature (human and nonhuman) as an object of scientific knowledge, an object that can be visually known, represented in realist terms, named, catalogued, and preserved in the annals of natural history or psychiatry. The poem follows the conventions of natural history – precise, visual description offered by a narrator with intimate knowledge of the creature's habits and habitats – while applying them to a fantastical creature. Moreover, Bishop builds on a favored surrealist technique, manipulations of and even violence to the eye as a mean of signaling the inadequacies of realist vision. Some famous instances of this practice include the scene in Buñuel and Dalí's "Un Chien Andalou" (1929) when a razor cuts into a woman's eyeball, and the final scene in Man Ray's "Emak Bakia" (1926) when we see a woman's open eyes, only to realize as she opens her eyes that we had been gazing at false eyes painted on her lids. Many of Bishop's representations of encounters with animals, whether real or imagined, involve eyes and the potential exchange or refusal of looks, a means of probing the extensions and the limits of the human vision of nature.

Ending the poem with a hypothetical shared gaze between Man-Moth and reader indicates the possibility of realist knowledge of this creature, a possibility that Bishop quickly complicates in the manner of the Surrealists. The poem concludes:

> If you catch him,
> hold up a flashlight to his eye. It's all dark pupil,
> an entire night itself, whose haired horizon tightens
> as he stares back, and closes up the eye. Then from the lids
> one tear, his only possession, like the bee's sting, slips.
> Slyly he palms it, and if you're not paying attention
> he'll swallow it. However, if you watch, he'll hand it over,
> cool as from underground springs and pure enough to drink. (*P* 17)

Bishop's speaker positions the reader as a potential hunter of the Man-Moth, if only in the sense of the amateur naturalist who seeks realist knowledge of the rare or obscure. The narrator implies that this kind of human vision, aided by the power of the flashlight (signifying enlightenment reason) involves power over and possession of the animal: if the human viewer sees the Man-Moth's tear slip from his eye, then the creature must acknowledge this gaze and hand over his "only possession." But the Man-Moth also watches the human viewer, to see if he can swallow and keep his tear, and his slyness connotes nature's ability to survive in adverse circumstances.

The "tear" – with its ambiguous origin, role, and meaning – figures this complex relationship. It is not clear whether the Man-Moth tears up from the physical sensation of the bright light, from emotions (fear or shame or sadness), or as a self-protective mechanism. Tears connote the feminized culture of sentiment out of which Romantic lyric springs, and its elegiac, consolatory aim: to mourn and ameliorate the human rift from nature or to cultivate feeling for an endangered nature. In Bishop's early story, "The Last Animal," about a zoologist's treatment of one of the last surviving mammal specimens on earth, the mammal also sheds tears when caught, but does not survive its life as a caged specimen (*PPL* 552, 556). Bishop plays with the meaning of tear as a violent rip, to connote the bodily "possession" with which the Man-Moth does not wish to part. The description of the tear as "cool as from underground springs and pure enough to drink," also suggests a mysterious or rare elixir, the kind that the protagonist of the Brazilian fantastical poem, "The Riverman," seeks out in following "the river's long, long veins" (*P* 106). Finally, the tear may serve as a form of physical defense, "like the bee's sting." Costello points out that the sting is "painful to the receiver, perhaps fatal to the bestower," implying "danger associated with purity" (54–55; Colwell 62–63). The tear as a potential sting suggests protection provided by the Man-Moth's eye, in a kind of reverse violence inflicted on the human who seeks to visually know and possess it. Given the ambiguous meaning and function of the tear, the poem leaves the reader wondering whether the tear will harm, transform, or heal the person who receives it. Is the final exchange of looks a plea to the reader's sympathy or an instance of the Baudelairean address to the reader as an "Hypocrite lecteur!", a figurative sting?

The poem closes with an eye that we cannot "see" in the sense of penetrating or delimiting its meaning. By refusing to foreclose on the tear's meaning, Bishop implies that the ultimate violence is one of looking at nature, whether inner or outer, with the aim of defining, collecting, or cataloguing it in terms of its otherness (as animal, female, irrational). In challenging what I have called a scientific, realist vision, Bishop makes possible a different understanding of the human relationship to nature built on a respect for its difference, opacity, and mystery (Paton, "Beppo" 197; Colwell 62). The unreadability of the Man-Moth's eye reveals the investments of our gaze, much like the eye of "the Fugitive" that Ernst brought forth in his *Natural History* frottages (Figure 1), and the eye of the wood in Leonor Fini's "Sphinx Regina" (1946, Figure 2). Ernst's frottage reveals the designs of an external and internal nature that meets and defies our rational gaze, while the fantastical eye in Fini's natural landscape upsets her precise, quasi-photographic perspective. Similarly, Bishop unsettles the precise detail of "The Man-Moth" by focusing in on the eye of her fantastical subject. Her allusion to surrealist photography is not coincidental: the Man-Moth climbs up facades with "his shadow dragging like a photographer's cloth behind him"; his world is black and white and inverted, like a photographic negative; and the description of his eye connotes not only the unfamiliarity of an unknown creature, but the lens of a camera as it focuses: "It's all dark pupil, / an entire night itself, whose haired horizon tightens / as he stares back, and closes up the eye." From this perspective, the Man-Moth may photograph us, handing us a reflection of ourselves in the eye of the other, rendering us both man and moth.

Mullen comments that Bishop's poems "tilt, magnify and upset rational perspectives through the delineation of particular natural detail" (71), while Naomi Schor argues that the sexual hierarchies of patriarchal culture shape the field of representation, resulting in a feminization of detail (80). Through exaggerated attention to detail, Bishop upsets the gendered assumptions historically embedded in rational perspectives, involving the ability to visually know, control, or possess nature or its representation (on the importance of this issue to ekphrasis, see Bergmann-Loizeaux, DuPlessis, Halpern, Lundquist, Samuels). Thus, Darwin, with "his eyes

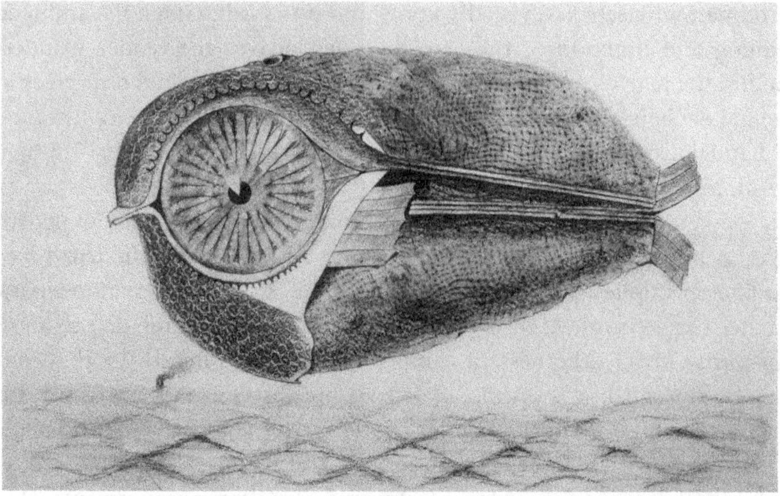

Figure 1. Max Ernst, "L'evade/The Fugitive" (1926).
(© 2013 Artists Rights Society (ARS), New York / ADAGP, Paris.
Reproduced courtesy of National Gallery of Art Library, Washington, DC.
Reproduction, including downloading of Ernst and Fini works is prohibited
by copyright laws and international conventions without the express
written permission of Artists Rights Society (ARS), New York.)

fixed on facts and minute details, sinking or sliding giddily off into the unknown," converges with grandmother's glass eye that looks sideways or heavenward: both appear to "catch a peripheral vision of whatever it is one can never really see full-face but that seems enormously important." By particularizing and blurring the rational, scientific gaze, Bishop brings an expanded view of nature, both human and nonhuman, to the fore: thus, the visual vertigo of Darwin appears often in Bishop's work, from Crusoe, who tallies the island's features by day and at night has nightmares of counting infinities of islands and "registering their flora, / their fauna, their geography" (*P* 182, 185); to the protagonist of "In the Waiting Room," eyes "glued to the cover / of the *National Geographic*," who suddenly experiences "the sensation of falling off / the round, turning world / into cold, blue-black space" (*P* 180); to the Sandpiper, who watches ("no detail too small") the sand shift beneath his feet: "As he runs, / he stares at the dragging grains. / The world is a mist. And then the world is / minute and vast and clear" (*P* 129) (Rognoni 246; Dickey 312–324; Millier 448; Pickard).

Bishop's presentation of this shifting focus on nature, seen through the eye of the Sandpiper and the poet, contributes to and can be productively illuminated by environmental, ecopoetic, and ecofeminist studies

Figure 2. Leonor Fini, "Sphinx Regina" (1946). Oil on canvas.
(© 2013 Artists Rights Society (ARS), New York / ADAGP, Paris.
Reproduction, including downloading of Ernst and Fini works is prohibited
by copyright laws and international conventions without the express written
permission of Artists Rights Society (ARS), New York.)

(Bate, Boschmann, Gilcrest, Keller, Rotella, Huang). Ecocriticism explores humans' ethical implication in natural systems and processes, and offers new conceptions of poetic form connected to poetry's ecological role (Buell, Bryson, Rasula). Bishop's oft-noted preference for a precarious stability within a moving, unstable world may articulate what Jed Rasula calls "poems as ecosystems, precariously adjusted to the surrounding biomass" (7). In 1962, Bishop read and praised Rachel Carson's *Silent Spring*, the book widely credited with starting the U.S. environmental movement (*OA* 415), and in a draft titled "The moon burgled the house" (*EAP* 110), she connected a dystopian vision to the exploitation of nonhuman nature: "the end of the world / proved to be nothing drastic / when everything was made of plastic." But this was simply a more explicit rendering of an environmental ethic that had guided Bishop's career-long interrogation of "nature" and "culture" as concepts that undergird diverse systems of thought and shape human treatment of the natural world. More pointedly, Bishop's adaptations of Surrealism and her Modernist departures from

Romantic nature poetry demonstrate that an ecological approach can help to account for the history of Modernism, and may re-orient our understanding of modernist experiments by women poets and artists in particular (Schulze, Rasula, Keller).

Guided by Darwin and her grandmother's glass eye, Bishop has left us with indispensable optical instruments through which to chart the vertiginious mixtures of modernity.

5

BONNIE COSTELLO

Bishop and the Poetic Tradition

Existing Monuments

What is the nature of Bishop's relationship to poetic tradition? The answer is various, ranging from homage to subversion, from allusion to parody; it includes verbal and aural echoes, thematic and structural parallels. No one would mistake her poetry for that of another era, certainly; the poetic tradition is not a formidable body of pristine originals to which she feels herself doomed to produce dim copies. She studied Greek in college and even attempted a translation of Aristophanes, but she would not say, with Alexander Pope, "Nature and Homer were … the same." But neither is Bishop driven to reject the past and "make it new," as Ezra Pound exhorted in 1934, to innovate in the way of radical Modernism. Bishop is more a poet of questions than of dogmas, and the question of the presence of the past, including the literary past, informs her work from beginning to end. She read Eliot's "Tradition and the Individual Talent" in college; she cites it in her essay "Dimensions for a Novel" (*Pr* 481), and she imagines it indirectly in her early fiction and poetry. "The Monument," for example, perhaps alludes to Eliot's idea of tradition. Eliot writes:

> The existing monuments form an ideal order among themselves, which is modified by the introduction of the new (the really new) work of art among them. The existing order is complete before the new work arrives; for order to persist after the supervention of novelty, the whole existing order must be, if ever so slightly, altered; and so the relations, proportions, values of each work of art toward the whole are readjusted; and this is conformity between the old and the new. (Eliot 5)

Both the crude nature of Bishop's image in "The Monument" ("it is of wood built something like a box") and the divided voice ("why did you bring me here to see it?") suggest ambivalence and skepticism about Eliot's "existing order," even as the present tense and imperatives affirm the presence of the past (*P* 25, 26). Bishop's comically cobbled-together structure of organic materials hardly has the dignified aura of the "ideal" order Eliot imagines. The poem follows no consistent meter, but it falls repeatedly into iambic pentameter in memory of poetic convention. Its memorial function is even less secure. The "artist-prince may be inside / or far away" (*P* 26). "The Monument" enters a long poetic debate about the nature of art's endurance, enters an "existing order" of *ars poeticae* that might include Shakespeare's Sonnet 55, Coleridge's "Kubla Khan," Keats's "Ode on a Grecian Urn," and Yeats's "Sailing to Byzantium." The makeshift monument Bishop describes (more Modernist assemblage than stately pleasure dome, more Calder than Coleridge) stands oddly within this august tradition. It absorbs Wallace Stevens's critical and antiauthoritarian meditations on statues in "The American Sublime" and "Owl's Clover," and his sense that art is "smeared with the gold of the opulent sun" (Stevens 129). We might hear Eliot's argument confirmed in her closing imperative to "Watch it closely" (*P* 27). The existing order is changed by the new work of art, and (Bishop would add) by all artworks' material existence in time.

Bishop also considers her relation to literary tradition in an early parable-like story, "The Sea and Its Shore," about a man named Boomer whose job it is to pick up the sundry papers that litter the beach each day. (Boomer is the phonetic sounding of Bulmer, the name of Bishop's maternal relatives, hence at least privately linking the persona to the poet.) Rather than merely discard what he collects, he attempts, like a *bricoleur*, to assemble and interpret the scattered fragments. This time there is no vertical monument, not even a heap of broken images; certainly there is no "order," only drift. The papers are "antimneumonics" rather than memorials, a mix of literary and nonliterary texts that obscure the surface of reality (*Pr* 14). Yet there is something heroic as well as absurd in Boomer's efforts to decode the fragments as if they could offer some clue to abiding truth. Bishop may be revisiting the theme of tradition as debris a few years later in her shore poem, "The Bight." "The bight is littered with old correspondences," although this time the litter, both personal and literary, has sunken down into the sediment beneath the surface, to be "dredged" up by the poet in a process that is "awful but cheerful" (*P* 59). The outside/inside ambiguity of the bight as a space reminds us that the literary past, like memory itself, is part of our reality, not just something we choose to encounter.

Appropriations and Revisions

Bishop's *North & South*, more than any other volume, shows her direct engagement with particular poets and poems of the past. She is apprenticing her art to masters, but also answering the past as she searches to find a voice for her own time. In this sense at least she is, as John Ashbery famously said of her in the early 1970s, a "poet's poet's poet." Many of the poems in the volume can be read as appropriations of nineteenth-century poems. Some are refigurations, as in "The Imaginary Iceberg," which borrows Melville's "The Berg" as a metaphor for the mind's longing for the absolute; some offer cultural critique, as in "The Fish," which revisits the great fish tale *Moby Dick* and offers an alternative to the quest for mastery.

Bishop often evokes iconic poems of the past to reassign their images and update their values for her own time and experience. Thus, in "Casabianca," a poem that alludes sardonically to Felicia Hemans's poem "Casabianca" (also known as "The Boy Stood on the Burning Deck"), Bishop mocks Victorian values such as heroic self-sacrifice and creates a meta-poem that points out the culture of mindless recitation that promotes those values. But more importantly, she transfers the narrative of naval duty to the realm of obsessive erotic love. Hemans's poem is a long ballad recounting the heroic story of the faithful son of an admiral (Bishop's poem takes his name and the first line of the poem) as he stood by the ruined ship in the Battle of the Nile: "A creature of heroic blood, / A proud, though child-like form" (Hemans 396). Unlike the figure in Hemans's poem, she can only "stammer elocution" and the result is less heroic than disastrous.

Similarly, Bishop both mocks and appropriates Tennyson's "The Lady of Shalott." "The Gentleman of Shalott" is a parody, but also a serious meditation on the split psyche of the artist. As a figure merging not only Tennyson's Lancelot and his Lady, but also mirror and world, the gentleman reflects many of the ontological and artistic issues Bishop would explore throughout her career with her own "sense of constant re-adjustment" toward the past and her own tentative figurations of self (*P* 12). Bishop would continue this practice of revisiting classic texts from a modern and often gender-conscious perspective. So, for instance, another mirror poem, "Insomnia" from *A Cold Spring* can be read in relation to Philip Sidney's Sonnet 31, "With how sad steps, O moon, thou climbst the skies." Like Sidney, Bishop explores the logic of inversion, but adds several turns – formal and narrative – to the inversions of Sidney's conceit. Hence, instead of the sonnet form (which she used often), Bishop creates mirror inversions with an *abba* rhyme scheme that suggests the chiasm of reflection. Bishop's moon offers no ideal place of love, nor is it a fellow abject with whom the poet can commiserate. Rather, the moon is distant and haughty, able to dwell in solitude in a way the suffering poet cannot.

The Bible was a major source of the tradition – literary and cultural – that formed Bishop as a poet, the "heavy book" of her childhood and the foundation of much of the literature she loved (*P* 58). If she was "not religious" she was nevertheless drawn not only to chapter and verse of the Bible, but also to the hymns, rituals, iconology, parables, and poems that constitute its afterlife (*Conversations* 23). In "Over 2,000 Illustrations and a Complete Concordance," she becomes restive in the "grim lunette" of the great code (a lunette is a crystal case for the host in Catholic ceremony) that seems at odds with the reality of her "travels," and she turns her attention to the fluent, unordered sequence of memory fragments (*P* 57). But the separation of text and world is not so absolute; the snapshots have Biblical analogues and if in memory "everything is connected by 'and' and 'and'" in contrast to the book's "diagram," Bishop is nevertheless reminding us that the Biblical narrative (unlike the illustrations) is similarly paratactic (*P* 58, 57). At the end of the poem she returns to take up "the heavy book," which continues to present an image of human longing for innocence and wholeness. But the "Old Nativity" has none of the authoritarian rigidity of the earlier engravings; rather, it becomes an ecumenical or even secular "family with pets" associated with the ordinary life, but transfigured as art (*P* 58). In Bishop, then, we have the paradox of a religious skeptic who found endless inspiration in the rhetoric of religion and in the Bible and its afterlife. "Genuine religious poetry," Bishop wrote in her notebook, is as "far as poetry can go" in the search for the spiritual in the material, "and as good as it can be" (VC). She would draw on this poetry not only to question the paradigms of the past, but also to give shape and meaning to her own personal and modern experience.

We find Christian symbolic tradition in the "rainbow, rainbow, rainbow!" suggesting Noah's covenant in "The Fish" (and the fish itself with its five wounds); in the "melancholy stains, like dried blood" on the cross-like rusted capstan of "At the Fishhouses"; and the old medieval carving of the cock in "Roosters," where it figures the Christian society's betrayal of its own foundational values (*P* 62). "Roosters" is one of Bishop's most direct responses to Biblical tradition and it quotes from Matthew 26:58, "Peter followed him afar off unto the high priest's palace, and went in, and sat with the servants, to see the end" (King James version), but it is not an anomaly. Bible stories and images are everywhere: the story of the Magi at the Nativity in "Twelfth Morning; or What You Will"; Genesis in "Santarém" – "Hadn't two rivers spring / from the Garden of Eden? No, that was four"; the parable of the Prodigal Son from both the Old and New Testaments in "The Prodigal" (*P* 207). Bishop does not just borrow these stories and images; she updates and reconsiders them, carries on a conversation with a tradition that has profoundly shaped her view of the world even as her experience draws her away from its patriarchal values and magical beliefs.

So when Bishop set out to tell the story of Robinson Crusoe and sought to do so "without all that Christianity" (*Conversations* 88), she created an image highly conscious of what it omits. If the absence of Christianity as a faith distinguishes "Crusoe in England" from *Robinson Crusoe*, Christian forms remain, to be refigured for a modern secular age still unmoored by any structuring belief. Crusoe is, as he was for Defoe, a latter-day Adam – Adam alone. But there is little evidence of God's plan for him, or of his special dominion or power of naming, even as the rationalized Adam of the Enlightenment. *Robinson Crusoe* is also a foundational text for the development of the novel in English, so that her poem implicitly addresses the narrative of heroic individualism, adventure, and mastery that characterize that tradition.

There are, of course, many ways to read "Crusoe in England" and biographical readings have prevailed. But if the poem's characters and landscape link to experiences in Bishop's life, it is a mistake to read the literary allusions and borrowings as a mere mask of autobiography. Whatever its intimate themes may be, the poem is also a reflection on the discontinuity between the cultural past and the present, the sense of an inheritance that does not provide for modern man and may even have misguided him. Defoe's Crusoe cannot reconstitute the culture from which he has been shipwrecked. But at the same time, he is a product of that culture, a post-Enlightenment rather than a modern man. At the end of the poem, the discouraging image of relics in a local museum suggests a view of the past as dead and irrelevant to the present. "How can anyone want such things" (*P* 186)? But Bishop is not Crusoe, neither Defoe's nor her own persona. She has, in fact, salvaged a great deal off the shipwreck of the past, and refashioned it to her particular experience and time. Again, then, we see Bishop both critiquing the work of the past and finding images and narratives within it that she can use to describe her world.

In adopting Crusoe as a persona, Bishop is certainly offering a critique of the Enlightenment past (especially its rational Christianity, social atomism, and scientism; its way of putting everything into an economic model; its hegemonic relations to others). One feels strongly the contrast between Defoe's confident, rational mastering hero and Bishop's world-weary, hopeless figure; a contrast made more intense by the overlap in details of setting and circumstance. But Crusoe is not only Defoe's character. By the time Bishop reinvents him, he has been an archetype for two centuries; a figure for the very condition of being cut off from the moorings of society and culture, having to "make do in a pinch," as she said of him in one of her notebooks (VC). Crusoe was thus a favorite figure of Rousseau who saw the castaway as a Romantic hero close to nature and outside society.

In adopting an archetypal fictional persona, Bishop follows a long-established literary convention. In fact, there is something of Tennyson's Ulysses in Bishop's Crusoe – the old wanderer restlessly looking back over his past adventures. And there is something of Eliot's Prufrock or Gerontion, not only in Crusoe's jaded tone, but also in the representation of modern consciousness, in which inner and outer landscapes are permeable, and timespace coordinates ambiguous. The measurable, rational world of Defoe's Crusoe is a dim memory.

One of the more playful disjunctions in Bishop's "Crusoe in England" comes when this character from the eighteenth century tries reciting to his iris beds a nineteenth-century poem: "'They flash upon that inward eye, / which is the bliss...' The bliss of what? / One of the first things that I did / when I got back was look it up" (*P* 184). Bishop reminds us here that, although poetic tradition may not be timeless, neither is it chronological in cultural memory. Defoe's Crusoe has no active "inward eye," of course. The anachronism here is playful, but in trying, in this "cloud dump," to remember the line from Wordsworth's "I wandered lonely as a cloud," Bishop's Crusoe opens the poem to a consideration of the legacy of Romanticism itself, its image of human imagination and spirit (*P* 182). By leaving out the word "solitude" from the recitation of Wordsworth's poem, Bishop draws our attention to it. *Is* solitude bliss, as Wordsworth proposed? Or is solitude really just loneliness? Is the human soul best realized in private communion with nature, or does the self crave connection with another human being? Bishop's Crusoe is unsuccessful as a Romantic hero – nature rejects his metaphoric projections; indeed, they do violence to nature. Memory does not transport him to a transcendent reality but displaces him, filling him with unsatisfied nostalgia. The Romantic "voice" of nature is unintelligible noise and the poem reverts to metonymy. Just as the structures of Enlightenment empiricism fail Crusoe, so also Romantic idealism, and its language of metaphor, leaves him disillusioned and homeless.

But if Bishop in "Crusoe in England" questions Romantic idealism and the egotistical sublime, she also points to the importance of Wordsworth. Other Romantic poets take their place in Bishop's consideration of the past. The little bird in "The Sandpiper" is a "student of Blake," looking for eternity in the grains of sand (*P* 129). The "artist-prince" of "The Monument," who may be from "Asia Minor or from Mongolia," alludes to Coleridge's Kubla Khan. Her either/or conclusions are more than a little reminiscent of Keats. But she returns most often to Wordsworth. In a letter to Robert Lowell, Bishop wryly described herself as a "minor female Wordsworth" (*OA* 222). Certainly she shares his interest in mysteries awakened in the contemplation of nature, and in the power of memory to untether us from time. We may interpret Bishop's Wordsworthian moments as occasions to challenge a masculine tradition, or more broadly as invocations of the Romantic legacy in the spirit of modern skepticism (as is often the case in Frost). Either way, it is clear that in many of her poems, Bishop positions herself within the Romantic transcendentalist line from Blake to Hopkins and from Emerson to Frost, even as she questions its metaphysical assumptions. This is particularly clear in her second book, *A Cold Spring*. The title poem owes as much to Keats as to Hopkins, whose "nothing is so beautiful as spring" is the epigraph qualified, but ultimately affirmed, as the poem unfolds the hard-won beauties of the season. Like Romantic poets, Bishop is often searching, as she wrote in her notebook, for "the spiritual in the material" (VC). But she sensed that the Romantics had distorted this effort, imposing the spiritual on the material. Her descriptive poems probe the landscape for metaphysical openings; anti-mimetic moments give a quality of strangeness and otherworldliness to the material world. But the poems often swerve from Romantic epiphany. In "At the Fishhouses," for instance, a poem that critics such as Willard Spiegelman and Charles Rzepka have associated with Wordsworth's "Tintern Abbey" and "Resolution and Independence," Bishop gives the material surface of the landscape a translucent, luminous character that readies the imagination for revelation; and indeed, in a visionary moment the water rises "above the stones and then the world" (*P* 63). These visionary experiences are enhanced by a Wordsworthian extended syntax and submerged iambic pentameter. But the poem concludes not with a confidence in nature's transcendental guidance, but with a feeling of "the cold hard mouth / of the world," and a skepticism about how much metaphysical truth the human mind can grasp: "our knowledge is historical, flowing, and flown" (*P* 64). If "Crusoe in England" seems to belie Wordsworthian idealism, other poems of *Geography III* such as "The Moose," "Poem," and "The End of March," do more to revise than reject the Romantic tradition, modifying and updating rather than repudiating its visionary project. Like Stevens and Frost, Bishop checks Romantic inflationary rhetoric but leaves room for a subjective relationship to nature, in which mystery and hope are maintained. But whereas Wordsworth invests this hope in moments of solitude, when man's soul communes with a higher spiritual power, for Frost (in a poem such as "Two Look at Two,") and for Bishop (in "The Moose," which seems cognizant of Frost), the connection to nature has its source in human association. Hence, the conclusion of "The Moose" when "the smell of moose" exists alongside "an acrid / smell of gasoline" (*P* 193).

Best Friends

Although Bishop eschewed confessional poetry and the exploitation of private autobiographical details for poetic profit ("you wish they'd leave some of these things to themselves," she remarked of the confessionals; "art just isn't worth that much"), she did not share Eliot's separation of the poet from his poetry; she was certainly interested in the lives of writers from the past (Cory and Lee 69; *OA* 562). She even offered a course in poets' letters. And despite resistance to autobiographical readings of her own poetry, she often stated that the best way to understand a writer's work was to read biography. Poems were not merely "texts" for Bishop, they were sometimes messages in a bottle that could convey comfort across distances of time and space.

Bishop's engagement with the devotional tradition and particularly with metaphysical poetry did not come from a strong sense of faith, but from the psychological directness of the work, and its masterful handling of language and form. George Herbert, perhaps more than any other poet, provided Bishop with an artistic model and a spiritual guide. Bishop first read Herbert when she was fourteen, and he remained her most cherished precursor. (He is "one of my favorites, if not my favorite" she wrote.) The simplicity and directness of Bishop's language, its colloquial diction and "naturalness of tone" undoubtedly owe something to contemporary models such as William Carlos Williams, as well as to the songs and ballads of Blake and Wordsworth (qtd. in Merrin 52). But in Herbert she found a combination of intimacy and wonder, and a drama of spiritual struggle. She was fond of citing his "Colossians 3.3." which declares that the Lord "taught me to live here so that still one eye / Should aim and shoot at that which is on high." (Bishop humorously linked the line to a Nova Scotia relative with one glass eye, but Herbert's concept of the "double motion" of life has relevance to her work.) Bishop's drama of thought and her self-correction, too, are traceable to Herbert. She studied his work so carefully that she dreamed about it, as she records in her notebook; the dream makes clear how important meter was to her craft: "Dreamed I had a long conversation on meter with George Herbert: we discussed the differences between his and Donne's and touched upon Miss Moore's, which was felt, in the dream, to beat Donne's but not his" (qtd. in Merrin 39). In the rhythms of poetry, Bishop heard the heartbeat of the poet – meter not only measures, but also marks the emotion and inner drama of the poetry. In her draft essay "Writing poetry is an unnatural act," she quotes Herbert's "The Sacrifice" at length for its "spontaneity, mystery, and accuracy, in that order" (*Pr* 328). Bishop may be responding to the rhythm here ("Arise, arise, they come. Look how they runne!"), iambic pentameter made turbulent with caesura and exclamation, the compulsion echoed in Herbert's triple rhyme, with the beholder separated by a pulled-in fourth line and slant rhyme "sunne" / "mine." It is difficult to track the influence of meter from one poet to another, but when Penelope Laurens finds in Bishop a deep emotionality in the meter of even the most apparently impersonal voice, we sense Herbert is a model. Herbert's rhythms, phrasing, and metaphysical conceits turn up often in Bishop's early poetry. Herbert's "The World" provides the porch for "A Miracle for Breakfast"; from "Affliction IV," "my thoughts are all a case of knives," Bishop takes the image of the sea in "Wading at Wellfleet." As this phrase makes clear, the mildness of Herbert's voice is often in counterpoint to violent feelings and emotions. Bishop's dream poem, "The Weed," is a secular and psychological re-imagining of Herbert's "Love Unknown" and also draws from "Holy Baptism I." Even though Bishop shared Herbert's feeling for the suffering and struggle of the psyche, she did not share his Christian faith. For her, the grotesque tortures of the heart find no relief in spiritual redemption. Yet Bishop has not simply turned Herbert's Christian allegory into a surrealist nightmare. The weed that divides the heart may seem more invidious and ambiguous in its signs than Herbert's God who tries the soul to strengthen it; yet the poet encounters the weed somewhat affectionately as it invades a grave-like garden of "final thought" (*P* 22). Bishop would often remark, quoting Herbert, that while life was full of trouble, the spirit must be made "new, tender, quick." In "The Weed," we see that Herbert is not just a stylistic example, but also a spiritual one, even for a poet without his faith, and perhaps precisely because Herbert's poems are dramas of a doubting and desolate soul recovering from its falls, Bishop found consolation in them.

Another "best friend" and early influence was Gerard Manley Hopkins ("Father Hopkins" and "dear Hopkins" as she calls him in prose and letters), who was crucial to Bishop's sense of great poetry even if "sometimes the point seems to be missing" (VC). She told Ashley Brown that she first read him in *Poetry* and saw a collection of Hopkins's work in 1927 (Brown 292). Hopkins's accurate descriptions of nature and visually startling metaphors clearly attracted her, but it was his "timing" and his auditory invention that had the most lasting influence on Bishop's work (*Pr* 468). Hopkins's timing helps "portray not a thought but a mind thinking"; it represents the mind in motion (*Pr* 473). Bishop's early essay on Hopkins's meter is the most sustained and subtle critical prose she would ever write, providing significant insight into her own formal choices. The essay makes clear "why using exactly the same meters and approximate vocabularies two poets produce such different effects" (*Pr* 468). Bishop had studied baroque prose in college and she applied the ideas of Maurice Croll to her reading of Hopkins's poetry. She quotes Croll: "Baroque art always displays itself best when it works on heavy masses and resistant materials; and out of the struggle between a fixed pattern and an energetic forward movement arrives at those strong and expressive disproportions in which it delights" (*Pr* 474). Bishop adds: "in all his form and detail, and above all in the moment he has selected for transference of thought to paper, Hopkins is a baroque poet" (*Pr* 474).

Hopkins's use of enjambment, coupled with a de-emphasis of end rhyme and an abundance of internal rhyme, served to break the supremacy of the line ending. Sprung rhythm freed up the number of unstressed syllables and allowed the line to expand or contract as the poet chose. Any number of syllables could comprise a line now, and anything from one to four syllables could contrive a foot. This, in addition to his use of *rove-over* lines and what he called *hangers* or *outriders* (syllables at the beginning of lines that are scanned as belonging to a foot beginning in the preceding line), allowed Hopkins to texture the poem as he saw fit, and allowed him to create swift, powerful rhythmic shifts within a line. As Bishop writes, "the poem can be given a fluid, detailed surface, made hesitant, lightened, slurred, weighed or feathered as Hopkins chooses" (*Pr* 473). All this, but still within the confines of a regular, predetermined number of stresses per line, should the poet desire.

We can hear Hopkins strongly in Bishop's early poetry, in "Anaphora," for instance: the lengthened syntax, internal rhyme and alliteration, sense of motion, stress over syllable count, enjambment and outriders, strong evocation of the senses at once visual and metaphoric, force of epiphany and sudden intrusion of the speaker's response.

> Each day with so much ceremony
> begins, with birds, and bells,
> with whistles from a factory;
> such white-gold skies our eyes
> first open on, such brilliant walls
> that for a moment we wonder
> "Where is the music coming from, the energy?" (*P* 52)

Bishop was also interested in Hopkins's unusual rhyming. "Hopkins is very fond of the odd and often irritating rhyme: 'am and ... diamond, England ... mingle and,' etc. These usually 'come right' on being read aloud, and contribute in spite of, or because of, their awkwardness, to the general effect of intense, unpremeditated, unrevised emotion" (*Pr* 473). Sometimes Bishop will use off-kilter rhyme for humorous effect, as in "Arrival at Santos" or "Pink Dog," but the "last, or"/"master" rhyme of "One Art" certainly seems in keeping with her observations of Hopkins's compelling awkwardness. Internal rhyme was crucial to the massive effect of the lines, and it is something we often find in Bishop. This line from "Little Exercise," for instance, demonstrates both Hopkins's surprising metaphors for the visual world, and his love of assonance: "little palm trees ... suddenly revealed/ as fistfuls of limp fish-skeletons" (*P* 42). Bishop is calling up Hopkins's example again in "Song for the Rainy Season," especially his love of alliteration, hyphenation, and sprung rhythm effects: "beneath the magnetic rock, / rain-, rainbow-ridden, / where blood-black / bromelias, lichens, / owls, and the lint / of the waterfalls cling, / familiar, unbidden" (*P* 99). We may even hear a tribute to Hopkins in Bishop's last poem "Sonnet," "caught – the bubble / in the spirit-level," which has many of the effects and images of "The Windhover" ("I caught this morning morning's minion / kingdom of daylight's dauphin, dapple-dawn- / drawn-Falcon") (*P* 214; Hopkins). Of course, Bishop's effects are less "baroque" than Hopkins's most of the time, but the memory of his dynamic intensity is everywhere in her work.

The third figure Bishop often cited as central to her ideal of accuracy, spontaneity and mystery was Baudelaire, seemingly a strangely profane third with Herbert and Hopkins until we recall how bizarre and uncanny are the narratives and metaphors of the two priest-poets. Bishop read French well and translated the Surrealist Max Jacob, but Baudelaire's "mystery" is a stronger influence. Ashley Brown noted that Bishop kept a photograph of Baudelaire near her writing desk. If Bishop was attracted to Herbert's cheerful natural imagery, "so cool so calm so bright," she was also interested in the "awful" side of things. As she remarked to Tom Robbins: "Poetry, as Baudelaire, Rimbaud and yes Shakespeare demonstrated, is as much a part of the brothel and the slaughterhouse as the garden and the glade" (*Conversations* 37). An element of the grotesque, of mortality mixing life and death, can be detected even in understated images. The iridescent flies in "At the Fishhouses," the rainbow in the oil spill in "The Fish," the image of "gooey tarts" as "red and sore" eyes in "Going to the Bakery" (*P* 173) are Baudelairean effects (effects Baudelaire drew from Poe, who also fascinated Bishop). As with Poe and Baudelaire, too, there are hypnagogic effects in Bishop's writing, moments when experience and dream converge and blur, sometimes through intoxication. This is particularly clear in a poem Bishop never finished, "Edgar Allan Poe & The Juke-Box," a Baudelairean argumentative response to reading Poe's poetics during a time when she often visited the local bars described as "cavities in our waning moon" (*P* 285). But these effects of dreamlike syntax and imagery are not just symptoms. Bishop introduces antimimetic elements that disturb our sense of the real. Baudelaire's trademark synesthesia adds to this dreamlike quality, as does a syntax that confuses the sense of transition from inner and outer worlds. Bishop's early, unpublished "In a Room" clearly shows this influence. Furthermore, Baudelaire offered, as Herbert and Hopkins and Wordsworth did not, an image of urban experience: its assaults on the senses, its confusion of the real and the unreal. Like Baudelaire, Bishop wrote several "window" poems, in which the subject looks out and blends the imaginary with the real – "Paris, 7 A.M.," for instance, shows the influence of Baudelaire.

Thus, when in "The Bight" we encounter the line "If I were Baudelaire," we sense that she has performed this thought experiment before, and that its significance to the poem goes beyond local detail (*P* 59). Baudelaire's name points to the synesthesia in "The Bight"; Bishop says the water "smells like gas," but imagines that Baudelaire would hear it "turning to marimba music" (*P* 59). However, the key to Baudelaire's connection to the poem is given near the end, where "the bight is littered with old correspondences" (*P* 59). Through a pun she alludes here to Baudelaire's "Correspondences" and the indeterminate "echoes" of the mind that resound from the contemplation of the physical world. Nature, he says, is a forest of symbols, but there is no symbol system or clear path through the forest; one is simply enchanted at the borderlands between the material and the spiritual. Bishop, for all her "accuracy" and descriptive precision, is a poet interested in the way experience can trigger metaphysical ideas and desires, directing us from surfaces to the unknown, the otherworldly.

Models of Modern Poetry

The young Bishop's relationship to what was, for her, contemporary poetry is of a different order from the aforementioned dialogues with tradition I have described. Eliot lectured at Vassar where Bishop interviewed him for the *Vassar Quarterly*. She was already reading Marianne Moore on her own when a Vassar librarian (a Moore acquaintance rather than a Moore fan) arranged for them to meet. Stevens's *Harmonium* she "learned by heart" as a college student, and he had of course been a notable visitor to Key West shortly before she lived there. Bishop's critical writing, especially "Time's Andromedas" indicates the deep interest she took in Gertrude Stein's innovative "auditory imagery ... making a direct effort to express one sense in terms of another" (*PPL* 658). We can see her adopting some of Stein's object lessons in *Tender Buttons* as she imagines her desk as a war zone in "12 O' Clock News." These figures offered various models of what it meant to be a modern poet, although her "Visits to St. Elizabeths," which depicts Ezra Pound as "the tragic man / that lies in the house of Bedlam," suggests what had become of Modernism's absolutes by the 1950s (*P* 131).

In her first two books, we can see Bishop working through these influences. Eliot's poetic theory offered an idea of tradition and of the poet's relation to his poetry; his practice modeled techniques of impersonality and symbolic abstraction. Bishop's "exteriorizing of the interior" as Moore described it, was certainly influenced by Eliot's efforts to reveal the peculiar timespace of subjective consciousness (Moore 364).

Eliot also offered a powerful image of the urban subject, isolated and yet embedded in an oppressive social reality and denatured landscape. Bishop's "Love Lies Sleeping" is directly traceable to Eliot's "Preludes," with its image of the polluted streets and lonely inhabitants. But Bishop refuses Eliot's despair and alienation, turning in "Love Lies Sleeping" toward, rather than away from, the social reality, and ending with anxious benediction rather than irony. In this way she reveals another influence, one even closer to her own generation, that of W. H. Auden. Bishop's "social conscience poem," "A Miracle for Breakfast," owes something to Herbert, as we have seen, but it owes much to Auden's example of the social sestina, "Paysage Moralisé," which deals with hunger and the destructive patterns of history. Bishop attempted an essay on Auden (it quickly became nothing more than a collection of quotations) called "The Mechanics of Pretense" in which she could be describing herself when she comments on his way of pretending to be the poet he would only later become. Auden showed Bishop's generation how to return to traditional forms and rhetoric, popular as well as literary, and still be modern. It may be to Auden that Bishop owed her famous "master/disaster" rhyme, which appears in Auden's "Letter to Lord Byron."

But Bishop told Ashley Brown of her college years: "I think that Wallace Stevens was the contemporary poet who most affected my writing then" (Brown 294). Dana Gioia tells of sitting in Bishop's class at Harvard: "She knew dozens of Stevens' poems by heart and would quote them casually in conversation" (*Conversations* 145). Bishop's title *North & South* owes something to Stevens' dialectical mapping, and even though she did not know him personally in Florida, she shared his interest in the Florida landscape. Stevens pops up in surprising places, such as in the epigraph to her college essay, "Dimensions for a Novel," "the lines are straight and swift between the stars" (*Pr* 480). Bishop rarely *sounds* like Wallace Stevens. She does not adopt his philosophical rhetoric or his abstraction; she does not write pure poetry or experiment with near nonsense. Hers is rarely a theoretical poetry, although the predicament of "The Gentleman of Shalott" and his fantastic figuration suggest Stevens more than Tennyson. Like Stevens, Bishop is a poet of transitions and of dynamic positioning within both physical and metaphysical dimensions of reality. Bishop was surely drawn to Stevens's meditations on the loss of religion and search for a supreme fiction, but she approached these subjects through description. In this light, we might think of Bishop's "Over 2,000 Illustrations and a Complete Concordance" as a continuation of Stevens' meditation in "Sunday Morning" or her "At the Fishhouses" as sharing something with "The Idea of Order at Key West."

Marianne Moore's role in Bishop's poetry and career holds a special status, as she was not only an important stylistic influence, but also a mentor and friend, and the major woman poet of the day. The progress of that relationship, from their early meeting at the lions in front of the New York Public Library, to their growing awareness of differences, is beautifully documented in their much-discussed correspondence and in the public appreciations they wrote of each other. Bishop saw the presence of Moore in her life as "one of the great pieces of good fortune in my life" and if she gradually pulled away from Moore's heavy-handed sponsorship and editorial meddling, she never ceased to appreciate the older poet for her art and her friendship (*Pr* 401). Inevitably, her descriptive practice influenced Bishop, and the two women were often compared. Randall Jarrell noted: "When you read Miss Bishop's 'Florida,' ... you don't need to be told that the poetry of Marianne Moore was, in the beginning, an appropriately selected foundation for Miss Bishop's work" (Jarrell 488). Moore offered an example of how that description might have ethical and spiritual significance, even if the didactic model would prove the wrong one ultimately for Bishop. We see Bishop adapting Moore's influence clearly in "At the Fishhouses," which owes something to Moore's "A Grave." Moore, of course, did not invent the fable form, but her menagerie, which paid homage to the particulars while allowing the fabulist's inventions, clearly invited Bishop to pursue this technique and adapt it to her own aesthetic preferences. Their letters share an interest in the devotional tradition, despite their differing vantage points of belief and skepticism. Some have read Bishop's tribute to Moore, "Invitation to Miss Marianne Moore" as ambivalent or even subversive, but we might rather say that it is a tribute aware of their different temperaments and perspectives. This is not so much an invitation as an invocation; indeed, Moore is a kind of aerial spirit bringing light and rectitude to a dark, disturbing world. Although the specific form of the poem derives from Pablo Neruda, "Invitation" is full of sensitive tributes to Moore's style: the "inaudible abacus" of her syllabics, her "dynasties of negative construction" and "unnebulous" imagery (*P* 80–81). The Protestant poet of manners and morals, Moore, and the skeptic poet of mystery and psychology, Bishop, approached life and language from separate vantage points, but their enduring friendship centered in the intersection of their angles of vision.

Inherited Forms

My focus has been on Bishop's relationship to individual talents in the poetic tradition, but her carefully crafted poems reflect her attention not only to the voices, but also to the forms and modes of her art. To write a sonnet or ballad or a pastoral elegy, she knew, was to call up other poems in those forms, to place her work within a history that she carries forward and alters. We are most aware of Bishop's attention to form when she chooses elaborate fixed forms such as the villanelle. "One Art" has received a great deal of attention because of the many extant drafts that show how Bishop's thought and feeling developed as she moved from free verse lines that register the chaos of feeling, to the pneumonic discipline of tight formal rhymes and repetitions. The counterpoint of form and subject matter in "One Art" (a narrow strictness in the treatment of uncontrollable loss) adds to the poignancy if also to the tonal ambiguity of the work, and many have noted how the pressure against containment heightens the emotional drama. But this is also part of the history of the form – before Bishop wrote "One Art," she likely read Dylan Thomas's "Do Not Go Gentle" and perhaps even Theodore Roethke's "The Waking," both treating inchoate and emotional material within the tight rules of the villanelle. In writing "Sestina," a poem that conveys the simplicity of a child's language and the complexity of unspoken awareness, Bishop may be following Ezra Pound's sestina in the voice of Bertrans de Born ("Sestina: Altaforte"), which employs an elaborate form for a colloquial voice.

Bishop experimented with the sonnet early in her career and returned to it often. She seems to have been drawn to the psychological drama and rhetorical invention possible within its narrow strictness. Her early "Three Sonnets for the Eyes" explores a classic conceit of the love sonnet, but treats it with a metaphoric violence reminiscent of Donne's religious poetry. Bishop's late poem "Sonnet" puts the traditions of the form under extreme pressure. Is a dimeter meter still a sonnet? What if the rhyme scheme divides the poem into six and eight instead of eight and six? Of course, as always, Bishop has used the form not as an arbitrary container, but as an embodiment of themes and emotions – the dimeter becomes a metrical register for a being "undecided," and the inverted rhyme scheme suggests a mirror inversion. But Bishop likely also knew that she was not the first to write an inverted sonnet. There is the example of Coleridge's "Work without Hope," for instance. Bishop understands that the formal conventions of poetic tradition have always been opportunities rather than mere constrictions – that as soon as formal rules were invented poets began to bend them.

Bishop sometimes drew on particular traditional forms because her subjects suggested them. When she witnessed a crime chase in Rio, it was the ballad that naturally came to mind – the form that puts the public in vicarious witness to the saga of strong emotions and even the violence of the individual (as in "Frankie and Johnnie" or "Stagger Lee"). When she wanted to memorialize Robert Lowell, it was not just the elegy, but the pastoral elegy that she chose, in part because Lowell himself had imitated Milton's "Lycidas" in one of his most famous poems, "The Quaker Graveyard in Nantucket." Poetic tradition was, for Bishop, not an intimidating "ideal order," or even a set of conventions to which she must submit, but a resource from which she could draw personal and aesthetic models and adapt them to her unique contemporary experience.

Her impact on the poetry that has come since – on writers as diverse as John Ashbery and James Merrill, including her contemporaries like Robert Lowell, Sylvia Plath, May Swenson, Adrienne Rich, and more recent poets like Amy Clampitt, Mark Strand, Henri Cole, Mark Doty, Elizabeth Spires, and Jane Shore, for instance – is immeasurable. Her reach extends to British and Irish poets as well, to Seamus Heaney, Eavan Boland, Paul Muldoon, and Tom Paulin, for instance. She has been translated into many languages and is thus making an imprint on poetry around the world. She is forever part of "poetic tradition."

PART II

Major Works

6

SANDRA BARRY

In the Village: Bishop and Nova Scotia

Knowledge is generally defined as the awareness or understanding we gain through our experience with the world. Experience is defined as direct engagement with the environment, with events and activities, and with each other. Elizabeth Bishop's art is an expression of her experience, her exploration of its complexities, her attempt to understand the nature of knowledge, and to describe what she knew or thought she knew about the world. The principal realms of experience for Bishop included sensation, emotion, memory, dream, and imagination. Experience began with her five senses (sight, hearing, taste, touch, smell), which were entangled in conscious and subconscious ways with revelation, contemplation, speculation, questioning, and qualification. These realms and actions combined in a seemingly infinite number of ways to produce different kinds of knowledge: historical, cultural, familial, geographical, physical, and aesthetic; none of which can, in the end, be separated from each other, that is, they relate to and inform each other in myriad ways. Bishop's final description of life, of lived experience, and the accumulation of knowledge is found on her gravestone in Worcester, Massachusetts: "All the untidy activity continues, / awful but cheerful" (*P* 59). Living and creating are eminently messy and ongoing processes.

In her poem "At the Fishhouses," written on the south coast of Nova Scotia in 1946, Bishop wrote: "It is like what we imagine knowledge to be" (*P* 64). This "it" was the sea: a source/site of life and death. The sea, knowledge, and, one could argue, imagination itself, are alike as "dark, salt, clear, moving, utterly free." She acknowledged with challenging semantics that knowledge is hard won and mysteriously real and unreal: "forever, flowing and drawn," and, finally, "flowing, and flown." This poem evokes the elemental nature of what Bishop sensed, remembered, dreamed, imagined – that is, knew – about her past, about her birth, childhood, family, and home, and how experience and the resulting knowledge ebbed and flowed throughout her life. This chapter explores some of Bishop's experiences and the knowledge she gained during her early years living in Great Village, Nova Scotia with her maternal Bulmer-Hutchinsons family, and shows how she embodied them in her art.

Looking at the arc of Bishop's poetry, from her first book, *North & South* (1946), to her last book, *Geography III* (1976), the impression is that the poems gradually become more autobiographical, more overtly drawn from or about her life. Thomas Travisano in *Elizabeth Bishop: Her Artistic Development* and Robert Dale Parker in *The Unbeliever: The Poetry of Elizabeth Bishop*, for example, set up Bishop's poetic development and career in three "phases" or "stages": "Prison," "Travel," and "History" (3) or "wish," "where," and "retrospect" (ix), respectively. The early poems ("The Imaginary Iceberg," "The Man-Moth," "The Weed," "The Unbeliever," and "The Monument") are conventionally read as brilliantly faceted surfaces about ideas, conceits, and abstractions, where personal experience is hidden, even absent. Some revision of this view has occurred (for example, Victoria Harrison's *Elizabeth Bishop's Poetics of Intimacy*), but this perception of "less to more" autobiographical incorporation and revelation in the poems persists. Some reasons for the persistence of this view are the privileging of Bishop's poetry over her prose, the general ignoring of her juvenilia, and the fact that the bulk of Bishop's oeuvre is unpublished (although this latter circumstance has changed with the publication of *Edgar Allan Poe & The Juke-Box: Uncollected Poems, Drafts, and Fragments*, resulting in more revision).

Another general observation about Bishop's poetry is that it is not confessional (McCabe xvi; Lombardi 31; Doreski 55). She herself made public and private statements about the emergence and practice of "confessional poetry" in the mid-twentieth century – most famously observing, "You just wish they'd keep some of these things to themselves" (Schwartz and Estess 303). Travisano has written extensively about Bishop's relationship with confessional poetry in *Mid-Century Quartet: Bishop, Lowell, Jarrell, Berryman and the Making of a Postmodern Aesthetic*, concluding insightfully that what she and these peers were up to was exploring the self rather than baldly confessing it; that they were creating a Postmodern narrative about the self. What this characterization points to is the complexity around Bishop's use of her life (her experiences and knowledge) in her art. This chapter augments this characterization of Bishop as explorer rather than confessor by suggesting that the experiences of her childhood were not only things that "really happened" to Bishop, but that the essence of these experiences was also aesthetic; that is, they produced the knowledge that life was like or, even more fully, was actually art itself.

That Bishop was a precocious child is amply testified to in her prose. Read together, "In the Village," "Primer Class," "The Country Mouse,"

"Gwendolyn," and "Memories of Uncle Neddy" form a memoir of her childhood and reveal that early in her life, she was intensely aware of the world around her. (There are important unfinished prose pieces that extend this published narrative; for example, "Reminiscenses of Great Village," "Homesickness," and "Mrs. Sullivan Downstairs," although the last two have now appeared in print.) The reasons for this heightened sensitivity are far too complex to explicate here, but Bishop's precocity was the result of her temperament, environment, and experiences (the intricate interplay between nature and nurture). Written and published during her adulthood, these stories remember, reconstitute, and revise the past from a higher or longer vantage point – from an adult perspective. By and large, Bishop chose to write most overtly about the facts of her past in autobiographical prose. Poetry was used for the distillation and compression that turned the personal and particular into the transcendent and universal. Yet separating Bishop's genres from each other, privileging poetry over prose, is something that Bishop herself did not do (she was writing both from the start). Bishop's art is also amazingly self-referential; she recycled regularly, so much so that the temporality (that is, the chronology of creation) feels non-linear. Even as Bishop suggested "Everything only connected by 'and' and 'and'" (*P* 58), one thing (fact, memory, trope) did not simply follow another and another in an orderly fashion, but surfaced and resurfaced, swirled and settled, in surprising ways.

Drawing from her Nova Scotian and familial past, expressing and exploring the knowledge she learned from that time and place and those experiences, Bishop began writing about her childhood experiences during her adolescence at school. Moreover, as soon as she began writing, putting her emerging world view into words and on the page, she began publishing some of it, offering some of her views to a public audience. Her poetry and prose appeared in *The Owl* (North Shore Country Day School) and *The Blue Pencil* (Walnut Hill School) in the late 1920s, when Bishop was in her mid-teens. How much lived experience and knowledge could she have accumulated at that age? A great deal. Even before she was born, circumstances set up a trajectory that provided her with more drama in the first decade of her life than many people have in a whole lifetime. Bishop learned about life and death, presence and absence, love and loss, home and exile, time and space, tradition and modernity (all of which became abiding themes in her art) during her early childhood. She experienced an "immense, sibilant, glistening loneliness" ("In the Village," *Pr* 71) and a "sweet / sensation of joy" (*P* 193). As described in "In the Waiting Room" (*P* 180), she learned the paradox of being at once an "*I* ... an *Elizabeth*" (that is, herself alone) and "one of *them*" (that is, inextricably linked to humanity). Late in life she defined this knowledge as a "dazzling dialectic" ("Santarém," *P* 207), acknowledging that boundaries between experiences (and selves) are fluid, even illusory, yet still real and abiding.

What was it about her childhood world that afforded her this view so early in life? Bishop claimed to have the capacity for total recall, at least at times, which she described as a Calvary, a burden. Even so, Bishop wrote about only a fraction of her experiences and knowledge. It is not possible to explore the entirety of her world even in a full-length biography. Yet that entirety had a direct and indirect influence on her art, even if she could not write about it all. The remainder of this chapter offers glimpses of the Nova Scotia part of Bishop's childhood world, describing some of its aspects and elements, the kinds of knowledge Bishop gained from her experiences, and how it became embodied in her art.

Elizabeth Bishop was born in Worcester, Massachusetts in 1911. Her father, William Thomas Bishop, was a wealthy businessman from that city. Her mother, Gertrude May Bulmer, a nurse, was from Great Village, Nova Scotia. This couple's demographics emerged not only from personal circumstances, but also point to the deep historical reality of the long-standing geographical, cultural, and political connections between the Maritime Provinces and the New England states. These links were complex, ever-shifting conditions, but at the turn of the twentieth-century, they remained firmly in place. In 1902, like hundreds of young women from the Maritimes, Gertrude went to the "Boston States" to train, where she met William and married him in 1908. Although they lived in Worcester, they regularly travelled to Great Village and Gertrude's family regularly visited her. Her oldest sister chose to live in Massachusetts and two younger sisters and two nieces also trained as nurses in Boston. The family's itinerant practice reflected the wider paradigm.

From birth, Bishop was not only part of a private drama, but was also caught up in historical forces; she was not only affected by intense family dynamics, but was also acted upon by larger cultural processes over which she had no control. One immediate consequence of all this intimate and public reality was mobility in the form of migration; not only back and forth between the two sides of her family, but also back and forth between two regions (her first North and South), between two nations (represented as Empire and Republic), and between the urban and the rural.

The impact of this mobility, this migration, on Bishop's life and art was pervasive and abiding. Her great themes of travel and geography can be located in this earliest conditioning (it is more than likely that she began moving between Massachusetts and Nova Scotia in utero). Bishop's first decade was spent moving around. This mobility has led some critics to argue that Bishop was homeless or rootless (Lombardi 86, 107; Doreski 80–81; McCabe 194–195, 203; Goldensohn 102). Throughout her life, she herself pondered states of being such as orphan, exile, and expatriate, and contemplated the ambiguous idea of home. But Bishop's mobility was not gratuitous – it was rooted in historical and personal causes that gave Bishop profound experiences – thus, knowledge – early in life. Bishop never settled for simple or reductive characterizations (so much in Bishop's art is equivocal, qualified, questioning, even as it settles on the page), and part of the reason why is because her earliest experiences were astonishingly complex and energetic. In 1978, she told Alexandra Johnson, "I've never felt particularly homeless, but, then, I've never felt particularly at home. I guess that's a pretty good description of a poet's sense of home. He [*sic*] carries it within him" (102).

Bishop was aware of the importance and power of mobility early on. In "In the Village," she pondered the mysterious movement and stasis of all manner of people and objects. The story can be read as a contemplation of motion. One of her most poignant evocations of her mother embodies this mobility in the potent metaphor of tide (a natural choice because of Great Village's proximity to the Bay of Fundy, known for its phenomenal tides): "First, she had come home, with her child. Then she had gone away again, alone, and left the child. Then she had come home. Then she had gone away again, with her sister; and now she was home again" (*Pr* 63). This passage takes basic facts (it is an exact chronology of Gertrude's movements between April 1915 and June 1916), the events Bishop experienced, and turns them into metaphor; that is, existential knowledge about how our lives ebb and flow in mysterious ways. The adult remembering the facts looks back and tries to order and transform the impact. In the story, however, Bishop seeks to reproduce the child's perspective; to recall the moment in time and reclaim the actual lived experience in all its mystery. The fact is, the experience itself was not only the foundation for memories, but also held the magic of revelation, which compelled its eventual transformation into art. The knowledge Bishop gained from her experience – of the historical and cultural imperatives, of the geographical setting, of her mother's behavior – was not only epistemic (what constituted reality; that is, events, actions, objects, and relationships), but it was also aesthetic (how the reality emerged; that is, its intrinsic character, energy, or nature).

One of Bishop's most direct statements about migration occurred in an essay she wrote in 1933 at Vassar College, "Time's Andromedas," an essay about the use of time in novels. Provoked by witnessing the migration of a large flock of birds (maybe Canada geese?) "going South," Bishop contemplated how each bird moves alone, has its own "individual rubato," yet is also part of a "time-pattern, or rather patterns, all closely related, all minutely varied, and yet all together forming the *migration*" (*PPL* 642). It is not difficult to locate the origin of her fascination with "an *idea* of the world's time, the migration idea" (*PPL* 643): her own migration experiences and her efforts to make sense of what they were, why they happened, and how they affected her – thus: she looked at, paid attention to, and, ultimately, wrote about the world in certain ways because of how she experienced it in the earliest years of her life. Bishop knew that she was her *self* alone, yet she was also part of patterns that governed her life, especially her childhood, when her ability to choose was more circumscribed. It was so for her ancestors, her family, her community; thus, it was so for her. This understanding was vividly expressed in her late poem "In the Waiting Room," where motion/mobility is the falling into consciousness and questioning: "*Why* should you be one, too?" (*P* 180). "Time's Andromedas" was written in the early 1930s; "In the Village," about experiences in 1916, was written in the early 1950s; "In the Waiting Room," about experiences in 1918, was written in the early 1970s – proof of a lifelong engagement with and practice of writing about formative experiences.

The major global event Bishop experienced during the first decade of her life was World War I, the Great War. Nova Scotia and Massachusetts were far from the trenches in Northern Europe, but even so, the "home front" was caught up in and affected by the tragedy of distant events. As a child, Bishop was acutely aware that "The War was on" (*Pr* 95; *P* 181), a phrase that appeared in "The Country Mouse" and "In the Waiting Room" (that is, both prose and poetry). The impact of this cataclysm prompted Bishop to observe to Anne Stevenson in 1963, "I often feel myself to be a late-late Post World War I generation-member, rather than a member of the Post World War II generation" (*PPL* 846). In *Stein, Bishop & Rich: Lyrics of Love, War, & Place*, Margaret Dickie writes insightfully of Bishop's preoccupation with war, but she focuses on the effect of World War II. Camille Roman also explores in depth the impact of war on Bishop's world view in *Elizabeth Bishop's World War II–Cold War View*. Yet the first war Bishop experienced, in the formative years of her life, was World War I, a bewilderingly complex event that helped set the foundation of Bishop's sense of self and world.

The impact of this war, like the meta-experience of "migration" (mobility), pervaded private and public realms. World War I produced a profound tension between two big ideas: tradition and modernity. The unprecedented brutality and loss undermined traditional values, beliefs, and practices of the nineteenth century, propelling forward a disillusionment, a fractured melancholy, and a heightened uncertainty. Technological development and its concomitant industrialization, which had begun in the late nineteenth century, was fueled and rapidly advanced. The result was not an overthrow – that is, tradition was not abandoned completely; modernity was not adopted absolutely – rather, the old and the new began the most intense dialogue they ever had, which lasted until World War II generated another cataclysmic shift. For Bishop, a child in the 1910s, the experience was one of intense ambiguity and open-endedness, which provoked serious questioning (additionally, because she was a child of two countries with different approaches to the war, the duality and dialogue was amplified and even more fraught). As an adult, Bishop had a deep respect for certain traditions (cultural, social, aesthetic) and practiced them; but she was also intrigued by and engaged in the contemporary and experimental. Her lifelong modus operandi was to hold these realms, conditions, and forces in a fluid balance; not to choose one or the other, but to have them mediate each other, and, at times even, to merge them together.

In "Cape Breton," the aeroplanes, motorboat, bulldozers, and bus coexist with "little white churches ... like lost quartz arrowheads," "brown-wet, fine, torn fish-nets," and "the closed schoolhouse," with its "rough-adzed pole topped with a white china door knob" (*P* 65–66). "Manners" literally sets up a dialogue between the horse-drawn wagon and speeding automobiles, which in "Filling Station" are "high-strung" (*P* 126). This dialogue continued in Brazil. In "Under the Window: Ouro Prêto," this dialectic is between donkeys and trucks, conversations at an ancient fountain, and transistors and bumper stickers. In "Questions of Travel," "the broken gasoline pump" and "the whittled fantasies of wooden cages" (*P* 92) spark a profound questioning.

In the midst of these large events and forces, private lives were lived. The first decade of Bishop's life comprised the first and perhaps greatest losses (in terms of abiding impact): her father died, her mother was hospitalized, and she was removed from Nova Scotia. William Bishop tragically died in October 1911, eight months after Bishop's birth. Gertrude was grief-stricken – suddenly, she was a new mother and a widow. She struggled with an underlying medical condition: hyperthyroidism. Bishop's infancy (birth to four years) was spent mostly with her mother. This brief synopsis holds within it *real* time (days, weeks, months, years), intensely complex experiences and interactions, and powerful emotional responses – all of which reverberated throughout Bishop's life and about which she wrote directly or indirectly.

Bishop had remarkably vivid memories of these earliest years, one of which found its way into one of her most memorable poems, "First Death in Nova Scotia." This poem can be read in many ways. One of the most obvious involves the nature of Bishop's relationship with her mother. "First Death in Nova Scotia" presents a tableau in which Gertrude initiates her daughter into the rituals around death: trying to teach her how to say goodbye, that is, to let go of what is lost. In the way of magical thinking natural to children, the young Bishop is fascinated by the whole scene, the experience, and innocently yet imaginatively questions how the dead baby (her cousin) can leave this world in the depth of winter. This "first death," which actually occurred in May 1915 (perhaps it was "A Cold Spring"?) during the first year of the First World War, was a profound existential experience that helped trigger in Bishop one of her lifelong artistic practices and poetic strategies: questioning. From "The Map" ("is the land tugging at the sea from under?" – the first poem in her first book) to "Five Flights Up" ("What has he done?" – the last poem in her last book), questions and questioning abound: "Why couldn't we have seen / this old Nativity while we were at it?" (*P* 58); "Should we have stayed at home, wherever that may be?" (*P* 92); "Why the extraneous plant? / Why the taboret? / Why, oh why, the doily?" (*P* 125); "Why, why do we feel / (we all feel) this sweet / sensation of joy?" (*P* 193); "Which is which?" (*P* 197).

In April 1915, Gertrude brought Elizabeth to Great Village to live. Although Bishop had been there before, this arrival marked the point when Great Village became home. It also marked the beginning of her second early loss: the hospitalization (that is, disappearance) of her mother. The place where Bishop came to live for the next three years was itself yet another major force that shaped her world view. Great Village was a vibrant community at the turn of the twentieth century. Still benefitting from the wealth generated by decades of shipbuilding in the second half of the nineteenth century, Great Village offered myriad cultural, social, religious, educational, and commercial activities. Being a port (the Great Village River flows into Cobequid Bay, part of the vast Bay of Fundy), the village had a remarkably cosmopolitan outlook, as ships from far-flung places delivered people and goods, and ships from Great Village sailed around the world. In 1966, Bishop observed to Ashley Brown, "In some ways the little village in Canada where I lived was more cultured than the suburbs of Boston where I lived later" (Brown 291).

Even though Great Village was directly affected by World War I and its global economic, technological, and political trends – exhibited in daily practices and discourse regarding the tension between the past and the future – the village remained a deeply traditional place. Resource industries (farming, fishing, lumbering) predominated. People still made many of their own goods (from butter to quilts), and if they bought goods, by and large they were produced nearby (there was a creamery, lumber mill, tannery, blacksmith, shoemaker, milliner, dressmaker, and tailor). Today, we call this kind of activity "local sourcing." Then, it was simply common practice. The village also had a wide range of mercantile, financial, and service businesses (that is, a booming commercial life). There were two churches (Presbyterian and Baptist) that governed not only faith and worship, but were also key influences in the overall social life of the village. A remarkable number of organized arts and sports activities (chamber orchestra, theatre troupe, literary society, baseball, horse racing, tennis) added to a lively and diverse cultural life. The village had a school that went from primary to grade eleven, with high pedagogical standards. It was said that the biggest export from Great Village was teachers.

What is drawn here is a sketch of village life, the barest general outlines, minus the details (Bishop loved details, "no detail too small" [*P* 129]), the colours and textures, the very things and qualities that so deeply impressed themselves on Bishop's precocious young mind. Some of the details can be seen in poems and stories, especially the memoir pieces: "In the Village," "Primer Class," "Gwendolyn," and "Memories of Uncle Neddy." As important as the details were, however, Great Village gave to Bishop more than subjects (quaint, colourful particulars) to write about. Her experiences in the village (as a whole and in its parts) gave her a way to write about them. The village was not simply a "what"; it was also a "how." For example, in the 1910s, Great Village remained a strongly oral culture. As vital as the written word was for Bishop her whole life (indeed, she learned to read and write in Great Village), her early experience with the powerful orality of Great Village influenced her artistic development. Orality was, again, not only a thing to describe, but it was also a force that affected *how* Bishop described things, experiences, and the knowledge she acquired from them. Orality was knowledge (historical, cultural, and aesthetic).

Oral culture manifested in many ways, for example, through oral tradition (the lore and story of the collective past); through performance (the village was a site of virtually daily organized public oral performance: recitations, sermons, lectures, speeches, teaching, singing); and through idiomatic speech and colloquialism. Bishop was fascinated by the voice of the village. She described herself as "a little pitcher with big ears" (*Pr* 151). This saying was part of the expressive orality of her childhood. Bishop did not simply hear all sorts of people speak; she paid attention to what they said and how they said it. One of the direct consequences of this acute mindfulness was the emergence of her own way of speaking (and writing). Bishop the poet was in possession of her "voice" at a remarkably early age. Even as she read and experimented with poetic predecessors (for example, her "Shelley phase" at Walnut Hill; her "imitation Hopkins" at Vassar), Bishop's "individual rubato" can be seen, heard, and felt in her juvenilia. For example, the Bishopesque poem, "Ballad of the Subway Train," written when she was sixteen, sounds like the Bishop of "Five Flights Up," in *Geography III*, even to the reprimand from a powerful, disembodied male voice and the concluding exclamation mark!

Voice is not simply about "style" (a direct, unadorned diction; a conversational tone; a penchant for concrete detail and modifiers; the use of formal, one might even say old-fashioned, poetic form), it is also about sensibility (the capacity for irony, humor, reticence, compassion, self-doubt, confidence), and interests (the preference for sensory or phenomenal memory mixed with allusion, fantasy, fable, parable, dream). "Ballad of the Subway Train" and "Five Flights Up" speak to relationship, transgression, and consequences by employing all these strategies and qualities, and they do so in a characteristically Bishop way.

Great Village's oral culture operated in a realm of communal custom, an aspect of the larger idea of tradition. A customary practice that profoundly affected Bishop was courtesy. Seamus Heaney identified this influence in his essay, "Counting to a Hundred: On Elizabeth Bishop," describing Bishop's experience of Great Village's customs of courtesy as "an early apprenticeship to reticence" (167). Most overtly, this apprenticeship is described in "Manners," a poem that makes it clear that the teaching to her of good manners by her beloved maternal grandfather occurred in the oral realm. As he told her, so he showed her – he practiced what he preached (although his tutorial was decidedly nondogmatic).

In 1963, Bishop observed to Anne Stevenson, "I think one can be cheerful AND profound! – or, how to be grim without groaning ... It may amount to a kind of 'good manners,' I'm not sure." She believed that a good artist "assumes a certain amount of sensitivity in his [*sic*] audience and doesn't attempt to flay himself to get sympathy or understanding" (*PPL* 864–865). Bishop's reticence is famous and has been regarded as both a strength and a weakness. When Bishop's earliest experiences in Great Village are considered, the origin of reticence is found in the custom of courtesy. Good manners operate like poetic form, as a foundation or framework from which to create and through which to enter art. It is not a distancing from or avoidance of emotion, but a humane way of handling it (especially intense, overwhelming emotion). In her adolescence, she further learned this lesson from one of her poetic heroes, Gerard Manley Hopkins. In her young adulthood, she witnessed it in her mentor Marianne Moore and explored it in "Efforts of Affection: A Memoir of Marianne Moore."

Elizabeth Bishop's maternal grandparents, William (Pa) and Elizabeth (Gammie) Bulmer, were exemplars of many aspects of Great Village life for

Bishop. They were purveyors of its oral traditions. They represented the "home-made," a way of life that required active, daily creativity (artisanship), hard work, and sustained effort. Pa was a tanner, currier, shoemaker, and farmer. Gammie was the quintessential wife, mother, and homemaker. She embodied, quite literally, all things domestic and private for Bishop, expressed most poignantly and hauntingly in "Sestina," a poem filled with Gammie's ordinary objects, which possess magical abilities, including a direct connection to her orality: "*It was to be*, says the Marvel stove, / *I know what I know*, says the almanac" (*P* 121), words that could also be spoken by Gammie *and* her granddaughter. Bishop shared a deep grief with her grandmother – they experienced the sorrow of private and public loss. This experience gave them existential knowledge about the world (fatalism? cynicism? stoicism?) and ways to express it: the grandmother makes tea and she laughs to hide her tears; the child listens, watches carefully, and draws "an inscrutable house." In that kitchen, the child becomes an artist.

A number of Bishop's poems about her maternal grandparents remained unfinished during her life, but have appeared in *Edgar Allan Poe & The Juke-Box*: for example, "Syllables," "For Grandfather," and "The Grandmothers." Each in its own way evokes the spoken and idiomatic, the oral expressiveness in which Bishop was immersed in Great Village. Her late poem, "The Moose," also embodies the abiding oral nature of her childhood experiences, with the "Grandparents' voices / uninterruptedly / talking, in Eternity," and all those life stories, the "deaths, deaths and sicknesses." For Bishop, what mattered most was their "Talking the *way* they talked" (emphasis added). She distills or compresses the whole universe of this spoken and heard world in one expression: "'Yes ...' that peculiar / affirmative. 'Yes ...' / A sharp, indrawn breath, / half groan, half acceptance, / that means 'Life's like that. / We know *it* (also death)'" (*P* 191–192).

The most important influence on Elizabeth Bishop during the first decade of her life is the one least acknowledged in the many books, essays, articles, and reviews written about her – that is, her mother. The occasional exception (for example, Harrison's sensitive and comprehensive analysis) proves the rule of this practice. If it was only a matter of ignoring Gertrude, that would be unfortunate; but when she is mentioned at all, it is generally to dismiss her as an insane, absent woman who played no active (certainly no positive) role in her daughter's life, let alone her art. Carole Doreski refers to Gertrude as "a shrill perversion of the nurturer" and an "omnipresent phantom" (77–78). Goldensohn simply refers to her as Bishop's "biological mother" who "died in an asylum after years of confinement" (144). Walker speculates on Gertrude's "pathological sense of guilt" (12) and claims she is the cypher for the insane Amos in "The Moose" (140). Travisano observes,

"Gertrude disappeared almost without a trace. In effect she became an un-person in Bishop's world" (*Mid-Century Quartet* 97). These characterizations are the norm and result from an ignorance about who Gertrude actually was.

While Gertrude's physical absence and its impact were real in Bishop's life, her emotional presence and its impact were equally real. Gertrude appears directly only rarely in Bishop's published poetry ("First Death in Nova Scotia," "One Art"), but somewhat more often in the unfinished poems ("Homesickness," "A Drunkard," "Swan-Boat Ride," "A mother made of dress-goods"). She appears vividly and directly in the published prose ("In the Village" and "Memories of Uncle Neddy") and the unfinished prose (most notably in "Reminiscences of Great Village"). But Gertrude's influence and impact are, in fact, everywhere. She hovers over, haunts, and inhabits published poems such as "The Map" ("women feeling for the smoothness of yard-goods" [*P* 5]), "Insomnia" ("By the Universe deserted, / *she*'d tell it to go to hell" [*P* 68]), "At the Fishhouses," "Cape Breton," "Visits to St. Elizabeths," and "In the Waiting Room"; in juvenilia such as "Three Sonnets for the Eyes," "Hymn to the Virgin," and "The Reprimand"; and in unfinished poems such as "The walls went on for years & years ...," "Where are the dolls who loved me so ...," and "Dear, my compass."

Except for a short period in early 1914, Bishop and her mother were very much together during the first four years of Bishop's life. During the early Great Village years (1915–1917), Gertrude was still present, coming and going; but illness was taking a toll and resulted in hospitalization at the Nova Scotia Hospital, Dartmouth, Nova Scotia, in late June 1916. It must be remembered that no one could foresee that she would remain there for the rest of her life (eighteen years; she died in May 1934). The family hoped for her return for years. In September 1917, Bishop's paternal grandparents, John and Sarah Bishop, arrived in Great Village to claim their son's daughter, John Bishop being her legal guardian (the probate, guardianship, custody, and other legal issues are too complex to describe here). For the six-year-old Bishop, being taken from home, the place where she believed her mother would return, was bewildering and engendered the fear that she would never see her mother again. Brett Millier observes that this removal "sealed little Elizabeth's sense of loss to a permanent condition" (20). Bishop remembered her removal from Nova Scotia in her memoir, "The Country Mouse": "I felt as if I were being kidnapped, even if I wasn't" (*Pr* 87). The ultimate effect of this well-intentioned but ill-advised action by the adults in her life was illness.

By the spring of 1918, Bishop was seriously ill. The Bishops transferred her to her mother's older sister Maude Shepherdson, who lived with her husband George in Revere, Massachusetts. Bishop's time with her maternal aunt and uncle were evoked in the unfinished poems "Salem Willows" and "Dicky and Sister," and the story "Mrs. Sullivan Downstairs." After Maude's death in 1940, Bishop tried to write an elegy, "For M.B.S., buried in Nova Scotia"; but, as with other attempts ("For Grandfather" and "Aubade and Elegy" for Lota), she was unable to get beyond a poignant, potent fragment.

It took a year for Bishop to recover and in the summer of 1919, she was brought back to Nova Scotia. For the next decade (the 1920s), Bishop migrated back and forth between Massachusetts and Nova Scotia. She never again lived permanently in Great Village, but the long summers she spent there during the second decade of her life reinforced and intensified her earliest experiences. This decade also brought the gradual realization – the tragic fact – that Gertrude would not recover and return.

Bishop's relationship with her mother was the most complicated and fraught of all her childhood experiences. Her efforts to understand what happened to Gertrude and herself, and to come to terms with its impact, was lifelong. Gertrude literally and metaphorically embodied the formative forces discussed in this chapter: mobility (migration, travel, singularity, and communal connection – what it means to be alone and a part of something); temporality (past, future, presen[t]ce, tradition, modernity – what it means to hold onto something for too long, to let go of something too quickly); orality (story, custom, performance, idiom – what it means to speak within and beyond accepted discourse). Gertrude was tide. Gertrude was time. Gertrude was voice. Bishop learned about ebb and flow, now and then, sound and silence from her mother. The love at the heart of Gertrude's life and relationship with her daughter rippled out in Bishop's own life and art. The loss of this love was a painful legacy and a strange liberation for Bishop – their relationship was complex, fraught, contradictory, and mysterious; it cannot be reduced to a vague speculation or reductive conclusion.

Bishop adopted and eschewed, integrated and abandoned myriad practices and beliefs – she acquiesced to and rebelled against customs and expectations, sometimes confidently, sometimes doubtfully. This modus operandi was a programme for living life and creating art: untidy yet compelling. It could make Bishop indecisive (even produce artistic paralysis), but it also made her deeply human, humane, and, at times, astonishingly comprehensive in an understated way. The curious non-linearity of Bishop's creative process – its sometimes mysterious prescience – was generative of poems and stories that are powerful literal memory and profound philosophical contemplation. This way of being and creating came about in part because Bishop held onto and let go of her mother, over and over again.

Bishop needed Gertrude to be a mother, but when that was no longer possible, she claimed her for art. There was nothing simple or easy in this choice and effort, nor perfect or complete, but it was a necessary and genuine process. "In the Village" begins: "A scream, the echo of a scream hangs over that Nova Scotian village" (*Pr* 62). Gertrude's scream hovers "forever" beside the healing "*Clang*" of the blacksmith's hammer, settles down to earth with the mysterious "*Slp*" of the river, and is caught in a "skein of voices" belonging to all the other women in her family. Her scream is lost and found, like all of Bishop's Nova Scotia childhood experiences, loved ones, memory, dream, imagination – like knowledge.

7

BETHANY HICOK

Becoming a Poet: From North to South

Elizabeth Bishop's movements from north to south and back again amount to an important geographical, intellectual, and aesthetic axis in her poetic development. These are not essentialist terms in Bishop's work; rather, they go beyond describing simple geographical destinations to assume diacritical significance. Bishop's poetry of the North often investigates various nativity scenes and childhood memory ("Cape Breton," "Over 2,000 Illustrations and a Complete Concordance," and later, "In the Waiting Room"), whereas southern sites more often become a realm for erotic self-discovery ("Late Air," "Pleasure Seas," "It is marvellous to wake up together"), perhaps because they are distant from the site of biographical nativity. At both poles, Bishop openly situates herself in the position of the traveler ("The Moose," "Questions of Travel") in order to ask important ethical questions about encounters with the other. In her first book of poems, *North & South* (1946), Bishop literally moves from a northern landscape with its imaginary iceberg, its "northerly harbor of Labrador," and its lonely and alienated characters, to the beaches of Florida, "the state with the prettiest name," with its vocal alligators and tropical lushness. In Florida, where Bishop lived for nearly a decade, she writes poems that express the intimate, literary, and racially mixed community of 1930s Key West. Bishop's second book, *A Cold Spring* (1955), moves from north to south but is dominated by northern topoi. As she moves into her mature phase with the 1965 *Questions of Travel*, South and North have become the organizing principles of the volume, which is divided roughly between the Brazil poems and those that explore the psychic spaces of a northern childhood.

Many of Bishop's major career tropes are in place in the early poems of the North: home, identity, travel, dislocation. But these poems are more likely to take the form of imaginative fable ("The Gentleman of Shalott," "The Man-Moth") or create Surrealist landscapes, as do some of her Paris poems ("Sleeping on the Ceiling," "Sleeping Standing Up," "Cirque d'Hiver"). These poems show Bishop's early homage to playful Modernist abstraction, as opposed to her later gravitation toward the loco-descriptive. The first two poems in *North & South* represent an emerging preoccupation with imaginative travel. "The Map" (1935) anchors the reader in a metaphor that links the science of cartography with the art of poetry; this is not geography, but a playful mapping of the creative process. Although the mapmaker, like the poet, is not entirely free, this poem imagines the poetic license such an imaginative cartographer might be able to take with shading and color: "The names of seashore towns run out to sea, / the names of cities cross the neighboring mountains / – the printer here experiencing the same excitement / as when emotion too far exceeds its cause" (*P* 5). The poem is humorous: "Are they assigned, or can the countries pick their colors?" The speaker's experience of the map (as aesthetic object) is tactile, sensual ("we can stroke these lovely bays"), open to possibility, imaginative, and provocative. The cartographer has a certain freedom within the boundaries of the map: "More delicate than the historians' are the map-makers' colors" (*P* 5). The science of cartography served Bishop well as a metaphor for the imagination, but, ultimately, she may, like Eavan Boland, have found it "limited" because she would turn to history and geography in later poems that would be anchored in the precise description of places she had seen (Boland 5).

The volume's second poem, "The Imaginary Iceberg" (1935), sets spinning an idea of travel that Bishop would return to in later volumes, offered here as a statement: "We'd rather have the iceberg than the ship, / although it meant the end of travel" (*P* 6). In "Questions of Travel" (1965), the idea is formulated as a question: "Should we have stayed at home and thought of here?" But, as the title suggests, this iceberg is imaginary, an abstract creation of the poet's mind. "The Imaginary Iceberg" seems to want to leave behind the iceberg or caution us against icebergs, or both. Bishop tells us that the iceberg of the imagination "cuts its facets from within. / Like jewelry from a grave / it saves itself perpetually and adorns / only itself" (*P* 6). This gorgeous Dickinsonian image tells us something about what the imagination might achieve on its own, and yet there are limitations to the isolated imagination, as Bishop's ending suggests, because the speaker chooses the ship, not the iceberg: "Good-bye, we say, good-bye, the ship steers off," leaving the iceberg behind "fleshed, fair, erected indivisible" (*P* 6). In a 1940 letter to Marianne Moore, Bishop reveals the iceberg metaphor to be part of the "furniture" of the poet's development and symbolic of her own struggle to create a sense of movement in her poetry and to move past the symbolist influence on her earlier work. She writes of "that continuous uncomfortable feeling of 'things' in the head, like icebergs or rocks or awkwardly placed pieces of furniture. It is as if all the nouns were there but the verbs were lacking" (*OA* 94).

In Bishop's stunning urban fable, "The Man-Moth" (1936), the hybrid creature of the title negotiates the vast urban spaces of an unnamed and ghostly city (undoubtedly inspired by New York); "he returns / to the pale subways of cement he calls his home" and makes contact with the human world only if we "catch him" (*P* 16–17). That is not to say that these poems are emotionally barren – far from it. The final lines of "The Man-Moth" are filled with pathos; Bishop effectively placed us in the Man-Moth's shoes, as it were, so that readers are likely to feel compassion for this strange and shy creature at the end and congratulate themselves for being among those who pay attention.

Bishop's poems of the North are often witty, playful and, at times, poignant, but when she moved physically and imaginatively south to Florida – where she eventually bought a house with Louise Crane and made extended trips for nearly a decade – the change seems to have initiated a significant shift in her art that cannot be accounted for just by referencing the poet's own maturity. Moving to Florida in late 1936, as Thomas Travisano has already suggested in his 1988 monograph, was a "catalytic event" for Bishop (19). Travisano has argued that with her move south, Bishop became a poet of history, as well as of the imagination; when she became a traveller, she also became an amateur naturalist and geographer who studied the plants, animals, people, politics, and industries of the regions where she lived. Bishop's South begins with the 1939 "Florida," which marks a definite shift from Bishop's early work in its precise descriptions of the topography, bird, animal, and reptilian life of Bishop's newly discovered state. Drawing on close observation and a visit she made to the naturalist E. Ross Allen, who wrestled alligators and could reproduce their various calls, Bishop begins to read the landscape as a possible mirror of culture.

The opening movement of "Florida" initially takes its cue from the early "Map" so that "the state with the prettiest name ... floats in brackish water, / held together by mangrove roots," but it quickly moves into a different scale, creating a multi-tonal composition on the state and how a visitor might perceive it (*P* 33). We have representation – how Florida appears on a map, jutting out into the Atlantic, as well as a description of its natural characteristics (swamp); and the name, which it received from the Spanish *Pascua Florida* or feast of flowers. But Bishop uses the occasion of this descriptive poem to explore what we do *not* see reflected in Florida's picture postcards and pretty name – the decay and death, for instance, that dominates the poem's imagery, so that the living mangrove roots "bear while living oysters in clusters," but when they die, they litter the "white swamps with skeletons"; "enormous turtles, helpless and mild, / die" on the beaches, leaving behind "their large white skulls with round eye-sockets";

and "buzzards are drifting down, down, down, / over something they have spotted in the swamp" (*P* 33). "Florida" is a "careless, corrupt state ... the poorest post-card of itself" (34). Those postcard images would not include the plague of "mosquitos" that "go hunting to the tune of their ferocious obbligatos" (34), and certainly not the metaphorical skeletons of a buried and violent history, dredged up after a tropical rain when "a gray rag of rotted calico" turns up on the beach, identified as "the buried Indian Princess's skirt" (34). With this bit of cloth, Bishop reminds us of Florida's exploitation and the forcible removal of the state's indigenous peoples. She also reveals a new subject: an effort to speak the past. Bishop's imagery prepares us for this final attempt to speak by projecting it onto the state's outsize animal and bird life in previous lines: "unseen hysterical birds who rush up the scale / every time in a tantrum," "tanagers embarrassed by their flashiness," "the palm trees" that "clatter in the stiff breeze / like the bills of the pelicans" (33). Much of this auditory imagery now can be seen as contributing to incomplete efforts of speech, particularly in the poem's last lines: "The alligator, who has five distinct calls: / friendliness, love, mating, war, and a warning – / whimpers and speaks in the throat / of the Indian princess" (34). The alligator's primitive calls from the swamp – "nascent speech," as David Kalstone has called them (74) – turn into words that now can be spoken by the Indian princess. Bishop's acts of unburying allow something of the buried past to be, however obliquely, revealed.

Close observation and description of the natural world in Florida leads Bishop into a more intimate interaction with it, a shift marked in her much-anthologized poem "The Fish," with its dramatic opening line: "I caught a tremendous fish" (*P* 43). Here Bishop's famous observer's "eye" that we have seen developing in "Florida" joins the lyric "I" of the speaker, enabling the poet to engage more thoroughly in ethics and establish greater intimacy with the reader. When the speaker hauls the fish out of the water, she takes him seriously as another living creature, describing him in such minute and loving detail that we come to know this fish intimately as we (and our speaker) consider his fate. To win our affection, Bishop manages to make this fish both like us and not like us at all. On the one hand, he is "battered and venerable / and homely"; Bishop's use of simile enhances his hominess, for "his brown skin hung in strips / like ancient wallpaper" (*P* 43). On the other hand, he is alien: "his gills were breathing in / the terrible oxygen" (43). When the speaker looks "into his eyes," she does not find in them an answer to her look; the fish's eyes only "shifted a little, but not / to return my stare" (43–44). The speaker's final decision to let the fish go is an ethical one measured at the beginning of the poem by the "grunting weight" of the fish on her line. Once she has let herself "admire ... his sullen face, /

the mechanism of his jaw" (44), once she has weighed his life in the balance, then her decision is a serious rather than a trivial one. She does not let him go because he is "like" her, but because she has taken the time to consider him.

Bishop's use of the lyric "I" suggests a level of comfort and intimacy with the reader that I would suggest emerges out of her experience of Key West in the 1930s–1940s. The very geography of the island (Key West is only three miles wide by five miles long) made "separation a physical impossibility," according to Stetson Kennedy, and "intimate coexistence" an inevitability (3). It was a "social laboratory," Kennedy notes, that proved that different kinds of people could get along and even "share diverse cultures and ... enjoy one another's company" (3). When Bishop began making her visits there in 1937, Key West was a diverse, racially mixed community of Cubans, Bahamians, mainlanders, writers, musicians, and artists, which, because of its relative isolation, developed a "unique species of folklife and culture," Kennedy observes (1). In addition to close proximity, Bishop's interest in recording the lives of the people she met in Key West was very much in the air at the time. The Works Progress Administration (WPA) maintained a presence in Key West in the 1930s – Bishop promoted the work of the Key West "primitive" painter, Gregorio Valdes, through the WPA Art Project, for instance (*OA* 79). Additionally, writers and artists worked not only to turn out brochures for tourism but, like Kennedy, conducted interviews in order to record and preserve the "folk histories" of its residents.

Bishop's letters, notebooks, and poems of this period can be seen in this context. Miss Lula and her black servant Cootchie of the poem "Cootchie" (1941), for example, were part of Mrs. Pindar's boarding house circle at 529 Whitehead Street in Key West where Bishop rented a four-dollar-a-week room (Millier 138). Bishop's widening social circle included Pauline Hemingway (Ernest's soon-to-be ex-wife); Bishop's beloved Mrs. Almyda, whose precious verbal ejaculations fill Bishop's letters; Gregorio Valdes; Faustina Valdez, the black nurse/housekeeper/lottery ticket seller; the whores of the Square Roof brothel that Louise Crane and Bishop visited (Fountain 78); men wrestling alligators; and Rumba nights at Sloppy Joe's (*OA* 71). Key West was Bishop's first exposure to race relations up close, demonstrated in the nuanced first stanza of "Cootchie," which intricately interweaves images of black and white to reveal layers of racial inequality. When Cootchie dies, she "lies in marl, / black into white she went" (*P* 46). But Bishop indicates in the rhyme "went/spent" that this is a second burial for Cootchie because "Her life was spent" – literally wasted – "in caring for Miss Lula" (*P* 46). What we do not see in "Cootchie" is the role of the observer in the story.

Bishop's "Faustina, or Rock Roses," alternatively, is more complex in its confrontation with alterity because the observer ("the visitor" of the poem) *is* part of the scene – at first just sitting and watching, but later actually "embarrassed." Bishop began drafting this poem in 1943, although it was not completed until 1947. The poem reveals power relations to be complex; like Cootchie, Faustina tends to a white woman ("in a crazy house / upon a crazy bed"), but in this case, the poem stages a possible power reversal. Unlike Cootchie, Faustina has negotiated "the terms of her employment" with the white woman: "She bends above the other" (*P* 71). And she presents to this "other" a mix of contradictions: "Her sinister kind face / presents a cruel black / coincident conundrum" (*P* 71). The question, or conundrum, could apply to either (or both) the white woman or the black woman: "is it / freedom at last, a lifelong / dream of time and silence, / dream of protection and rest? / Or is it the very worst, / the unimaginable nightmare" (*P* 71–72). As in "Florida," the poem reveals a hidden history of violence, oppression, subservience, slavery – the master-slave dialectic on which this relationship depends.

Key West was a small, intimate place where everyone crossed paths and, as Kennedy argues, diverse people had to get along. Bishop's "Jerónimo's House" (1941) reflects a new level of intimacy with the lives of the people who lived there. Inspired by the small, perishable-looking houses that were built in the nineteenth-century for Cuban workers in the Key West cigar factories, Jerónimo's house is both a fragile and robust shelter, as well as a place for friends to gather. Yet even though this house is fragile, a "fairy palace" made "of perishable / clapboards with / three rooms in all," a "gray wasps' nest / of chewed-up paper / glued with spit," it is Jerónimo's "home," his "love-nest" (*P* 35). Even Bishop's side-by-side arrangement of the stanzas on the page seems architectural, perhaps inspired by Bishop's love of George Herbert and such shape poems as "The Altar." Bishop's poem becomes a sort of spiritual container for its own "ad hoc domesticity," as Susan McCabe has called it (85), and then invites us in: "Come closer," Jerónimo beckons (35). Jerónimo's gesture might be read as a metaphor for Bishop's own attempts to draw closer to the places and lives she was encountering on her travels.

It is also likely that Key West's combination of tolerance, intimacy, rich night life, and tropical beauty, far away from the site of biographical nativity, led Bishop to a new realm of erotic self-discovery. Angus Cleghorn credits Bishop's "geographical shift" to Florida with an "erotic awakening" (69) that we can trace through the Florida poems. In "Late Air," for instance, the poet refers in the first stanza to "the radio-singers" who "distribute all their love-songs / over the dew-wet lawns," but "on the Navy Yard aerial" she has found "better witnesses / for love on summer nights" in the "five remote red lights" that "keep their nests" there (*P* 45). High up there, "where the dew cannot climb," these lights are "Phoenixes / burning quietly" (45). These are strange, incongruous witnesses to love, but one suspects it is their indifference that is important for a lesbian poet finding ways to speak an alternate line of desire in the heterosexual world represented by the radio singers. "Pleasure Seas" (1939), not published in *North & South* but which dates from that period, explores that alternate seam through the medium of water: "The sea is delight. The sea means *room.* / It is a dance-floor, a well-ventilated ballroom" (*P* 279). Despite the space, "Love," sun-like in this poem, fails to connect. Even though "Love / Sets out determinedly in a straight line, / One of his burning ideas in mind, / Keeping his eyes on / The bright horizon," he/it "suffers refraction / And comes back in shoals of distraction" (*P* 279–281). With the new editions we can see that Bishop's exploration of this theme seems to be developing in at least two distinct strands: one follows the "mechanical pleasures" that Key West's honky tonks, bars, and dance halls provided ("Edgar Allan Poe & The Juke-Box," "The Soldier and the Slot Machine"); the other strand is celebratory, as is the case with Bishop's erotically charged aubade, "It is marvellous to wake up together," which dates from the late-1930s to early-1940s during Bishop's love affair with Marjorie Stevens. In Bishop's version of the aubade, or lovers' morning song, the lovers are awakened not by the dawn, but by a spectacular electrical storm common to Florida, alerting us to the possibility of a divergent path for desire, but, unlike "Pleasure Seas," this one hits home: "It is marvellous to wake up together / At the same minute; marvellous to hear / The rain begin suddenly all over the roof" (*P* 283). The lovers are lit up in a bird cage of lightning (a humorous riff on love birds in cages). And in their transported delight, the whole "world might change to something quite different, / As the air changes or the lightning comes without our blinking, / Change as our kisses are changing without our thinking" (283).

Although moving geographically from north to south influenced Bishop's approach to her subjects, the poems of *North & South* remain a movement from north to south, rather than a dialogue between north and south. Bishop's approach to geography and landscape changes markedly in a few of the major poems of *A Cold Spring*: "Over 2,000 Illustrations and a Complete Concordance," "Cape Breton," "The Bight," and "At the Fishhouses" – four of Bishop's most important career-changing poems. She won the Pulitzer Prize in 1956 for the combined volume *Poems: North & South – A Cold Spring*. In these poems, Bishop begins to engage in a spatial practice that she herself described as a "geographical mirror" in the margins of drafts for "At the Fishhouses" (Millier 182). Millier glosses this usage as Bishop's "attempt to find herself reflected in the land and the sea" (182), which is true to a point, but what makes Bishop relevant for us today is that this spatial metaphor is not a mere reflection, but rather, the beginnings of a poetics that thinks historically – a process that James Clifford reminds us, involves "locating oneself in space and time" (11).

In "Over 2,000 Illustrations and a Complete Concordance," two kinds of cultural encounter structure the poem: 1) the speaker's "reading" of the illustrations in a child's Bible and 2) her travels from north to south, including Newfoundland, Rome, Mexico, and North Africa. In turn, the Bible and its Christian worldview, "God's spreading fingerprint," structures the traveller's response to the other during her travels. The poem conveys a view of history and culture that emphasizes corruption and spiritual bankruptcy. In a letter to Marianne Moore from Mérida, for instance, when Bishop was traveling in Mexico in 1942, she wrote, "I *feel* the corruption" (*OA* 110). The poem's title, opening lines ("Thus should have been our travels / serious, engravable"), and printing and engraving lexicon indicate that the poem is structured around the speaker's perusal of a child's Bible. The title of the poem ironically refers to what might have been a kind of sales pitch for this child's Bible, used to lure possible buyers by emphasizing the Bible's illustrations, not its content. Through that irony, Bishop establishes from the beginning her skepticism over that religious document's doctrinal authority, while at the same time acknowledging its power over us – that is, our difficulty in resisting the overall sales pitch of religion. One of the underlying investigations of the poem is to understand how these scenes, and particularly the Nativity scene at the end, have shaped Western (Christian) identity and civilization and thereby influenced our search for meaning.

With its opening comparison (our travels should have been like the engravings in this book), the poem initiates a dialectic between religious iconography and scenes from the poet's travels in its search for meaningful experience. Meaning is allusive and illusive. This speaker is no longer a child looking through the Bible for the first time, but rather an adult whose sight has become jaded, so that the Seven Wonders of the World "are tired / and a touch familiar," and full of judgment as the adult speaker notes "the squatting Arab, / or group of Arabs, plotting, probably, / against our Christian Empire" (*P* 57). The "Arabs" come from events Bishop recorded in letters and notebooks about her travels, as do many of the travel details in the poem, spanning several major trips Bishop took from 1936–1941, including her trip to Morocco in 1935 with Crane where they visited Tangier, Rabat, and Casablanca, and to Mexico in 1942 with her then partner, Marjorie Stevens, where she spent a month with Pablo Neruda and his wife in Cuernivaca and traveled throughout the country.

The rich experience of this poem is textual and textural. Bishop situates us with the speaker early on in the pages of this child's illustrated Bible: "The eye drops, weighted, through the lines / the burin made, the lines that move apart / like ripples above sand, / dispersing storms, God's spreading fingerprint" (*P* 57). Just as we sit with the child Elizabeth in the much later poem, "In the Waiting Room," looking over the pages of the *National Geographic*, these lines take us through the pages and skillfully lead us into our travels that move from north to south, east to west. The opening movement is followed by seven travel vignettes, often delineating an empty kind of tourism where the "natives" perform for the tourists. The speaker describes the machine-like "Collegians" in St. Peter's Square in Rome who "marched in lines, / crisscrossing the great square with black, like ants," or an Englishwoman who pours tea in Dingle harbor, as she passes on the trivial information that the "Duchess was going to have a baby" (58). In the "brothels of Marrakesh," the "pockmarked prostitutes … flung themselves / naked and giggling against our knees, / asking for cigarettes" (58). In each vignette Bishop focuses on scenes of corruption and decadence, offering up a mechanistic and empty spiritual landscape. And, thus, we arrive at the final vignette. It was "somewhere near there" – that is, the "brothels of Marrakesh" – where the speaker sees "what frightened me most of all: / A holy grave, not looking particularly holy" (58). It is "an open, gritty, marble trough, carved solid / with exhortation, yellowed / as scattered cattle-teeth; / half-filled with dust," but it is "not even the dust / of the poor prophet paynim who once lay there" (58). It is a space filled with death but emptied of meaning. Bishop provides a bit of comic relief after this (tragic?) scene, with her description of their tour guide, Khadour, who, dressed "in a smart burnoose," "looked on amused" at his charges (58). Whatever Bishop's intentions here, the comedy does not entirely alleviate the underlying sense of emptiness and loss. Bishop seems to be playing, Nabokov-like, with the reader's desire to find some meaning in these random scenes, so she brings us to the brink of a "holy grave" that is empty. I cannot help thinking that Bishop is Khadour here, laughing behind her own burnoose. Bishop brings us to a point of rich cultural encounter: the empty grave and the absent "poor prophet paynim," tourists looking in, and a Muslim tour guide looking on. Khadour possesses the controlling gaze, his look and laughter directing our response. Although Bishop might have been using the archaic word paynim (or pagan) to mean non-Christian (i.e., Muslim) solely for its alliterative qualities, the word also reflects the attitudes of the Westerner toward the Muslim prophet, as well as the Muslim guide, Khadour, to his tourist charges, presenting in these few lines a complex series of interactions over the Muslim "holy" grave, the penultimate stanza that leads into the Nativity scene of the poem's final movement.

The poem's last stanza defines the problem of the Postmodern traveler. How does she find meaning in a world where "everything" is "only connected by 'and' and 'and?'" (*P* 58). Is the answer here, in this heavy book, the child's illustrated Bible? We are instructed to "Open the book," and as we do, "The gilt rubs off the edges / of the pages and pollinates the fingertips" (58). If the play on words (gilt/guilt) is not immediately apparent, it will be after the next instruction: "Open the *heavy* book" (my emphasis). In its final lines, "Over 2,000 Illustrations" returns us to the humble origins of the Christian epiphany, the visit of the Magi to the Christ child in the stable in Bethlehem: "Why couldn't we have seen / this old Nativity while we were at it? / – the dark ajar, the rocks breaking with light ... and, lulled within, a family with pets, / – and looked and looked our infant sight away" (*P* 58). As Travisano has noted, Bishop emphasizes not "the divine qualities of the holy family" here, but the "domestic" – "a family with pets" (120). From the opening question of these lines ("Why couldn't we have seen?") to the poem's final nod to Wordsworth ("And looked and looked our infant sight away"), Bishop acknowledges, questions, and intertwines at least two traditions: religion and literature (Christian and Romantic) – neither of which can offer the secular traveler of the poem the meaningful experience, the "serious and engravable" moment of truth for which she longs. For Wordsworth, infant sight comes from God, "who is our home," and although that sight is lost forever as the child becomes a man, something of its glory remains behind, and Wordsworth is confident that "Our Souls have sight of that immortal sea / Which brought us hither." The secular poet of "Over 2,000 Illustrations" cannot find such compensation in a lost celestial home. She has only the representation of it (the heavy book that carries with it the weight of thousands of years of Western thought and Christian tradition). A new infant sight can only be found, perhaps, in a freshness of image – Khadour laughing behind his burnoose, the Nativity described as "a family with pets" – that jar the imagination out of received interpretations, tidy encounters, and easy answers to life's mysteries.

Bishop returned to the North in the summer of 1946 when she traveled back to scenes of her own childhood nativity in Nova Scotia. As Jonathan Ellis has argued, she deliberately retraced her own family's footsteps during this trip and in subsequent ones. She was, as Ellis has suggested, apparently looking for how family connections were linked to "a particular place" (*Art and Memory* 45). In the summer of 1946, she "read through her mother's medical records" at the Department of Health in Nova Scotia; in the summer of 1947, she visited Cape Breton, where (as she later revealed in letters to Anne Stevenson) her mother had taught school as a young girl of only 16; in the summer of 1951, during her last visit to Nova Scotia before leaving for Brazil, Bishop "asked permission from the Ottawa Lighthouse Authority to stay on Sable Island where her great-grandfather's schooner had been lost at sea" (Ellis 45). These trips to the North were deliberate steps into the past, and they demonstrate that geographical movement was not only important for the new experience that infused Bishop's work as a result of it, but also for its link to the past. In these visits north, it appears that Bishop was attempting to read the landscape of her ancestors as a way of understanding her own origins as a poet.

The description of bird life that begins "Cape Breton" follows on the heels of the naturalist description of the Florida poems. Here, "on the high 'bird islands,' Ciboux and Hertford, / the razorbill auks and the silly-looking puffins all stand / with their backs to the mainland / in solemn, uneven lines along the cliff's brown grass-frayed edge" (*P* 65). The anthropomorphized birds, like the ones from Florida, seem characteristic of their particular climate – in this case, northern. They look out to sea, marking the edge of their environment. But this poem travels deeper into personal history. The landscape is mysterious, full of ghosts, holding a secret, as Ellis has suggested, in "those folds and folds of fir" (65). The poet traces only around the edges of these secrets, however, following "the wild road" that "clambers along the brink of the coast" (65). The abandonment of things stand in metonymically for the more painful loss of people and the helpless feeling of abandonment (a characteristic trope of Bishop's; consider the lost mother's watch in "One Art," to give just one example). So on the road "stand occasional small yellow bulldozers, / but without their drivers, because today is Sunday" (65), and, in the next image, "The little white churches have been dropped into the matted hills / like lost quartz arrowheads" (65). Bishop mixes Christian and native artifacts in this remarkable simile, creating the sense of memory as an archeological dig, which also reveals layers of historical memory. Finally, the poet concludes that, "The road appears to have been abandoned. / Whatever the landscape had of meaning appears to have been abandoned, / unless the road is holding it back, in the interior, / where we cannot see" (*P* 65). The line comes down heavily on the word "abandoned," and the poem's last line ("an ancient chill is rippling the dark brooks") hints at what the poet risks in her return to these nativity scenes of childhood – the ancient chill of abandonment, loss, death. But it is also the wellspring of the poet's life and art – the "childhood's river" of Bishop's elegy for her aunt, "For M.B.S., buried in Nova Scotia," or the "dark seam of the river" that runs in "A Short, Slow Life" (*EAP* 98, *P* 297).

"At the Fishhouses" explores in geography the knowledge of this ancient chill. Bishop began taking notes for this poem just after her trip to Portapique on Nova Scotia's south shore in 1946 (Ellis 77). Self-discovery does not tend to be erotic in these poems, as it was in some of the Florida poems; southern climes seem to invite warmer imagery and a deeper sense of erotic understanding. Northern climates yield a colder intellectual knowledge of the human condition and loss. The world of "At the Fishhouses" is both alien and strangely familiar. The poem is geographical in its careful description of the place, the natural world, the major industry (fishing), and the old man whose work it is to mend the nets and clean and gut the fish. His work is meaningful, valued. Bishop describes his artistry with the nets and the tools of his trade ("his shuttle worn and polished"), and the blade of "that black old knife" that scrapes the scales from "unnumbered fish ... is almost worn away" with use. Like the rainbow in "The Fish," iridescence is everywhere in the scales that line every surface: "There are sequins on his vest and on his thumb" (*P* 63). When the speaker and the old man share a cigarette (a Lucky Strike), the speaker establishes her first important connection: "He was a friend of my grandfather" (62). This is indeed a lucky strike, but Bishop's poem demonstrates that establishing such a connection does not lead to "complete comprehension," the desire of the traveler in "Arrival at Santos." Self-knowledge is far more elusive and, indeed, alien, as the speaker learns when, having established a tenuous bond with the old man, she turns to the natural world, where despite her comical efforts to "speak" to the seal by singing Baptist hymns to him because of their shared belief in "total immersion," the seal merely regards her; this element in which he lives is "bearable to no mortal" (*P* 63). But then she imagines what might happen, what could happen, if we try out this element (and its possible metaphorical connections to the dark past, what cannot be said, the space of absence and loss): "If you should dip your hand in, / your wrist would ache immediately, / your bones would begin to ache and your hand would burn / as if the water were a transmutation of fire" (*P* 63). The transmutation is complete in the poem's final extended simile that compares the alien watery element with knowledge. Knowledge is historical and, therefore, subject to change. The repetitions – "flowing and drawn," "drawn," "flowing, and flown" – echo the poem's incantatory lines, "Cold dark deep and absolutely clear," creating a lullaby that lulls us to sleep, or numbs us like the water, rocking us – producing a sensation that is strangely at odds with the coldness of this place. In the final simile, Bishop's language lulls us in the arms of what cannot sustain us and in so doing, comes powerfully close to the cold center of the past contained in the startling image of the "cold hard mouth" and "the rocky breasts."

It would take another move south to Brazil to reveal the full range of Bishop's north/south geographical and aesthetic axis. Indeed, *A Cold Spring* originally ended with two Brazil poems: "Arrival at Santos," which Bishop reprinted as the first poem in *Questions of Travel*, and "The Shampoo." "Arrival at Santos" prepares us metaphorically for what Bishop's next move south to Brazil would mean for her development as a poet with its final line: "we are driving to the interior" (*P* 88). As with Bishop's earlier move south to Florida, her geographical compass continued to point north – "Dear, my compass / still points north," as she has it in one recently published Brazilian poem (*P* 313) – and south. But with her dramatic dislocation to the southern hemisphere, she came to explore more deeply the culture, politics, people, and language of her newly adopted country, and she made a bolder move into the interior of her own psyche with a more sustained return to scenes of childhood, memory, and desire.

8

BARBARA PAGE

Home, Wherever That May Be: Poems and Prose of Brazil

When Elizabeth Bishop reached Brazil toward the end of 1951, she did not intend to stay, but soon her growing love for Lota de Macedo Soares, the prospect of a home, and her fascination with the exotic landscapes and provocative new culture led her to linger for nearly two decades. Frankly a tourist when she arrived, Bishop gradually came to know Brazil well, becoming a serious interpreter of her adopted country and a respected translator of Brazilian authors. Asked about the influence of Brazil upon her, Bishop distinguished between "the general life" there, which "had an impact upon me," and "the literary milieu in Brazil," which did not. Brazilian poetry, especially, had its *modernismo* movement, to be sure, but remained more formal and "farther from the demotic" than American modernist poetry. She insisted that even though she had been influenced by Brazil, "I am a completely American poet" (Brown 290). Even so, she came to be regarded, in the words of one Brazilian interviewer, as "an old friend of Brazil and things Brazilian" (*Conversations* 48). In recognition of her contributions, in 1971, the Brazilian government awarded her a high civilian honor, the Order of Rio Branco, for "services rendered to Brazil."

From the buffering distance of South America, Bishop's long meditation on home and homelessness branched into new considerations of what it means to be a lifelong traveler and led her to defend direct experience and local observations in preference to universalist claims of Romantic and Transcendentalist forebears and early Modernists – and to a mild-mannered dispute with Pascal at the conclusion of "Questions of Travel." Except for a handful of sketches, much of Bishop's Brazilian prose offers her reading of its history and culture, some of which proved controversial among Brazilian critics. Similarly, certain of her Brazilian poems, notably "Manuelzinho," "Brazil, January 1, 1502," and "The Burglar of Babylon" have drawn differing judgments of her sensitivity to questions of power, race, and class. Bishop's growing ambivalence toward Brazil colored much of her later work. Conversely, her late poem "Santarém" was suffused with *saudades* (generally referring to longing and nostalgia) for Brazil – a term Bishop associated with homesickness.

Bishop's life in Brazil falls into roughly three periods. From early 1952–1960, Bishop and Lota lived mostly in Samambaia, in the prize-winning Modernist house designed by Sergio Bernardes that Lota was building when Bishop arrived, nestled remotely in the mountains outside the old imperial summer capital, Petrópolis, north of Rio de Janeiro. These years were mostly happy and productive, by her own account, and the house at Samambaia was the second of three loved and lost houses mourned in her poem "One Art." Culminating this extended period of happiness and productivity was a dreamed-of trip she took down the Amazon from Manaus to Belém. Curiously, the only writing it inspired was a fragmentary draft, "On the Amazon" (*EAP* 124–125), until her late brilliant poem of reminiscence, "Santarém" (*P* 207–209), and her posthumously published story, "A Trip to Vigia" (*Pr* 110–116).

After the 1960 election of Lota's friend and neighbor Carlos Lacerda as governor of Guanabara (the state around Rio), Bishop's life changed for the worse. Lota was appointed chief coordinator of a project to build a three-mile-long park covering a stretch of landfill by Guanabara Bay – her inspiration – and was obliged to move to her apartment in Rio. In the increasingly chaotic strife-laden atmosphere of Brazilian politics leading up to the imposition of military dictatorship in 1964, Lota became preoccupied with urgent events and agitated by professional rivals – notably her erstwhile friend, landscape architect Roberto Burle Marx. When left behind at Samambaia, Bishop felt lonely; in Rio – a city she never liked – she felt neglected and grew restless. In the mid-1960s, she purchased a decaying eighteenth-century colonial house in Ouro Preto, in the mountains of Minas Gerais, and began to renovate it. She named it Casa Mariana, partly in tribute to poet Marianne Moore and partly because it lay on the road to the nearby town of Mariana. It became the third of her loved houses in "One Art." Owing to wild inflation, both she and Lota found themselves short of funds, and against Lota's wishes, Bishop took her first teaching position – a semester at the University of Washington. An ill-advised affair begun there led to a serious break between the two, exacerbated by Lota's declining physical and emotional health. This period ended with Lota's 1967 suicide in New York City, to which Bishop had decamped on the advice of Lota's psychiatrist.

The third and final period begins with Bishop's return to Brazil, where she discovered to her dismay that many of Lota's friends blamed her for Lota's death. Even so, she thought she might stay in Brazil, living part time in Ouro Preto. Gradually, she came to realize that life in Brazil without

Lota was untenable. Moreover, she needed the money she could earn by her appointment to teach at Harvard. For several years Bishop divided her time between Ouro Preto, where she hoped to write in peace, and Cambridge, where she taught and reconnected with northern friends. The balance was tipped by a warming relationship with Alice Methfessel, the last great love of her life. Although the house in Ouro Preto remained unsold in her lifetime, she moved with her possessions from Brazil in 1974. Bishop's last projects, cut short by her sudden death in 1979, were to be a collection of pieces about Brazil and an elegy to Lota, which survives only in notes and a few fragments (*EAP* 149, 219–221).

Although Bishop's Brazilian work is informed by her deepening knowledge of the country and colored by altering conditions of her life there, its sequence of publication reflects both her esthetic decisions and the long gaps between publication of individual works and books. "Arrival at Santos" and "The Shampoo" conclude Bishop's second volume of poems, *North & South – A Cold Spring* (1955). They thus mark her transition from the North and South of her first collection to the deeper South of Brazil. In "Arrival at Santos," Bishop writes quasi-naively as a tourist disembarking at the bustling commercial port near São Paulo. Only at the poem's end does the comedy and discomfiture of travel open into metaphoric resonance: "We leave Santos at once; / we are driving to the interior" (*P* 87–88).

"The Shampoo" was written during Bishop's first year in Brazil, but was not published until 1955, after being rejected by the editors of *The New Yorker*, who were baffled by its subtle celebration of domestic happiness in middle-aged love. It is Bishop's first poem in which, as Jonathan Ellis notes, love is not associated with loss ("Aubade" 167). Bishop had known Lota casually in New York in the 1940s, and when the two met again in Brazil, each was shocked to find the other had aged. To early drafts of "The Shampoo," Bishop had given the title "Gray Hairs," (VC 57.6), underscoring the fact of age, but in the alchemy of the finished poem the gray has transmuted into "shooting stars in your black hair." The awful anxiety and disarray of "Days and Distance" in *A Cold Spring's* "Argument," vanish in the freighter's wake bringing Bishop to a new landscape and new love (*P* 79).

"The Shampoo" is a construct of circles – lichens, rings around the moon, the moon itself, the big tin basin. Against the usual urgency of Time in poems such as Andrew Marvell's "To His Coy Mistress," here the mistress is the hasty one, whereas Time is amenable, suiting Bishop's own famous preference not to be rushed. For all its metaphorical extravagance, the scene is domestic, intimate, even homely. In later years, Ashley Brown, a visiting scholar and friend in Brazil, recalled observing the "great ease" of Bishop and Lota with one another, and that Bishop made a ritual of the shampoo (Fountain and Brazeau 142). With her delicately erotic invitation – "Come" – the poet draws the circle close, joining the ever-symbolic moon to the battered shiny tin basin.

By the time Bishop selected poems for her 1965 volume, *Questions of Travel*, the import of "Arrival at Santos" had deepened, becoming now a point of departure for her long meditation on time, home, and travel; she placed it first in the "Brazil" section of this book, adding to it the date January 1952. David Kalstone groups together her first three poems – "Arrival at Santos," "Brazil, January 1, 1502," and "Questions of Travel" – as "poems of method, shucking off habitual notions of culture and history" (214). The "Brazil" poems offer, in Kalstone's words, "a sequence about participation" representing "self-location," whereas the poems of "Elsewhere" and Bishop's story "In the Village" present the materials of memory and of childhood recollected (220, 218). A large gap in time and experience now yawns between the sensibilities of the tourist in "Arrival at Santos" and the narrator of the next poem in Bishop's sequence, "Brazil, January 1, 1502" – a learned poem, informed by aesthetics and history, that spans more than four centuries. As Guy Rotella argues, following Kalstone's lead, this poem especially extends Bishop's "ideas about the limitations and powers of knowledge and art" (224).

"Brazil, January 1, 1502" has drawn disagreement among critics over the degree to which a modern-day traveler like Bishop is implicated in the violent appropriations of the colonizing Portuguese. Although some may regard the traveler Bishop as implicated in imperialism, Rotella contrasts the Portuguese belief ("[c]onfident that their cultural assumptions were divinely warranted facts," which results in "imperialistic appropriation and destruction") with Bishop's view that our assumptions are provisional and historically limited: "Bishop does not attempt to take possession of the scene" (224–25). Rotella notes a crucial simile in the poem – the nature that greets our eyes looks "fresh *as if* just finished / and taken off the frame" (*P* 89; Rotella 225; italics mine). But nature is not reducible to our picture of it. Although the colonists, wrapped in "an old dream" of outdated culture, "ripped away into the hanging fabric," the Indian women, alive within nature, elude them, "retreating, always retreating" behind the illusory fabric dreamed of by the invaders. Lorrie Goldensohn notes that when the adolescent Bishop read W. H. Hudson's *Green Mansions*, she, in her own words, "was filled with the longing to leave for South America immediately," hoping to glimpse the bird-woman Rima, an Indian featured in Hudson's book, "slipping away among the moving shadows." As a caution against some readings arguing that Bishop's speaker identifies with the Indian women,

Goldensohn observes: "It is ... not *as* Rima but as *a seeker* of Rima that Bishop comes to South America" (203–204).

"Questions of Travel," third in this sequence, clarifies Bishop's distinction between the fixed assumptions of imperialists and the relative innocence, even lack of imagination, of Bishop's tourist/traveler. Bishop wrote to that homebody Marianne Moore explaining, or defending, her habit of going about: "Travel heightens sensation by dismantling old ideas; close observation becomes a source of renewal and reinvention." Bishop underscored "that uneasy heightening of sensation" as "essential to travel" (Costello 130). Bonnie Costello usefully contrasts Bishop's view of travel with that of the Transcendentalist Thoreau, who "assumes the stationary prospect of the mastering gaze" (149). In his essay "Walking," Thoreau described his ideal traveler as one who "having no particular home [is] equally at home everywhere." Emerson admired in Thoreau's writing "the power of the imperial mind over all nature's plurality." In Thoreau's mind, wrote Emerson, "[e]very fact lay in glory, ... a type of the order and beauty of the whole." Costello, however, regards Thoreau's "model of awareness [as] atemporal and unitary, the very antithesis of travel" (149). In contrast, for Bishop as a traveler, "it does not at all follow that, 'having no particular home,' one is 'at home everywhere,' or may take dominion" (143). Her consciousness "is travel-bound, temporal, and particular." Costello concludes that Bishop "replaces transcendence and mastery with pleasure in discovery and surprise .... The knowledge gained in these poems pertains less to things in their relation to the 'order and beauty of the whole' than to history and to the beholder's desires" (149–150).

In Costello's framing, then, the three opening poems of *Questions of Travel* are not only poems of method, as Kalstone says, but poems defining Bishop's fundamental outlook and her difference from the American Transcendentalists. These poems bear out and expand Bishop's vision of "what we imagine knowledge to be" in "At the Fishhouses" (*P* 64). In this light, Bishop's meditation on home in "Questions of Travel" no longer looks like the complaint of a displaced orphan. Instead, home appears now to be provisional, changeable, uncertain – difficult, even harsh perhaps, but immersed in life. It is not a lack of imagination after all that sets off the traveler, but rather a quest for knowledge that is historical and grounded in experience, not metaphysical. The "childish" voice of the traveler, complaining that the extravagant landscapes of Brazil are too much, seems initially wilful, pressing forward toward the next novel sight: "the tiniest green hummingbird," a bit of "inexplicable old stonework." Incrementally, a defense of travel emerges with the wheedling words, "But surely it would have been a pity" not to have seen *these* scenes and *these* things, including the history recorded in "the weak calligraphy of songbirds' cages." Finally, the traveler is prepared to take a stand of sorts: "No." Pascal, if not wrong, might "have been not entirely right." Anything but imperialist, Bishop's traveler acknowledges that one's choices are "never wide and never free." This traveler, whose knowledge flows through time and space, must suffer the uneasy sensation of motion sickness and its disorientations. The answer to Pascal is not Thoreau's – that home can be anywhere – but a question of continual orientation and reconsideration: home, "wherever that may be" (*P* 91–92).

Despite her happiness with Lota, Bishop's feelings toward Brazil remained equivocal: "I have had some rather bleak stretches in which I wonder, my god, what am I doing *here?* " (*OA* 275). With Lota's help, and her library, Bishop began to read Portuguese writers and poets and soon could follow conversations. She was charmed by a Brazilian children's classic, *Minha Vida de Menina*, the diary of a girl living in the mountainous interior toward the end of the nineteenth century, and set about translating it. She saw in *The Diary of "Helena Morley"* as it was called in English, a parallel narrative to her own stories of her Nova Scotian childhood (Ribeiro 17). As an introduction to this translation, Bishop composed a long account of life in Diamantina, the mining town of "Helena Morley's" childhood, after visiting there in 1956. She sent a copy to João Cabral de Melo Neto, one of Brazil's most distinguished poets, whose early poems share with some of Bishop's a surface simplicity of subject and form. He responded: "I consider your description the best appreciation ever done of a Brazilian colonial city's atmosphere" (VC 10.10).

From time to time, for the rest of her career, Bishop translated works of writers she admired, but only when she thought they would go into English, including the musical elements of rhythm and rhyme. Judging by Bishop's translations in her co-edited *Anthology of Twentieth-Century Brazilian Poetry* (1972), she was also drawn to themes of rustic families and childhood recollected, such as Carlos Drummond de Andrade's "Viagem Na Família" / "Travelling in the Family," Cabral's "Morte e Vida Severina," / "The Death and Life of a Severino," and Joaquim Cardozo's "Cemitério da Infância" / "Cemetery of Childhood." Perhaps recalling her flirtation with Surrealism in her early career, Bishop also translated three of Clarice Lispector's unnerving moral fables, "The Smallest Woman in the World," "A Hen," and "Marmosets" (Lispector 500–511).

Despite these achievements, Bishop, by her own acknowledgment, never mastered written or spoken Portuguese: "After all these years, I'm like a dog: I understand everything that's said to me, but I don't speak it very well" (Brown 291). Her Brazilian translator Paulo Henriques Britto, unlike Cabral, believes that this limitation led Bishop to misunderstand her adopted country: "Unable or unwilling to learn Portuguese properly, Elizabeth Bishop was a most ineffective (and reluctant) cultural intermediary; in fact, all she asked of Brazil was a home – a place where she would be loved and understood and where she could write in peace" ("Cultural Intermediary" 496). Fair enough, although Bishop did want to write about Brazil and worked hard against the temptation to represent it as exotic; of her projected book, never completed, she said, "I'd like to make Brazil seem less remote and less an object of picturesque fancy" (Brown 302). In judging that what Bishop sought in Brazil was a home, Britto may have overlooked the forever provisional nature of home in her way of thinking. She remarked tellingly to a Brazilian interviewer, "from time to time I go back to the United States, returning to my linguistic sources, like a diver coming up to the surface" (Ribeiro 14–15). She knew she was out of her element in Brazil. Home as a place remained equivocal, whether in the North or the South. She was at home, metaphorically, only in the English language.

The next four poems, as Bishop arranged them in *Questions of Travel*, are set in the subtropical mountains of Samambaia and saturated with the atmosphere of the rainy season. The first two, "Squatter's Children" and "Manuelzinho," present, first, a long view and then a close-up of a family living on the Samambaia property. Manuelzinho – "[h]alf squatter, half tenant (no rent)" (*P* 94) – lived and worked on the Samambaia property for many years, and "Squatter's Children" is about his family. Given the abjectness of the children's storm-threatened "specklike" house, the poem's elevated diction – "effulgence," "unwarrantable," "echolalia" – may at first seem peculiar, but as Costello astutely argues, "Squatter's Children" can be read as a challenge to "Wordsworth's notion in the Immortality Ode that nature is God's mansion" (167). If so, Bishop here redresses Romantic optimism with darker irony, just as she had redressed Thoreau's Transcendental mastery in "Questions of Travel" with earthbound knowledge. Nevertheless, the children's "laughter spreads / effulgence" (radiance) "in the thunderheads" – evoking but reversing Milton's "on thee / Impresst the effulgence of his Glorie abides" (*Paradise Lost* III 387–388) and countering the mother's voice, "ugly as sin." The children's play and laughter escape, precariously, either biblical allegory (their ark is unwarrantable – unauthorized) or the law of the land. However, they are warranted only in the soluble "rooms of falling rain" (*P* 93). Responding to the children's laughter, the voice of the rain is mere "echolalia," meaningless repetition. In Bishop's natural mansions, the landlord (God) is absent.

With the next poem, "Manuelzinho," Bishop's observing eye moves in close even while she places herself outside the drama, speaking in the voice of "a friend," Lota, as she acknowledged (*OA* 315). Although recognized as a great achievement of tone and color – Randall Jarrell judged it a masterpiece (*WIA* 590) – it has drawn the fire of some American and Brazilian readers for what they see as insensitivity to Manuelzinho's painful social and economic condition. Stung by a reviewer's objection to the poem, Bishop retorted that she had been "misunderstood" in "the social-conscious days." Actually, she wrote, "Brazilians like 'Manuelzinho' very much. I've had several English-reading friends tell me, 'My God (or Our Lady), it's *exactly* like that'" (*OA* 479). Friends of Lota's upper-class social set, that is. Poet Frank Bidart recalled Robert Lowell saying that, under Lota's influence in Brazil, Bishop became unattractively conservative. Bidart disagreed for the most part, finding her Brazilian poems "often radical in perception and feeling," but he thought "Manuelzinho" was the exception, "with its whiff of noblesse oblige" (Fountain and Brazeau 140–141). Bishop's translator Britto sees in "Manuelzinho" "the caricature of a Brazilian 'primitive,'" with Lota's voice capturing "the exact mixture of helpless exasperation and condescending affection that characterizes the feelings of Brazilian patricians for their servants" ("Cultural Intermediary" 493). Lota was patrician, and usually proud of it. In this poem, however, the speaker regrets exercising her superior wit at her gardener's expense. Manuelzinho has painted his straw hat green: "I called you the Klorophyll Kid. / My visitors thought it was funny. / I apologize here and now" (*P* 97).

Although for Lota, at her most "precipitate and pragmatical," Manuelzinho is "the world's worst gardener since Cain," for Bishop he is an artist of sorts, exercising creative imagination under hard conditions, painting his hats and edging his cabbage beds with red carnations. In this regard he joins the Samambaia cook, who took up painting and produced work Bishop genuinely admired (*OA* 243). Applying her own well-stocked literary imagination, she further refigures Manuelzinho into an imaginary realm of mystic three-legged carrots, and Dream Books for accounting, where his deceased father is not really dead and "the meek shall inherit the earth – / or several acres of mine," as Lota sarcastically remarks. Yelled at, Manuelzinho vanishes as if he'd "been a gardener / in a fairy tale all this time."

It is apparent that Bishop is not simply recording her observations of scenes and activities around Samambaia. She is engaging several kinds of shifting perspective and signification for aesthetic effect, to be sure, but also for moral purpose. To critics of Bishop's "Manuelzinho," such displacements evade hard facts of social inequity; as English poet Charles Tomlinson tartly remarked, "the better off have always preferred their poor processed by style" (Tomlinson 89). Thomas Travisano disagrees, arguing that Bishop is not concealing social barriers between rich and poor, but examining them (*Artistic* 146). Comparing Bishop with Flannery O'Connor (a writer Bishop admired), George Lensing goes one step further. In O'Connor's story "The Displaced Person" and in Bishop's "Manuelzinho," he argues, the "narratives register a subtle truce between the social classes, ... allowing the system to function in the quotidian world each inhabited" (194). The balance of evidence in Bishop's work does not suggest, however, that she favored a truce with unjust social systems. Although her poems generally avoided explicit politics, judgments are implicit: the squatter's children *should* inherit mansions in heaven; Manuelzinho *deserves* to inherit, if not the earth, certainly a good piece of it. Her art does entail distancing, displacements, and, yes, style, but it does not conceal or sentimentalize social conditions. For Bishop, Manuelzinho is not a social problem, or not only that, but an indispensable presence of weight and meaning, composing and creating life at Samambaia, in that time, in that place, living aslant, as the draft poem "Gypsophilia" has it, on an iron mountain (*EAP* 129).

With "Electrical Storm" and "Song for the Rainy Season," Bishop turns her eye from the property and occupants around Samambaia to the domestic interior of her home there. Both poems were published in 1960, but the first and fourth stanzas of "Song for the Rainy Season" were composed in 1954 (Millier 304); its mood of intimate happiness therefore spans a long stretch of Bishop's life at Samambaia. Travisano describes both as love poems, and calls "Song for the Rainy Season" "this hotbed of surprising intimacies." Noting Bishop's longstanding "instinct for enclosure and safety," he finds here "a more satisfying form of hermeticism, since the (unnamed) beloved is *inside* rather than *outside* enclosure" (*Artistic* 149, 151). The house, in fact, is not enclosed but open to creatures and atmosphere; although "hidden, oh hidden," it is not defended (*P* 99). The two poems are paired by more than their sequential position in *Questions of Travel*, for the openness of the house and expansiveness of spirit in "Song for a Rainy Season," as Angus Cleghorn observes, "answers to the repressive short-circuiting of the 'Electrical Storm'" ("Wiring" 76). A number of readers, notably Cleghorn and Goldensohn, have connected the many electrical storms and wires in Bishop's poems with eroticism (Cleghorn "Wiring"; Goldensohn 28). This linkage is most explicit in the complete but withheld love poem from Key West, "It is marvellous to wake up together," in which lovers are awakened – and aroused – by an electrical storm (*P* 283; Goldensohn 28). In "Electrical Storm," the natural world is as hostile and unpleasant as certain human encounters: the thunder banging on the roof is as "spiteful as a neighbor's child" and the hail looks like artificial pearls, "diplomats' wives favors / from an old moon party" (*P* 98). Bishop's beloved cat Tobias – a transitional animal between external nature and the domestic interior – is driven in, terrified by the storm, and takes to the warm sheets of the bed left by its human occupants. Lightning from the spiteful storm has struck the house; the wiring is fused, the telephone dead. At the literal level, the poem presents a scene of the often fierce subtropical world Bishop wanted her readers to experience. For years, Bishop and Lota had lived at Samambaia without electricity or telephone, at times almost cut off from the outside world by a rough mountain road. These touches of civilization were hard-won and precarious. For Bishop, however, isolation in rude conditions had its compensations in the sequestration she often sought and in domestic intimacy. Displacing fright onto the cat, the threat recedes to miniature. The mood is not severe.

We are thus prepared for the sheer lyricism of the next poem's opening: "Hidden, oh hidden / in the high fog / the house we live in." Here seclusion is not removal from life but intensification of it, where the house and its occupants are open to natural fecundity, and even the touches that damage and tarnish are warm. The thunder banging on the roof of "Electrical Storm" gives way to the stamping of "the ordinary brown / owl." The place teems with life and seems blessed "beneath the magnetic rock, / rain-, rainbow-ridden." In this poem, Bishop's habitual personification of nature suffuses house, cloud, and creatures with erotic warmth. The open house is receptive to "membership / of silver fish, mouse, / bookworms / moths" and provides "a wall / for the mildew's / ignorant map." It celebrates a secular version of the Miltonic paradox of the fortunate fall: the life of mortal love is maculate and its very blemishes are cherished: "rejoice!" "Song for the Rainy Season" is certainly a love poem, but it should be noted that the speaker is in love, not just with a person, but with *it all* – her little world of the fog-hidden house and all its creatures, in a state of almost transcendental happiness.

Almost. Having achieved a pinnacle of celebration – "rejoice!" – Time, briefly amenable in "The Shampoo," reasserts its inexorable power. Change is inevitable "(O difference that kills)," the rock, unmagnetized, will no longer wear the clothing of delight, the owls will fly off, the waterfalls shrivel (*P* 99–100).

In "The Armadillo," the owl does fly off, as this very decline is enacted in an allegory of natural innocence violated and destroyed, in part by the very ignorance implied in innocence within mortal and moral life (*P* 101–102). A piece of Brazil's cultural history is in play with the colorful celebration of that country's most popular saint's day, the June 24 festival of Saint John. From Samambaia, Bishop wrote to Anny Baumann of the fireworks and bonfires all over the valley: "Fire balloons are supposed to be illegal but everyone sends them up anyway ... They are so pretty – one's of two minds about them" (VC 23.3). In fact, they were so dangerous that Lota had fire extinguishers installed on the roof of the house – Bishop's loved house.

Bishop's ambivalence is captured in the poem by the shift from detached observation to the urgent outcry of its italicized ending, an internal critique of all that precedes: "*Too pretty, dreamlike mimicry!*"

Two of the animals of "The Armadillo" have a precursor in the draft poem "The Owl's Journey" (*EAP* 91) from a dream dating as far back as Bishop's college days; almost until "The Armadillo" was finished, its working title had been "The Owl's Nest," bringing Bishop's long-gestated symbolic animals home to roost, so to speak, in Brazil. Finally, however, the shrieking owl and panicked baby rabbit yield place to the armadillo, whose body itself shapes an archaic protest – "*a weak mailed fist / clenched ignorant against the sky*!" The cause of the poem's suffering and protest is the children of the valley, raising tribute to a saint represented as a child. Cosmic or spiritual yearnings are strongly rebuffed in "The Armadillo," a tragedy of innocence and harmful ignorance. The suffering is real; our sympathies are engaged with the weak, but in this scene, there is nowhere to turn for redress.

Quite early in her residence in Brazil, Bishop began to consider putting together a volume of travel writing and sketches about her adopted country. Soon, however, more serious consideration of conditions there began to press upon her. In 1958, when the new capital, Brasília, was under construction, Bishop tagged along on a trip to the interior with visiting British novelist, Aldous Huxley. They flew to Brasília, a dusty plain of half-finished futurist constructions designed by architect Oscar Niemeyer within the plan laid out by Lúcio Costa, then on to visit an Indian settlement along the Xingu River. Under Lota's tutelage, Bishop had learned a good deal about Modernist Brazilian architecture, and in fact had helped translate Henrique Mindlin's *Modern Architecture in Brazil*, but she found Brasília dreary. Huxley, "remote and silent," supplied little by way of human interest, and their visit to the Indians was brief and superficial. Still, with the famous novelist's name as the hook, Bishop wrote up the trip as "A New Capital, Aldous Huxley, and Some Indians," and sent it to *The New Yorker* (*PPL* 365–401). Although Lota and her friends adamantly opposed what they regarded as President Juscelino Kubitschek's ruinously extravagant plans for Brasília, in her essay Bishop strove to be even handed and descriptive. But when *The New Yorker* turned it down, with relief she went back to writing, as she said, "something more my natural bent" (*OA* 369).

A first result of Bishop's return to poems, was "The Riverman," a remarkable success especially as it was not inspired by observation but by a book, *Amazon Town*, an account of native Brazilian life by anthropologist Charles Wagley. Airing her doubts about it, she wrote to Lowell, "You don't have to like the 'Riverman' poem. Lota hates it, and I don't approve of it myself but once it was written I couldn't seem to get rid of it" (*WIA* 315). She was reassured by his response: "I wouldn't worry about the Amazon poem – it's the best fairy story in verse I know. It brings back an old dream of yours, you said you felt you were a mermaid scraping barnacles off a wharf-pile. That was Maine, not Brazil" (*WIA* 321). He later remarked percipiently that "The Riverman" was "a very powerful initiation poem that somehow echoes your own entrance in Santos" (*WIA* 591).

Bishop had long been preoccupied with borderlines between land and water, between waking and sleeping, between fantasy and everyday life. A dream she had while living in Key West of following a fish into the sea toward "some sort of celebration" anticipates the riverman more closely than the anxious mermaid Lowell recalled (VC 75.3a, 15). In "The Riverman," Bishop drew these formative themes together with her deepening experience of Brazil, creating for the first time, as Goldensohn notes in her excellent examination of the poem, "a first person compound of Brazilian legend from within North American diction and feeling," in a poem that "touches on central thematic preoccupations" with "estrangement and communality" (208). No longer positioned at a distance from an observed scene or in a state of bemused ambivalence with domesticity, Bishop gives the voice of her apprentice *sacaca* the humble but firm confidence of the truly enchanted. For the duration of the poem, Bishop's habitual ironic detachment is banished, as it must be for the magic to survive. Bishop invests elements of her own dream life and experience in the voice of her riverman – an admission, perhaps, that she was no longer a mere visitor in Brazil. The riverman's underwater travels have separated him from his former life, as he leaves his sleeping wife and notes his difference from his unknowing godfathers and cousins above.

In "At the Fishhouses," knowledge is "drawn from the cold hard mouth / of the world" (*P* 64); similarly, the riverman reasons that the river "draws from the very heart / of the earth" (*P* 106). But even though the new element has changed him – "the river smells in my hair" – he still hovers between the old and new life. His enchanting tutelary spirit, Luandinha, speaks to him in a language he only begins to know: "I understood like a dog, / although I can't speak it yet" (*P* 104). Here Bishop infuses her own experience most directly into the voice of the riverman, as we can see when she uses the same doggy figure to describe her imperfect mastery of Portuguese (Brown 291). The riverman is not a stand-in for the poet, however, but for her belief that where folk art and legend still shape and express lives, a fresh feeling for life, as in childhood, endures. Bishop – reader, traveler, observer, resident of Brazil – through her riverman, has moved within the frame of the story begun with Hudson's *Green Mansions* and continued through the curtain of landscape in "Brazil, January 1, 1502."

In the early 1960s, Bishop's happy life at Samambaia was severely disrupted. When newly elected governor of Rio state Carlos Lacerda appointed Lota to head the project to build a "people's park," Lota found an outlet for her formidable talents, but she quickly became absorbed in pushing the project through snarls of political connivance and competing artistic egos. Her success in building Parque do Flamengo (which remains today) came at the cost of her health and peace of mind, and because she spent most of her time in Rio, Bishop felt obliged to join her there, unhappily exchanging the slow pace of Samambaia for the hectic, dilapidated city. Moreover, President Kubitschek's forced economic development, and the construction of the new capital in Brasília, ignited wild inflation; therefore, when the editors of the *Life* World Library offered her a substantial sum to write a volume on Brazil, she reluctantly accepted. By then, Bishop knew a good deal about the country and outlined chapters on its history, natural settings, culture, and arts under tantalizing titles including "Paradoxes and Ironies," "Vegetable, Mineral, and Animal," and "The Unselfconscious Arts" (*Pr* 164). As Cleghorn shows in his thorough comparison of the two texts ("The Politics of Editing Bishop's 1962 *Brazil* Volume for Life World Library"), the *Life* editors laid heavy hands on the book, imposing their cheery Cold War story of a developing country progressing inevitably toward liberal democracy. Embittered, she all but disowned it.

On the eve of the quatercentenary of Rio, Bishop accepted a commission to write an article for the *New York Times Magazine*, "On the Railroad Named Delight" (*Pr* 342–351). Noting the swelling numbers of the "very poorest Brazilians" from the Northeast filling Rio's *favelas* (slums), she acknowledges the decline of "the intellectual capital of the country" (344) to the status of a provincial center (351) beleaguered by governmental inefficiency and inflation. More cheerfully, she describes Carnival, which she enjoyed and attended nearly every year, and her delight in the annual samba lyrics, translating several of them. She concludes by favorably comparing race relations in Brazil to the segregated United States (351), but found herself misunderstood and excoriated by a local journalist as an American paternalistic racist (Castro). This was unfair, as Bishop had plainly disparaged race relations in the United States, not Brazil. However, Bishop did misjudge effects of the 1964 military coup, declaring prematurely that "the press is free" and "[t]alk about police and army brutality and torture has died down" (350). As Bishop's letters from the mid-1960s attest, she was slow to recognize growing repression under military rule, and drew sharp criticism from Brazilians who suffered under the twenty-year dictatorship (see Regina Przybycien in Goldensohn 206–207; and Caetano Veloso 6). In poems, Bishop gave more effective voice to her sympathies and protest against injustice, notably in "The Burglar of Babylon," finished in time to be included in her 1965 *Questions of Travel*, and "Pink Dog" (in drafts called "Farewell to Rio" or "Rio Blues"), begun in this period but not published until 1979.

From Lota's apartment in Rio, overlooking the *favela* called "Babilonia," Bishop observed soldiers tracking down a notorious criminal and then followed the story in newspapers. In a matter of days, she wrote off an inspired response, "The Burglar of Babylon," shaped by both her childhood love of traditional balladry and her pleasure in Brazilian folk poetry. Brazilian journalist and critic Léo Gilson Ribeiro immediately recognized a resemblance to Brazil's *literatura de cordel* (literature on a string), folk poetry narrating sensational events of the day (15), so named because they were produced as booklets, strung up, and sold from kiosks in cities of the Northeast. Bishop relished and collected these *cordel* poems as examples of a living folk art.

The "Burglar's" opening and closing scene – "On the fair green hills of Rio / There grows a fearful stain: / The poor who come to Rio / And can't go home again" (*P* 110) – evokes Brazil's tragic history of Northeastern poverty and inequality enforced by crushing governmental power, the source of the growing tide of immigrants swelling Rio's *favelas*. Bishop knew this history well through her travels and reading of Brazilian classics such as Euclides da Cunha's *Os Sertões* (*Rebellion in the Backlands*). And in Mícuçu, she found a sadly diminished contemporary parallel to the Northeastern bandit Lampião, a popular hero of Brazilian stories and songs, sometimes likened to Robin Hood. In "The Burglar," pathos – not satire – is the tone, as Travisano remarks (*Artistic* 163), voiced by Mícuçu's helpless auntie and witnessed with tacit self-reproof by "Rich people in apartments" (*P* 113). Here, the poet's habitual remoteness from her subject is not a matter of aesthetic distance but, as she confessed, of shaming implication in the gap between rich and poor: "*I* am one of the 'rich with binoculars!'" (Goldensohn 6). George Monteiro, however, reports that some Brazilians were offended by the narrator's "standoffish vantage point," and argues that in choosing the ballad form, Bishop kept her distance from the hard reality of her story (*Brazil and After* 62). To Lowell, it was a triumph, like Bishop's "Visits to St. Elizabeths": "It's surely one of the great ballads in the language, and oddly enough gives more of Brazil somehow than your whole Life book" (*WIA* 560). The "Burglar," he thought, "tells a lot about your own judgments on your society, obliquely" (*WIA* 591).

It is perhaps just as well, in view of Bishop's Brazilian critics, that her "Pink Dog" was not published until 1979, for it gives no quarter to Rio's beauty and charms. If, in her "House Guest," Bishop enacts a sad comedy of a misbegotten, complaining Fate, and in her prose-poems of "Rainy Season;

Sub-Tropics," she displaces a mood of self-pity and discomfiture onto her oversized and strayed toad, crab, and snail (*P* 163–63), then in "Pink Dog," disenchantment distills into Swiftian irony. Although Monteiro reasonably regards its rhyming tercets as like Dante's *terza rima* (*Brazil and After* 75), its more immediate antecedent in tercets is Bishop's own "Roosters," another poem of angry rejection, arising from the overrunning of Key West by the military at the outset of World War II. In both, violence and aggression prompt real anger beyond the despairing, helpless protest of her armadillo fleeing a firestorm. In "Pink Dog," no room remains for ignorant innocence: vicious reality is the stuff of "all the papers," how "they deal with beggars" by drowning them in the tidal rivers (*P* 212). Here direct address keeps the poet close: "Didn't you know"; "Yes"; "Now look." In Bishop's angry disenchantment, even her much-loved Carnival becomes complicit in monstrous civic heartlessness toward the poor and helpless: "A depilated dog would not look well. / Dress up! Dress up and dance at Carnival!"

By the mid-1960s, "Rio," Bishop remarked, "was getting on my nerves badly" (*OA* 436), but Samambaia was too lonely without Lota. Bishop was drawn to the slower pace of the old colonial towns of Minas Gerais, especially Ouro Preto, which she liked "because everything there was made on the spot, by hand, of stone, iron, copper, wood" (*OA* 440). She also liked her host there, Lilli Correia de Araújo, the Danish widow of a Brazilian artist, staying at times at her inn, Chico Rei, but longer at Lilli's old four-square colonial house on the road to Mariana. From her second floor bedroom, Bishop overheard conversations of passersby gathered around an old fountain, which she put into a poem, "Under the Window: Ouro Prêto," dedicated to Lilli (*P* 175–176), its mood remarkably different from that of her Rio-born poems of complaint. It is a celebration of another maculate world – rusted, oily but cheerfully carrying on, a relief from the queasy, ill feeling suffusing Rio.

Within sight, down and across the road, stood another old colonial house with gardens on both sides and a commanding view of the town in the valley below. By September 1965, Bishop bought it, her third loved house of "One Art," Casa Mariana (*OA* 440). Behind this story lay two other poems unpublished in her lifetime, both love poems and one of them certainly private testimony to Bishop's brief, giddy infatuation with Lilli, her "darling Dane," and "Dear Aurora Borealis" (VC 112.2). Under the spell of her "dearest blue eyed fair-headed" Lilli, she composed and illustrated two versions of "Dear, my compass still points north," enumerating nostalgically their shared northern roots (*EAP* 140; *P* 312–313). Lloyd Schwartz rightly comments that, "with typical obliqueness, it is even *about* Brazil – or, rather, what Brazil is not" ("Annals" 86). The second poem, "Close close all night," from this time and mood, is intimate but ambiguous as to the sex of the closely entwined lovers. Bishop eventually gave it to an Ouro Preto friend, artist José Alberto Nemer, who illustrated it in celebration of his own wedding (see Quinn *EAP* 332–336.)

The interlude of relief and renewed happiness in Ouro Preto proved fleeting. By the end of 1965, Bishop departed for her first teaching job: a semester at the University of Washington. Returning, she made a trip down Brazil's second-largest river, the São Francisco, and afterward wrote up a glum report of the experience (VC 55.3). There would be no repetition of the dreamlike joy of her trip down the Amazon. The affair Bishop began with a young woman in Seattle, Roxanne Cumming, was clumsily concealed and soon discovered by a devastated Lota. From there Bishop's long, rich life in Brazil with Lota careened to its disastrous end with Lota's suicide in New York City in 1967.

In the aftermath, Bishop thought perhaps there would be no more poems, but slowly she began to recover, returning to a poem she had been working on in the mid-1960s, "Crusoe in England," which in many readers' eyes retrospectively became a tribute to her lost life and love in Brazil (*P* 182). Restlessly, she moved for a time to San Francisco and back to Ouro Preto, then after the break up of her affair with Cumming, moved back and forth between Boston and Ouro Preto. As she resettled in North America, part of her mind cast back to Brazil. With Emanuel Brasil, Bishop co-edited *An Anthology of Twentieth-Century Brazilian Poetry*, which ends with mid-century poets, but declined Brasil's invitation to edit a second volume, of concretist and other contemporary experimental poets, with whom she had little affinity. Finally, among her last great poems, appeared "Santarém" (*P* 207).

The poem was begun soon after Bishop's trip but not completed and published until 1978, giving, as Millier has remarked, almost comical import to its opening lines: "Of course I may be remembering it all wrong / after, after – how many years?" (534). Like "Poem," "Santarém" is a meditation on "life and the memory of it." "Poem" anchors memory in Bishop's childhood home in Nova Scotia; "Santarém" floats it at the literal midpoint of Bishop's dreamlike journey down the Amazon River, and at the midpoint of Bishop's long life in Brazil, a place from which finally she had to move on, as surely as if summoned by the ship's whistle in the poem (*P* 208). Both are poems of aftermath, of long experience and hard-learned knowledge, where the weight of all those yesterdays may sometimes be "almost impossible to lift" (*P* 203), but at fortunate moments may be measured – "about the size of our abidance" (*P* 197) – or simply recounted, as in the fragment "Syllables": "Whatever there is, or was, of affection / may it be said" (*EAP* 101). We can see that the golden mood of "Santarém" was an attainment of time, of the sort that "resolved, dissolved" painful memories of guilt and loss, now as remote as "literary interpretations" of the Garden of Eden. In a fragment composed soon after Lota's death, Bishop addresses her companion on the trip down the Amazon: "oh that was a nice day, Rosinha, wasn't it ... / one of the nicer ones. OH I hate memories / sometimes" (*EAP* 147). But now, later on, they can be gathered and cherished, "touching in detail" (*P* 197).

Miss Breen, of "Arrival at Santos," and Mr. Swan, of "Santarém," bookend Bishop's questions of travel in Brazil. Neither is an antagonist; the poet and Miss Breen disembark from the same tourists' deck, and Mr. Swan, we are assured, is "really a very nice old man" (*P* 209). The distance between them, however, is lit by the experience of life lived immersed – like the riverman – in another element: Brazil. Leaving home was really never a question for Bishop, as it may have been for Pascal. A tender fragment recalling Nova Scotia, as a "pocket of Time," close and warm, abruptly ended when Time, capricious, not at all amenable, "reached in, / and tumbled us out" (*EAP* 103). Compensation for Time's caprice is aqueous memory – the source of knowledge – like the Nova Scotian "Fishhouses'" ocean and Brazil's Amazon; flowing and flown, perhaps, but moving – where loss reconciles with life.

The gain is precarious. The repeatedly misidentified "church, the Cathedral, rather," is fair warning to Bishop's readers. In "Santarém," its spire was struck by lightning, a menace without harm, while the priest, "*Graças a deus*," was away. Visitors to the historical place learn that there is no evidence of its cathedral having been struck by lightning. Was this incident instead an artifact of another memory, from Nova Scotia, recorded in "Syllables"? "That steeple – I can't remember – wasn't it struck by lightning?" (*EAP* 101). But in the dreamlike watery journey, a place, an object of that place, can still the passage of time, if only momentarily. In "Poem," the very water, as she remembered it, is "*still* standing from spring freshets" (*P* 197; italics mine). Such "details" as apparently slight as "the yet-to-be-dismantled elms, the geese" of "Poem" or the wasps' nest of "Santarém" invest memory with totemic significance. Mr. Swan, ironically of Philips Electric, is in the dark: "What's that ugly thing?" To Bishop (the necessary traveler), the wasps' nest secures – assures – the life now lost except to memory. When Crusoe removes from exile to "another island," the tokens of his former life shrivel: "How can anyone want such things?" (*P* 186). For Bishop, however, the golden sands of Santarém, its zebus ("*blue*, with down-curved horns and hanging ears"), and the wasps' nest ("small, exquisite, clean matte white") reconcile the poet to loss. In memory, they – and Brazil – live.

9

LLOYD SCHWARTZ

Back to Boston: *Geography III* and Other Late Poems

Six months before her sixtieth birthday, Elizabeth Bishop returned to her "origins" – or close to them. Born in Worcester, Massachusetts in 1911, she moved to Cambridge, Massachusetts in 1970 to teach at Harvard, replacing her friend Robert Lowell, who had left for England to be with his new wife. She had lived mainly in Brazil since 1951, and although that connection was unraveling, it was still not quite over. Harvard was putting her up in a barely utilitarian apartment in Kirkland House (where Alice Methfessel was the house secretary, and soon became Bishop's friend and partner). The poet, who suffered from chronic asthma, was also assigned a dingy classroom in a damp basement. Early that fall, she gave her first reading as a Harvard faculty member, at Emerson Hall, in Harvard Yard. That was where I first met her, introduced to her at the reception following the reading by my friend Frank Bidart, who had met her before through Lowell.

"Miss Bishop, I enjoyed your reading," I told her, "and I've admired your poems for many years."

"Oh," she replied, "thank you."

And that was the end of our first conversation.

What I then took to be cool politeness, I later understood to be an almost morbid self-consciousness about her work. And I couldn't yet know that emotions she had learned to repress or understate in her poems were already beginning to surface with surprising directness. It would take nearly three years before we could consider ourselves friends. Good enough friends for her not only to allow me to make her poems the subject of my doctoral dissertation (I had virtually given up on a previous topic), but to generously offer to meet with me and answer any questions I had about her writing – a subject virtually off limits to even her close friends. I now suspect that a certain motherly instinct to get a young graduate student to complete his degree outweighed her reluctance to discuss her work. "I would have been such a nervous, over-devoted mother probably," she wrote to Robert Lowell (*WIA* 342). But would any of the numerous younger writers Bishop "nurtured" have thought of her in these terms at the time? The one exception she made about discussing her work was in her letters responding to the questions posed to her about her poems by Anne Stevenson, the young American poet who was living in England and writing the first book-length monograph on Bishop.

She wasn't very happy in Cambridge, although there were a few people around whom she liked, including Bidart, and, for a time, William Alfred, the playwright and Harvard professor of Old English, a good friend of Lowell's. And of course, Methfessel. In letters to her friend Linda Nemer in Brazil, she complained that she didn't like American coffee, and sent her the only poem (at least, her only extant poem) that she wrote in Portuguese (VC September 1970) – a bit of darkly comic light verse about "mixers" at Harvard, in which she uses the Portuguese word for "Mixmaster" for these social gatherings. Of course, it's also a poem about her discomfort with America and the odd "mixture" of improvements and miseries in America as compared to her life in Brazil. Here are a couple of stanzas in a translation by Barbara Page and Carmen Oliveira that's probably better than the Portuguese original (Brazilians are generally disparaging of Bishop's attempts at Portuguese) and sounds more like the "real" Bishop:

> The water is so hot
> that I burned my hand.
> All the lights work.
> The bed is soft; the pillows
> give me asthma.
>
> This evening there is something
> called "a mixer."
> Students, male and female,
> mixing and mixing
> in the large dead rooms.

Of course, no one but Linda Nemer ever saw this poem before Bishop died on October 6, 1979 in the Boston waterfront condominium to which she had by then moved.

The first new poem *everyone* saw, after she returned to Boston, was the first poem she published in the three years since her last unsettling Brazilian poems of the later 1960s ("Going to the Bakery" and "House Guest") and the oddball New York poem raising, but not answering, the implicit question: "Why does a chicken cross the road?" ("Trouvée"). The new poem, "In the Waiting Room," appeared in *The New Yorker* in the summer of 1971; *The New Yorker* had held it for more than a year, so she had arrived in Cambridge having written but not yet published this poem she felt a little nervous about – one that included lines that no one, maybe not even she herself, could have predicted she was capable of writing:

> But I felt: you are an *I*,
> you are an *Elizabeth*,
> you are one of *them*.
> *Why* should you be one, too? (*P* 180)

The elusive poet of privacy and reticence was suddenly, startlingly, more openly personal, more overflowing with the expression of personal feelings than her readers had ever seen. What no one could have known before her death was that "In the Waiting Room" (*P* 179) was based on an unpublished story, a slightly fictionalized memoir (it's sometimes hard to tell the difference between Bishop's memoirs and her stories) that she had been working on perhaps a decade before. She called it "The Country Mouse," and it was – like "In the Village" and "Gwendolyn," both of which she published in *The New Yorker* – a story about her childhood. This one is her *Paradise Lost*, dealing with the unhappy aftermath of her wealthy paternal grandparents uprooting her, practically abducting her, from her carefree quasi-farm life with her maternal grandparents in tiny Great Village, Nova Scotia. The story – which ends, "Why was I a human being?" – doesn't quite hang together, somehow lacking in compression and structural intensity. But she turned it into an astonishing poem that seemed remarkably fresh and thoroughly different, even to people who had been following her closely.

"In the Waiting Room" is one of those central Bishop poems, like "At the Fishhouses," "Roosters," and "The Man-Moth," that suggests what used to be called "a tragic view of life." It proposes a painful human dilemma from which no escape is possible. How can she not be part of the world, to be "one of *them*"? She may want intensely to escape from having an identity. But where does that leave her? Falling off the edge of the world "into cold, blue-black space" (outer space the standard color of ink). How convincingly Bishop relives her flash of insight about this Gordian knot just before her seventh birthday, as she shifts back and forth between her adult voice and her voice as a child, looking up at the "grown-ups" in the dentist's waiting room, "at shadowy gray knees, / trousers and skirts and boots / and different pairs of hands / lying under the lamps," letting us know (almost bragging) that she "could read," and how aware she was that in the winter "it got dark / early."

That line break is chilling. The accents in her three-beat line could easily have fallen on "*win*ter," "*dark,*" and "*ear*ly." One of her riskiest gambits in this poem, imitating a child's singsong narrative, is the opening series of five self-contained lines that fall neatly, almost monotonously into place, a list of simple facts, end-stopped, with no enjambments. Then suddenly, this unexpected enjambment, like a shift into a minor key, turns the simple statement of fact into an ominous, unsettling, heart-twisting discovery: "It was winter. It got dark / early" (*P* 179). All of a sudden, Bishop adds to the plain recitation of facts a third dimension of feeling. Perhaps not since her uncanny "At the Fishhouses" (*P* 62), with its final acknowledgment of the tragic double bind – the desire for knowledge and the pain of its necessity – had Bishop written a poem so thoroughly immersed in the complexity of human suffering.

Her next poem also returned, as she continued to do over and over again during these consolidating Boston years, to a subject she had been working on for at least six years, and it too probably hit closer to home in her new living situation than when she first began to think about it. "Crusoe in England" (*P* 182) is her deepest poem about loneliness and displacement, a profoundly autobiographical and overtly emotional poem (wasn't Cambridge, Massachusetts, this Crusoe's England, just as her lover in Brazil, Lota de Macedo Soares, had been her lifesaving Friday?) – although most of the details are not literally autobiographical.

Here is a famous character with whom Bishop could thoroughly identify – a character shipwrecked and isolated in an exotic environment, inhospitable yet lush and waiting to be mined. In a famous bit of fact-checking (*NYr* 325), *The New Yorker* questioned Crusoe's anachronistic attempt to quote the lines in Wordsworth's "I wandered lonely as a cloud" about "the bliss of solitude," lines Crusoe ironically can't quite remember – Bishop's nudge to the reader that the speaker isn't the "real" Robinson Crusoe. What saves Crusoe from his utter loneliness is the arrival of Friday, and their homoerotic attraction ("he had a pretty body") and their frustration about not being able "to propagate our kind" has all too evident autobiographical elements.

Of course, the central irony comes from the second and third words of the title. Rescue, *home*, being back "in England" (or America), is less than it's cracked up to be. Things that on the desert island once "reeked of meaning," like a knife blade or a handmade umbrella, no longer have any real or practical value. Which turns out to be worse: danger or civilization, isolation or rescue? Bishop's answer is none of the above. There is no solution. The poem eerily forecasts Bishop's posthumous celebrity, with museums eager to own and display Crusoe's objects, as if Bishop, so dubious about the value of any art, had deeply sensed and felt confident in the nature of her own achievement – but what good did it do her?

An unexpected occasion at Harvard forced Bishop once again to return to an unfinished poem. She was invited to be the Phi Beta Kappa poet for the 1972 Harvard Commencement, an honor not lost on her, and presenting a challenge for her to complete another poem. "The Moose" (*P* 189) first began to take shape some twenty-five years earlier, when some legal matter while she was living in Key West forced her to visit Great Village. By 1972 she had a substantial draft. As we know, living in Brazil opened the floodgates to her memories of Nova Scotia. Perhaps she could complete this poem that recalled so much of her earlier life only after she returned from Brazil.

In "The Moose," the difficulty was partly formal – her choice of six-line rhymed stanzas. With some helpful feedback from Frank Bidart, she completed a readable draft in time for the Harvard commencement (she was quite amused that the dean introduced her poem as "The Moos"). After the reading, she continued to revise the poem, not only before its publication in *The New Yorker*, but even afterward. Her last word on "The Moose" finally appeared in 1976 in *Geography III*.

Her nostalgia, a real homesickness for Great Village, had begun much earlier, of course, but it seems to have become more piercing after her return to Boston (and the action of this poem depicts a return bus ride to Boston, back in 1946). Bishop's beloved Aunt Grace, to whom "The Moose" is dedicated, was beginning to fail and she was beginning to fear her own slow dissolution, lingering illness, and the loss of memory. That sense of nostalgia is a major issue in this tender, achingly touching poem – Bishop explicitly compares the people falling asleep in the bus to her own grandparents in their old feather bed, looking back at their own families ("what he said, what she said, / who got pensioned; // deaths, deaths and sicknesses"). Suddenly a moose comes out of "the impenetrable woods" – "antlerless" ("It's a she!"), "otherworldly." "Why, why do we feel / (we all feel) this sweet / sensation of joy?" That mysterious joy goes back even further than home and grandparents, what Prospero in *The Tempest* called "the dark backward and abysm of time." "The Moose," however, ends on an ironic note. The past is past. We return to the present and its "acrid / smell of gasoline."

Nostalgia is also the central issue of another story about Great Village, "Memories of Uncle Neddy" (*Pr* 146) begun in Rio; a story triggered by the arrival there of two old portraits by an itinerant Nova Scotia artist of Bishop's mother and uncle when they were children. This is Bishop's only story in which she directly compares her life in Brazil with her childhood memories of Nova Scotia. She completed the story in 1975, three years after the Phi Beta Kappa reading, but to Bishop's great disappointment, it was turned down by *The New Yorker* and not published until 1977, when it appeared in *The Southern Review*.

Bishop once referred to herself in a letter to Lowell as a "minor female Wordsworth" (*WIA* 122), not as a poet of philosophical memory, but as a "Nature Lover." Along with "At the Fishhouses" and "In the Waiting Room," her most aching narrative of retrospection and her most comprehensive meditation on the nature and value of art are present in "Poem" (*P* 196), her vision (not, as she claims in the poem, "too serious a word") of early twentieth-century Nova Scotia seen through the medium of a little oil sketch by her great uncle, George Hutchinson who Bishop believed (wrongly) was a member of the British Royal Academy, "an R.A." The title imitates old-fashioned generic titles for untitled poems. But here, its modesty is also loaded because not only is this "Poem" about a painting, it's (like Keats's "Ode on a Grecian Urn") also deeply about poetry itself, and the way the writing of this poem, like the little painting of Great Village, captures "life and the memory of it." "Poem" also represents the ultimate fulfillment of her search for the quality she admired as an undergraduate in seventeenth-century prose; the quality that she also found especially in Hopkins (and very much a quality of Keats's Odes): the mind in action. In her undergraduate essay on Hopkins (*Pr* 473), she quotes M. W. Croll's essay on "The Baroque Style in Prose": "Their purpose was to portray, not a thought, but a mind thinking." That sense of the poem as depicting a drama is nowhere in Bishop more vivid than in her moment of discovery: "Heavens, I recognize the place, I know it!"

Readers generally agree that the last lines of "Poem" are among Bishop's most poignant. In her sixties, she'd become more conscious than ever of her mortality. The birds, flowers, and trees at the end of the poem are all natural things that are not going to survive in the natural world: "the munching cows" ("munching" is such a human term), the frail "iris, crisp and shivering," "the water / still standing," "the yet-to-be-dismantled elms." Aren't we all natural creatures facing our inevitable and impending demise, "along with theirs"?

With her small inheritance, Bishop was always aware of and careful with money. She encouraged Alice Methfessel to get the best possible price for her papers. Does art, like the "old-style dollar bill" that measures the size of this little painting, help us measure the value of our lives? "How live, how touching in detail / – the little that we get for free, / the little of our earthly trust. Not much." This may be her most Keatsian poem in both its commitment to art and beauty and its questioning of their ultimate value.

Not every poem from this period is a backward look. Perhaps the most surprising is the mysterious "Night City" (subtitled "From the plane"), which appeared in *The New Yorker* shortly after "The Moose" (she let poetry editor Howard Moss know how unhappy she was with its being "relegated to the back pages" of the issue). It's a kind of stylistic throwback to her Surrealist poems of the 1930s and 1940s, a grim reminder of her status as a frequent flyer, and her vision of cities as Hell on earth ("The city burns tears ... The city burns guilt ... The conflagration / fights for air / in a dread vacuum").

Surprising, too, is another poem that she began years before, "12 O'Clock News" (*P* 194), partly in its form (prose paragraphs with side glosses), partly in its jokey tone (a circular typewriter eraser seen as a "unicyclist-courier"). Her own desk is here an image of a battlefield. Or is it a real battlefield pretending to be a writer's desk? That "typed sheet" of paper – is it "An airstrip? A cemetery?" Life and the memory of it, which is which? Bishop's occasional prose poems date back to her 1937 "The Hanging of the Mouse," which she published in her 1969 *Complete Poems* along with three more recent monologues in the voices of grotesque animals – "Giant Toad," "Strayed Crab," and "Giant Snail" – that make up "Rainy Season; Sub-Tropics," all thinly veiled personal references to her own character and situation (*P* 163–166).

Bishop kept her writing life very much to herself. Few drafts surfaced, even among her friends, until they appeared in print. She was a social animal, "a creature divided" between her very private writing and her fairly active social and professional life of concerts (Maria Callas, Ella Fitzgerald), movies, poetry readings (giving as well as going to), lunches, dinner parties (giving as well as going to), and her teaching. She continued to travel, mainly with Alice Methfessel, to Brazil, Scandinavia, the Galápagos, and Greece. And she summered regularly on North Haven Island, off the coast of Maine.

She was a regular guest at John Malcolm Brinnin and Bill Read's house near the ocean at Duxbury, Massachusetts (there's an amusing late photograph in which she's playing croquet with Richard Wilbur and seems to be threatening him with a mallet). "The End of March," dedicated to Brinnin and Read (its original *New Yorker* title: "End of March, Duxbury"), is set on a walk along the beach. Not a poem of nostalgia, it's both a kind of Horatian tribute to a host (not without some irony) and a poem about life choices. She has a fantasy about living all alone in an old green house she sees on the beach, "an artichoke of a house" – that impulse picking up a thread from some of her much earlier works: the 1929 essay "On Being Alone," from the Walnut Hill School magazine *The Blue Pencil*; her beach-comber story, "The Sea and Its Shore"; and the ambitious Kafka-esque story "In Prison." But here she knows only too well that this wish for isolation is "perfect! But – impossible." Loneliness is no longer seen as a matter of choice.

Not until the very last line does there seem to be much looking back in "Five Flights Up" (*P* 203), her poem of the previous year set in Alice

Methfessel's Cambridge apartment, where she often went to write. This poem ends with a parenthetical, almost shocking outburst of unexplained regret: "(A yesterday I find almost impossible to lift)." It's one of her rare poems about an animal in which she does not identify with the animal, here the puppy with "no sense of shame," who can, enviably, bring "Yesterday … to today so lightly!"

"Five Flights Up" had the important position of being the last poem in *Geography III*, which turned out to be Bishop's last book. It was not the last poem she completed before the publication of that book, nor did she originally intend it for that place. That location of honor she reserved for "One Art" (*P* 198), which is certainly now her most famous – dare one say most "popular" – poem. It seems to be the poem to which most readers connect, *the* poem about universal loss. The modus operandi is teaching herself the ironic lesson about how to be good at losing. It makes me think of another poem of deep, tragic irony in which the poet is teaching the reader how to find something most people would seem to want to avoid: Keats's "Ode on Melancholy." You want to be good at losing? Then "practice"! And because she has lost so much in her life – the immediate trigger for "One Art" was her desperate fear that her relationship with Methfessel was ending – she's the expert, the one who has the most experience.

Despite appearances to the contrary, much of the suffering in Bishop's life – genuine suffering, and starting early – was the source of her poetry. She might easily have been a happier person had her father's parents never removed her from her idyllic childhood in Great Village. Of course, "one never knows," as she was fond of quoting Fats Waller, "do one?" (*PPL* 715). Methfessel's impending marriage was a crushing blow. The first draft of the poem that became "One Art" insists that this loss is indeed a disaster. But like Keats listening to the Nightingale's song, Bishop's working on a poem, *this* poem, perhaps literally kept her alive, delaying her wish to die. The ending of the poem, as her revisions show, almost immediately became more complicated. She stumbles to the heartbreaking admission that this loss only "look[s] like … like disaster." And that her calling is to "*Write* it!"

"One Art" was the last poem Bishop completed and published before the publication of *Geography III* only a few months later. And while not every poem in *Geography III* appears in the order she wrote it, the order is close to being chronological. At the time, "One Art" seemed to her the inevitable last poem. But because the book was so short – something of an embarrassment to Bishop – the Farrar, Straus, and Giroux designer, Cynthia Krupat (the daughter of Bishop's old school friend, Frani Blough Muser), came up with an idea that Bishop liked: each poem would begin quite low on the page, so that even the shorter poems would require more pages. "One Art," a villanelle in six short stanzas, would take up two pages. The problem was that if it were to come at the end, then the first page (the right-hand page) would end just before the very last stanza; one would have to turn the page in order to read that one stanza. This was unacceptable to Bishop. She felt that the reader had to see the whole poem, on facing pages. But there was no way to accomplish this except by changing its location in the book. The decision was to place it between "Poem" and "The End of March," and that "Five Flights Up" would be moved to the end. In retrospect, this now seems the right choice – a quieter, subtler, way to end a book, with a sudden, larger looking back; as opposed to having the book end on the more melodramatic word "disaster."

There's one more poem in *Geography III,* and it was a poem that particularly benefited from the book's design. "Objects & Apparitions," dedicated "For Joseph Cornell," is a dazzling exercise in ekphrasis, an indirect description of Cornell's boxes (Bishop loved Cornell and actually constructed a box of her own on his model); boxes in which, the poem concludes, "my words become visible for a moment." The surprise facing the first readers of *Geography III* was that, when one turned the page, one discovered that the poem was not by Bishop, but a translation of a poem ("Objetos y Apariciones") by her friend Octavio Paz. Bishop loved this little joke. Paz did too, and he also regarded her translation as better than his original. It seems as much Bishop's manifesto as Paz's.

During this period in Boston, Bishop worked on other Paz translations, although "Objects & Apparitions" was the most substantial. She gave Frank Bidart her translation of Paz's philosophical love poem "January First" (a throwback, at least in its title, to her "Brazil, January 1, 1502") for the issue of the journal *Ploughshares* he was guest editing. Others appeared in the *Harvard Advocate.* Her major work in translating poems – masterpieces by some of the greatest twentieth-century Brazilian poets – was essentially done before she returned to Boston. She was in the process of completing, with her friend Emmanuel Brasil, the Wesleyan University Press *Anthology of Twentieth-Century Brazilian Poetry.* Two of her translations appeared in *The New Yorker* shortly after her arrival at Harvard, and one of these, Vinicius de Moraes's "Sonnet of Intimacy," gave her particular pleasure because it seems to have been the first poem published in *The New Yorker* to include (in fact, end with) a "four letter word." That word was the otherwise unshocking "piss," and it referred to a cow, but she was quite proud of her triumph over the then timid strictures of the magazine.

One of the key poems from this period is a poem Bishop never published, the short love poem "Breakfast Song," an aubade to Alice Methfessel that Bishop had essentially completed by the end of 1973. I saw it in Bishop's notebook when I was visiting her at Harvard's Stillman infirmary shortly after New Year's 1974 (she had fallen down a flight of stairs and broken her shoulder). I was shaken by its startling, almost bald intimacy – "Last night I slept with you. / Today I love you so" (*P* 327) – and even more moved by the singular candor with which Bishop confronted her death, a quality both entirely new to her yet also in a very large way the subject underlying all of *Geography III*. My own fear was that she might decide never to publish this poem while she was still alive, and I made an exact copy of her draft that I didn't show anyone until decades after her death. When I finally sent a copy of it to Alice Methfessel, her response was: "Oh, that poem." But no copy of the manuscript I saw has yet surfaced among either Bishop's or Methfessel's papers. What happened to it remains a mystery. Almost four decades after it was written, "Breakfast Song" (whose original title on a fragmentary draft in the Vassar archives is "Simple-Minded Morning Poem"), seems to me the most remarkable of all of Bishop's "morning-after" poems (including such early poems as "Love Lies Sleeping" and "Anaphora"), as well as the most positive. It's one of her late poems that signals a possible new direction in her style, albeit a direction she'd be nervous about.

One of the revelations after Bishop's sudden death in 1979 was that she had actually been working on a number of poems. Her will gave her literary executors, Methfessel and Frank Bidart, "the power to determine whether any of my unpublished manuscripts and papers shall be published, and if so, to see them through the press." There might have been less controversy over Bishop's posthumous publications had her will been more generally known.

The most serious of these unpublished poems from her years in Boston include her most explicit – and explicitly sexual – lesbian poem, "Vague Poem (*Vaguely love poem*)" (*P* 323), which recalls the image of rock roses from her 1947 Key West poem "Faustina, or Rock Roses." It's hard to tell whether Bishop was attempting a new, much looser, more conversational style or if this poem simply survives in a relatively early draft. We can't really know whether Bishop, who told Frank Bidart that she wanted "closets, closets, and more closets," didn't publish these poems because she didn't regard them as finished or because they were too graphic in their sexuality for her to feel comfortable making them public. I'd guess some combination of both.

Closer to being finished is "Salem Willows" (*P* 331), a poignant and dreamlike poem, a descendant of her early "Cirque d'Hiver," about riding "Around and around and around" on a mechanical golden carousel lion at a Salem amusement park while her Aunt Maude, like one of the Fates, sat waiting for her, knitting (almost the opposite of the timid and childlike

"Aunt Consuelo" whom the slightly older and wiser "Elizabeth" is waiting for in the dentist's office in "In the Waiting Room"). The lion here echoes the mythic "lion sun" in "The End of March." Salem also comes up in an unsettling autobiographical poem Bishop was working on shortly after she arrived in Cambridge called "A Drunkard" (*P* 317), a kind of etiological myth explaining that the source of her alcoholism might have been her mother's reprimand when the three-year-old Elizabeth tried to distract her mother from helping the victims of the devastating Salem fire of 1914. Equally nightmarish but more polished is "For Grandfather" (*P* 329), in which Bishop meets up with her dead grandfather in the frozen North – surely another premonition of her own death. "Grandfather, please stop! I haven't been this cold in years."

In a 1952 review of a memoir by Wallace Fowlie that Bishop published in *Poetry,* she referred to a childhood memory of a swan biting her mother on a swan-boat ride in Boston's Public Garden (*Pr* 266). That image recurs in several fragmentary late drafts, "Swan-Boat Ride" and "A mother made of dress-goods..." (*EAP* 155–157). Swans were not positive images for Bishop. They appear in the name of an inn in the fascinating but fragmentary "For Mr. and Mrs. Carlyle," which includes a disconnected final quatrain with one of Bishop's grimmest depictions of a relationship:

> One flesh and two heads
>   Engaged in kisses or in pecks.
> Oh white seething marriage!
>   Oh Swan with Two Necks (*EAP* 180)

Finally, there are the four last masterful uncollected poems that Bishop published in *The New Yorker*, completed too late for *Geography III,* but many years from a new volume. The two poems about Brazil, which she had started much earlier, are essentially opposites. "Santarém" *(P* 207), looking back to her trip to the Amazon in 1960, is an Eden ("perfect! But – impossible") of peace and harmony and good omens (lightning strikes the priest's house and brass bed, but "*Graças a deus* – he'd been in Belém"), with golden light suffusing the charmingly exotic and touching details, and its particularly uncanny image of two rivers, the Amazon and the Tapajós, flowing side by side – an image she is tempted but finally refuses to submit to literary analysis. "I liked the place; I liked the idea of the place." The poem finally becomes, like "In the Waiting Room," a poem of self-definition, when at the end, she returns to her boat with a prize: a matte-white stucco-like empty wasp's nest she admired so much when she saw it in a pharmacy that the pharmacist gave it to her. But practical-minded electronics CEO Mr. Swan, the retiring head of Philips Electric ("really a very nice old man"), doesn't have her imagination for oddities. His curtain line is "What's that ugly thing?"

On the other hand, "Pink Dog" (*P* 212), which she began around 1963 when she first contemplated leaving Brazil (one of its earliest titles was "Goodbye to Rio"), is her most savage poem, a bitterly comic social satire in syncopated samba rhythms and tilted triple rhymes. It's a wicked parody of her friend Vinicius de Moraes's phenomenally popular hit song from 1962, "The Girl from Ipanema." It's far from a gorgeous "garota" who is crossing the Avenida Atlántica on her way to the beach; rather, it's an ugly hairless mongrel bitch with whom Bishop, with her "dog hair," clearly identifies. Like "Crusoe in England," this is another poem about her sense of displacement. And like "One Art," it's a poem that ends with her giving advice ("You know I *love* to give advice," she wrote to Frank Bidart in a copy she gave him for Christmas of *Fannie Farmer's Boston Cooking School Cookbook*). In "Pink Dog," indirectly, it's once again advice to herself: "Dress up! Dress up and dance at Carnival!" Chilling advice she can neither follow nor accept. It was published in time for Mardi Gras in 1979 and would be the last poem she completed.

"North Haven" (*P* 210) was another response to a devastating loss: the sudden death of her dearest poet friend, Robert Lowell, in September 1977. The island was a place she loved, another Eden, where she could feel at ease in jeans, squatting on the grass picking lingenberries for jam, or wading in the tide pools gathering mussels, or just sitting in the den playing Boggle with Alice. Lowell, years earlier, had told her about his happy adolescence there, where he "learned to sail, and learned to kiss." The joy of their separate experiences there coincided.

The poem begins with one of Bishop's most hyper-real, dreamlike descriptions, in italics ("*I can count / the new cones on the spruce*") and set apart by extra space from the rest of the poem. This particular Eden is really a kind of Shakespearean pastoral, appropriate for an elegy to a great poet, with the names of flowers and birds in initial capital letters, some of the phrases directly from Shakespeare ("Daisies pied ... and more, returned, to paint the meadows with delight" – allusions to the song at the end of *Love's Labour's Lost*). When she saw the poem in *The New Yorker*, she was dismayed that she had allowed poetry editor Howard Moss to talk her out of the initial capital letters, and was eager to have "North Haven" reprinted as soon as possible as she intended. (And it was – shortly before she died, as both a broadside and in the Lowell memorial issue of the *Harvard Advocate*.)

> Nature repeats herself, or almost does:
> *repeat, repeat, repeat; revise, revise, revise.* (*P* 210)

She could tease Lowell, posthumously, about his manic revisions of his masterpieces. But she could also see some of that same impulse in herself. Hadn't Lowell famously teased her about the same thing?

> Do
> you still hang your words in air, ten years
> unfinished, glued to your notice board, with gaps
> or empties for the unimaginable phrase –
> unerring Muse, who makes the casual perfect?
> ("For Elizabeth Bishop 4" *Collected Poems* 595)

How lovingly they envied each other's gifts. How sad the inevitable end for both of these poets:

> "The words won't change again. Sad friend, you cannot change."

Bishop was again frustrated with *The New Yorker* that year because it had kept her little "Sonnet" (*P* 214) so long without publishing it (it finally appeared posthumously, on October 29, 1979, more than a year after it had been accepted). This is a poem virtually intended to seem posthumous, a portrait of her life in purely imagistic terms: the bubble in a spirit level and a compass needle (examples of things "Caught – "); a broken thermometer and the rainbow reflecting from the beveled prismatic edge of an empty mirror (examples of things "Freed – "). A virtual orphan shuttling between different sets of grandparents, and a lesbian, she, like the spirit level trying to find balance and stability, was always "a creature divided." As a lifelong traveler looking for a permanent home ("*home,*" she writes in "Questions of Travel," "*wherever that may be*"), what more appropriate image for herself than a compass needle, "wobbling and wavering, / undecided." And as someone who had suffered from chronic health problems all her life, how liberating to represent herself as a broken thermometer, or to stand, at last, before an empty mirror. How can we not see Bishop's version of freedom as poignant images of release – from suffering and from painful, self-conscious self-examination – that could come only in death?

As in many of her formal poems (like the villanelle "One Art"), here, too, she turns formal expectation on its head. This "Sonnet" reverses the traditional octave and sestet, the second part now longer than the first. And the usual pentameters are now reduced to dimeters. There are hard rhymes concluding each of the poem's four images: divided / undecided; away / gay. But throughout the poem are numerous internal rhymes and interlocking assonances (thermometer / mercury / bird). "Bubble" and "needle" are rhymes slanted off "bevel" and "level." In a poem consisting of only forty-one words, four present participles (wobbling / wavering / running / flying) practically create their own internal rhyme scheme.

And then there's that last word. Can we take Bishop at her word when she told her friends that she had hoped in this poem to restore that word – "gay" – to its literal meaning? Don't we, at least on one level, have to? That desire for gaiety was part of Bishop's spirit. Despite all her losses, her illnesses, and the terrible suffering of people she was close to, she wanted to enjoy her life. Those of us who were lucky enough to know her, knew that she sometimes did, and fully, and that her writing, however difficult for her, surely (so we hope) had given her profound satisfaction and even pleasure. Even if she regarded her return to Boston as some kind of failure or defeat, she must have seen that Boston also opened for her a new perspective. These new poems of retrospect were in turn unlocking some of the mysteries of her earlier poems. Her poems of self-advice embodied a new capacity for self-knowledge. This was a rare time in her life when she was producing poems at a surprisingly steady pace. She must have felt that these were all poems of unprecedented emotional power and freedom (even if she didn't want some of them published in her lifetime). She must have known, on some level and however reluctantly, that these poems were the culmination of her life's work.

10

SIOBHAN PHILLIPS

Bishop's Correspondence

When Anne Stevenson began the first full-length study of Bishop's poetry in the early 1960s, she wrote to her subject for clarification, and the inquiry yielded almost a decade of epistolary exchange (see Ellis, "Between," for a full analysis). One of Bishop's responses includes an explanation of the poet's aesthetic ideal. "What one seems to want in art, in experiencing it," she writes, "is the same thing that is necessary for its creation, a self-forgetful, perfectly useless concentration" (*Pr* 414). Justly famous, the passage reappears in editions of Bishop running from a 1983 volume called *Elizabeth Bishop and Her Art*, when Bishop's fame was only beginning to grow, to the 2011 collection of *Prose*, when she was recognized as the most important American poet of the late twentieth century (Orr). Changing citations of "the Darwin letter," however, show developments during that span. The 1983 book excerpts a paragraph of analysis, presenting it under a title as if it were a miniature essay (288). The 2011 volume includes the entire letter, presenting it under Bishop's opening notation of place and date and including Stevenson's messages before and after (*Pr* 410–417). Correspondence is no longer a negligible medium through which Bishop articulated her ideas; it is a distinct medium that exemplifies those ideas. Letters have moved from secondary source to primary document. This shift helps to constitute a wider development in Bishop criticism, which has gone from analyzing her great but scant output of lyric poems to considering those poems among a full range of her fine art, essays, fiction, translation, and other writing. In the case of correspondence, this attention must assess an ill-defined genre as well as assimilate newly discovered content. Full attention to Bishop's correspondence means clarifying the form of the letter itself, relating the properties of epistolarity to Bishop's aesthetic practice and cultural context.

Bishop's own reading and analysis demonstrate her interest in epistolarity as a distinct field, what Jonathan Ellis describes as her "faith in letter writing as an art form in its own right" (*Art and Memory* 142). Bishop took in letters by everyone from Horace Walpole to Anne Sexton – staying up late to finish thick volumes of Coleridge's, looking forward to an "old age" in which she would read all of Madame de Sévigné's, objecting to misrepresentations of Hart Crane's (*OA* 324; *NYr* 241; *WIA* 147–148). Ellis documents more than two dozen volumes of correspondence by authors and writers in the library she left, and that list leaves out collections by Fanny Burney, Charles Darwin, Sidney Smith, and Ivan Turgenev, among others (*Art and Memory* 156). "We've been reading Henry James's *Letters* ... all week," she writes in 1941, and "I've just been re-reading all the Hopkins letters all over again," she writes in 1965 (*OA* 103; *WIA* 572); in 1953 she is thinking about "acquiring" Mrs. Carlyle's letters "for myself," having read them "long ago," and in 1974 she responds to a gift of Edna St. Vincent Millay's letters with the admission that she already owns them (*OA* 272). Correspondence was the genre that spurred enthusiastic recommendation and near-addictive consumption: "Thank you for the Flannery O'Connor Letters," she writes in 1979; "I can't stop reading them – have until 2 a.m. for two nights now, to the detriment of my daily life" (*OA* 630). Bishop's interest in epistolarity helps to demonstrate the still-underappreciated breadth of her reading, as she ranges across categories of time, style, and type of writer in her admiration for the genre of correspondence.

Bishop's reactions demonstrate the acuity as well as the avidity in her epistolary reading, given that she explored the limits of correspondence as a serious or literary form. Her own "Darwin letter" proves that letters can contain valuable analysis. In her view, so did the correspondence of many she read. Keats in his letters, for example, "makes almost every other poet seem stupid" (*NYr* 228). Even correspondence that did not discuss weighty topics could make aesthetic claims. The one Harvard seminar Bishop taught that was not focused on poetry was titled "Letters: Readings in Personal Correspondence, Famous and Infamous, from the 16th to the 20th Centuries," and she writes to friends that she plans to consider "[j]ust *letters* – as an art form or something" (*OA* 544). With a proposed syllabus that runs from Keats to "a letter found in the street," Bishop's plans take ephemeral messages to be worthy of sustained analysis, and she later complains about a student who thought correspondence by Montagu, Walpole, and Byron was "too frivolous" (*WIA* 703). Still, the "just" in "just *letters*" betrays her own suspicion of letters' frivolity, and the same disquiet blooms in a never-finished review of Sylvia Plath's correspondence, several years later: "Of course one can't really 'review' letters, or criticise them – ," Bishop writes, "at least, not perhaps the way a play, a novel, or poetry can be reviewed and criticised" (Ellis, "Mailed" 13–14). Taken in tandem, Bishop's late-career reflections on epistolarity know that letters are "fascinating," but hesitate about setting their fascination next to that of fiction, verse, and drama. How does one treat letters as an "art form" while acknowledging, even crediting, their extra-artistic "something"?

Or how does one craft "a poetics of the familiar letter" when the letter's mark may be its "refusal of the literary"? These phrases come from Tom Paulin's 1994 review of *One Art*, the first and principal selection of Bishop's correspondence (3). At more than 600 pages that are far from a complete presentation, the collection celebrates Bishop's lifelong writing of the genre she so liked to read. The book, therefore, not only offered a wealth of content, joining Brett Millier's 1993 biography to provide details of Bishop's life story; it also pressed the issue of form, raising the question of what the letter allowed or developed in Bishop's art. Paulin's answer follows his subject's when he emphasizes the letter's dubious artistry: this ambiguity promotes an "unfinished completeness," Paulin writes, a composition that emerges "here and now as part of a process" (4). Epistolarity's moment-by-moment divagation thus manifests Bishop's overall preference for "a mind thinking" rather than "a thought" (*Pr* 473). One 1938 note, for example, moves from her "awfully nice" room to a view of "convicts in their black-and-white stripes" to a history of Key West to a recent lunch in New York to her views of Communism before concluding with plans for "joining the Anarchists" and "renting a catboat" (*OA* 68–69). Bishop writes in stages, noting when Friday in one spot becomes Saturday in another and recording the breaks for refreshment, conversations, interruptions, other work: "Time out to make *another* little coffee," or "Time out while a *tiny* boy … comes to the door with a suitcase of pathetic goods to sell, and sells them to me. I now have a crude potato-peeler, cruder flint gadget for lighting the gas-stove, a blue plastic barrel to keep *something* in" (*WIA* 363, 573). The result is a precision never fixed or finished: "Perhaps I shall get this mailed today or tomorrow," she writes at the end of a 1959 letter to May Swenson, "so I shall draw it to a close, and give up the hope of turning it into something brilliant at the last minute. The flock of parrots that comes every year about this time is back and I wish you could see them – their backs are bright green and their breasts bright yellow, so as they turn in the air the effect is very gay – and they never stop talking at the top of their voices" (May Swenson Papers I.103.4003). Last-minute brilliance makes the "close" of this letter into the continuation of experience. Bishop stops her written words only by yielding to a real world that never stops talking.

Epistolary process thereby dramatizes the accuracy that marks so much of Bishop's work, and that critics have noted from Randall Jarrell's early praise to Zachariah Pickard's recent reconsiderations (Jarrell 235). Letters support Bishop's tendency toward a reportage that keeps faith with its subject by remaining open to change – so that a poem like "The Monument" begins its looking with "Now" and continues via self-correction (*P* 25). With this, letters support Bishop's suspicion of any writing that strays too far from lived experience – what Paulin calls, in an allusion to Heideggerian *Dasein*, her sense of "being-in-the world." When Bishop writes to Robert Lowell, for example, about her idea of meter, she tells him that she has "loads of thoughts on the subject and I think I'll have to write again tomorrow," then goes on to sketch a "theory now that all the arts are growing more and more 'literary'... a late stage, perhaps a decadent stage ... If I were Shapiro I'd write a book about it. (And have you read *Art & Illusion*? by one Gombrich? – it is fascinating.) I find it is time to go to market" (*WIA* 335). As Bishop's "theory" resists the definitive with the prospective – "tomorrow" – it also resists the "literary" with the worldly, a trip to "market." Bishop's speculations thus exploit their epistolary difference from the prose in a book by Shapiro. She tempers aesthetic philosophy with quotidian practicality. This accords with her statements of creed in that "Darwin" letter, which move beyond "observation" to advocate a "living in reality" that understands "non-intellectual sources of wisdom and sympathy" (*Pr* 414): letters preserve these very sources. If Keats's epistolary intelligence could mix a report on his brother's health with his view of poetic imagination, Bishop's would leaven an analysis of decadence with household duties.

In this way, correspondence supports Bishop's career-wide attempts to integrate literary composition and ordinary living, to find forms adequate to the apparent formlessness of quotidian sensation. Such a preference, however, was not a disinterested one. Just as Keats used letters for his theorizing, in part, because his socioeconomic status denied him more formal prose outlets, Bishop used letters for her theorizing, in part, because she felt that her own position required complicated negotiations of authority – as a female, a lesbian, an expatriate, and/or a relatively unheralded writer who produced poems slowly. Langdon Hammer focuses on those complications in his seminal essay about *One Art*, showing how correspondence's status as ambiguously aesthetic allowed Bishop to control "her conflicted experience of professional obligation and achievement" (163). In the aforementioned passage about "decadence," for example, a movement between "meter" and "market" allows Bishop both to join and demur from the confident theorizing of established male critics like Shapiro, Gombrich, or even Lowell himself. Indeed, as Hammer shows, Bishop's conflicted sense of authority especially pervades the two longest, most involved correspondences of her life: with Lowell, a colleague who both championed and overshadowed her, and with Marianne Moore, a mentor whom Bishop both resisted and emulated. Bishop needed their assistance and encouragement; she enclosed poems to Moore, for example, with the request to "please tell me what you think," and she wrote to Lowell to get help with procuring fellowships, among many other promptly answered solicitations (*OA* 67; *WIA* 316). Yet Bishop also chafed at their guidance. She famously refused Moore's letter of suggestions about "Roosters" ("I know that esthetically you are quite right, but I can't bring myself to sacrifice ... a very important 'violence' of tone"), and wrote her own letter of correction about Lowell's French translations ("I don't think you should lay yourself open to charges of carelessness or ignorance") (*OA* 96; *WIA* 356). Bishop's ambivalence may be most patent in her late memoir of Moore, "Efforts of Affection," which was written at a time when her relationship with Lowell was also problematic – since she was considering writing a preface to a book about Lowell and taking on what had been his post at Harvard (*Pr* 117–140; *WIA* 656–678). But throughout Bishop's life, letters demonstrated and managed this difficult psychological content. They allowed Bishop a mixture of assertion and reliance that could both use and refuse other writers' influences.

The fact of influence itself, however, marks correspondence as a form. As Hammer points out (173), its distinctive, ambiguous place between life and literature joins its distinctive, ambiguous place between one author and another. Personal letters differ from other prose in that they are directed toward, and expect a reply from, a particular person (Altman 88–89). Bishop relishes this transitivity, despite its entanglements, as her letters continually reinforce their connection to others. The very description of her Harvard letters course, in fact, ends with a request for reply: "I need some ideas from you both," she tells her correspondents. She interweaves other speculation with similar expectations: Burroughs is "probably very much like Poe, don't you think?" she asks Lowell, or "I suppose you have read the Fiedler book?" (*WIA* 501, 317); "have you ever seen that wonderful Miró *Farm*?" she asks Moore, or "those articles they have been running in *The New Republic* about the miracles of science, etc.?" (*OA* 90, 101) "What do you think?" she asks May Swenson after a description of Robert Fitzgerald (*OA* 336). Such questions seem less about garnering someone else's ideas than reinforcing the structure of responsiveness that letters provide – which turns production into reception, consumption into collaboration, reading into writing. When she stayed up late with Coleridge's letters, for example, Bishop fell into an empathy so fervent that "his tooth-aches are *my* tooth-aches," as she tells Jarrell, recounting that "only the pleasant and relieving prospect of writing you can tear me away from that adorable man" (*OA* 324). Composing a message to Jarrell here stands in for composing a message to Coleridge, continuing the almost physical bond established by the latter's correspondence. Letters therefore make Coleridge "contemporary," Bishop writes in the same letter. If epistolarity forbids the disinterestedness of literature, it also precludes its distance, bringing together two people across gaps of time and space.

Togetherness was particularly important to Bishop, since she endured the loss of many people close to her and often felt the lack of any permanent home. Bishop's focus on correspondence supports a critical emphasis on her orphaned, outsider status. J. D. McClatchy's review of *One Art*, for example, is headlined "Letters from a Lonely Poet," and in a later, more subtle reading, Heather Treseler analyzes Bishop's unpublished letter-poems in the light of her need for reparative connection ("Dreaming" 88–90, 95–103). With specific phrases from her letters, as well as through their sheer volume, Bishop shows a steady fear of being cut off: "I hate to keep losing people," she laments to Kit and Ilse Barker, for example, and tells Moore that a message from her "lightened my sensation of being AN EXILE very much" (*OA* 250, 60). Letter-poems show similar anxieties: "Letter to N.Y.," for example – addressed and dedicated to Louise Crane, with whom Bishop shared a house in Key West – marks a distance from both place and person with its fervent "wish" for more news about goings-on in the city (*P* 78). Bishop's residence in Brazil, where she lived consistently from 1951–1967 and intermittently after that, made such wishes only more important and more vexed, as she despairs at "mailboxes [that] are never collected" and "glue machines which are frequently incapacitated by their own glue" (*OA* 237). Continual fuss about post and postage cloaks less practical anxieties about delivery.

This anxiety even becomes a compositional principle. As Hammer notes (178), Bishop's written letters often strive to maintain connection for as long as possible, in a self-perpetuating self-consciousness: "I've been entirely alone for 4 days and am just chattering without having anything at all to say" (VC I.24.4), she writes to Pearl Bell in 1954, for example, and asks Pauline Hanson, in the middle of a 1951 letter, "May I keep on talking to you for a while?" (VC I.32.1). The dynamics of this "keeping on" help to explain why so many Bishop letters begin with intentions of a brief message and pick up speed through several single-spaced pages of "chatter." Bishop's relish for such chatter capitalizes on a formal characteristic of correspondence, the "solecism of *two presents*" that Charles Lamb describes in one of the first considerations of epistolarity (105). Bishop does so, moreover, by emphasizing another peculiarity of correspondence: a conflation of writing and speech – most famously considered by Jacques Derrida in his musings on *La Carte Postale*, and usefully historicized by Eve Tavor Bannet in her consideration of eighteenth-century correspondence (Derrida 463–476; Bannet 46–49). It is a fittingly correspondent irony that Bishop sounds more conversational when typing than when talking, that she apologizes in one note for her "strangeness" of tone when "dictating" correspondence (*NYr* 324). Composing a letter in written prose allows the comforting fiction of being and speaking with another.

The *difference* between writing and speech, however, was just as important for Bishop, as she emphasizes with a contrast in her unfinished Plath review. "Writing letters, not telephoning," she writes, "is ... a bit like getting dressed up and going to the symphony concert instead of sitting at home in pajamas and listening to it on the radio: ... once one takes pen in hand, one has to make an effort; certain formalities are to be observed" (Ellis, *Art and Memory* 145). Correspondence requires the "effort" of a "formal" presentation, in Bishop's view; it does not simply indulge the ease of an informal intimacy. Her opinion on this point (especially when it comes couched in a review of Plath) might therefore clarify Bishop's use of epistolarity vis-à-vis her opinion of confessionalism. From her time to our own, critics have debated how "confessional" a poet Bishop really is, wondering if her well-known antipathy to the movement belied her own use of its methods (Rosenbaum, *Professing Sincerity* 193). Bishop's regard for correspondence could place her in the confessional camp: although she recommended, in a 1967 interview, that writers "keep some of these things to themselves" (Cory and Lee 68), she also praised Dorothee Bowie, in a 1968 letter, "because you are so beautifully Indiscreet & do tell one all the lurid details one is always dying to hear" (VC I.27.3). Since the letters of *One Art* provide information about Bishop's own experience, moreover, the book adds a potentially confessional valence to many poems, and the editorial choices of *One Art* further this idea by linking letters and poetry in the unified "one" of her "art." "The letters constitute her autobiography," Robert Giroux argues in his introduction, by offering "details of her little known private life" (Giroux vii). To those with the requisite knowledge, then, Bishop might be offering the same autobiographical details in her verse. Several early reviews support this idea in their focus on biographical material (Ian Hamilton and Pheobe Pettingell provide examples), suggesting that to read Bishop as an epistolary writer may be to read her as a confessional one.

Yet Bishop's musings on Plath's letters – as well as Bishop's practice in her own letters – oppose such a reading. She refuses the equation of epistolarity and autobiography as well as the related equation of correspondence and confessionalism: the "formalities" of the letter form mean writing toward another, and with another in mind, rather than writing for oneself, and about one's suffering. Indeed, that very suffering is to be resisted, Bishop feels: her chief objection to confessional "self-absorption," when she criticizes the trend in her "Darwin letter," is its failure of "good manners" and concomitant "*heaviness*" (*Pr* 417). Bishop's emphasis on the reverse is evident in poems like "The Bight," with its suggestive invocation of "old correspondences" and comparison of boats to "torn-open, unanswered letters." In this poem, first-person description avoids the despair of a psychological "dredge" (Treseler, "Dreaming" 95) to end with a summary of "awful but cheerful" activity (*P* 59). Like Keats, therefore, who would resist "feeling vapourish" by "adoniz[ing] as I were going out" before "sitting down to write," Bishop would use the "dressed up," "symphony-going" self-presentation of epistolary composition to resist her darkest moods. This was not always possible – Bishop sometimes writes, as she notes apologetically in one message, "selfishly, to unburden myself a little before I get up my courage to go out" (*OA* 536). But she also destroys notes that she finds too despairing to post, rewrites a message that is "too gloomy and weak-minded to send," and expresses relief when Lowell did not get a letter in which "I think I sounded rather gloomy and apologetic" (*OA* 509; *WIA* 158). She exhorts Lowell, moreover, to resist his own "*heaviness*" through epistolarity, recommending the "cheering" prose in Sydney Smith's collected letters (*WIA* 420). Such cheerfulness-despite-awfulness was a standard for Bishop's letter writing as well as a comfort in her letter reading.

That standard distinguishes her from other poets of her era – Lowell, for example, who was the major exponent of confessionalism. Their similarities and differences were most apparent in the second major publication of Bishop's letters: *Words in Air*, which appeared in 2008, provides both sides of the complete Bishop-Lowell exchange. It thereby offered critics occasion to note the two poets' changing reputations, which have reversed Lowell's previous dominance; one review of *Words* asserts Bishop's "sweeping posthumous triumph" over her "friend" (Hofmann 358). It seems paradoxical to promote a double-authored text as a "culminating book" for Bishop, since elision of Lowell's part in the exchange ignores the very dyadism that Bishop prized in epistolary method. But the revision may be fitting nonetheless, given that Lowell's failure to recognize dual authorship separates the two friends. In fact, it occasioned Bishop's most strenuous defense of letters – objecting to Lowell's 1972 collection *The Dolphin*, which quotes and alters correspondence from his estranged wife, Elizabeth Hardwick, without securing her permission. Bishop presses the fact of relationship as she recommends a correspondent ethics against her friend's confessional aesthetics: "One can use one's life as material," she concedes, "but these letters – aren't you violating a trust?" (*WIA* 708). Bishop also uses the evidence of other writer's letters, in this letter to a writer about his misuse of letters, by quoting correspondence from Hardy, Hopkins, and Henry James to prove her point. Lowell's decision violates a code of conduct that is, for Bishop, fundamentally linked to genre – not only by forgoing cheer for the "tragic, anguished" experience of a rejected woman, or by relinquishing accuracy for a "mixture of fact & fiction," but also, and more fundamentally, by appropriating another's writing as his own. Bishop's attention to epistolarity itself supports her aversion to Lowell's letter-indebted poems (Chiasson).

That distaste indicts more than *The Dolphin*, since Lowell's confessional appropriations only emphasize the first-person valence of lyric more generally. Bishop's attention to the forms of correspondence, therefore, clarifies her subtle attention, also, to the conventions of verse. Her epistolarity anticipates the "new lyric studies" of recent criticism, which would dismantle the fiction of an individual, even an abstracted, poetic speaker, disembodied from particular setting and expressing himself without the encumbrance of audience (Jackson). Letters provide an alternative model: *two* writers, set in a particular place and time, speaking to each other through responsive and responsible exchange. That situated back-and-forth, moreover, erases the supposed boundary between the "absolute privacy" (Warner 79) of the lyric and the violating publicity of its dissemination – a division that was particularly important in postwar America, and which confessionalism only emphasizes (Nelson 40). The letter assumes a sphere of action that is neither single nor general. Several critics of letters, including Mireille Bossis, Rebecca Earle, Liz Stanley, Eve Tanor Bannet, and Logan Esdale, have explored this epistolary space; and Heather Treseler analyzes its application to Bishop (Bossis 70; Earle 4; Stanley 209; Bannet 226–227; Esdale 104; Treseler, "Lyric" 24, 57, 75–76, 104–105). In a letter-indebted poem like "The Bight" or a postcard-indebted poem like "View of the Capitol from the Library of Congress," one can see how Bishop resists both the narrow privacy of self-reflection and the unfettered publicity of a general pronouncement. In Hammer's words, Bishop's correspondence enacts a space where "poet and reader" can be "alone together" (173). It is something like the "*estudio*" she describes in a letter to Lowell, a room that is neither institutional nor domestic and that she has lined with pictures of her friends – an area where she need not feel herself a "public figure," but might write in view of a familiar audience (*WIA* 161–163).

This space has particular uses for a feminist and queer poetics, and letters offer fruitful evidence for the evolving criticism of Bishop as a woman and lesbian. It is no accident that Bishop's objections to *The Dolphin* defended a female correspondent against male appropriation – as she did earlier, too, in her protests against William Carlos Williams's poetic use of letters from Marcia Nardi (*WIA* 38). To take correspondence seriously is to provide women with authorship and authority in their own right, to rectify the exclusion of women from traditional genres by enfranchising the supposedly nonliterary stuff of personal exchange. Bishop's proposed letters syllabus thus includes her own "aunt Grace" between Chekhov and Keats, and begins with "Mrs. Carlyle," a copious correspondent who went unpublished in her lifetime, rather than her more famous husband. Perhaps more important, correspondence also unsettles the relationship between women like Mrs. Carlyle and their correspondents, famous husbands among them, because epistolarity does not specify the terms of its dyadic intimacy beyond requiring the collaborative equality of two parties. Letters can thereby evade the strictures of heteronormative binaries, finding less conventional arrangements of friendly intimacy. Bishop's exchanges with Moore and Lowell test this very chance when she resists the patterns of mother-daughter or lover-beloved (Bishop could respond to Lowell's famous letter about wanting to marry her, for example, by ignoring the subject entirely [*WIA* 219–229]). Several astute discussions of Bishop's sexuality, therefore, use letters to describe queer negotiations of fixed roles: Treseler analyzes the gendered epistolarity of Bishop's and Moore's interchanges, for example, as she develops Kathryn R. Kent's analysis of "semi-public/semi-private" areas of lesbian identity formation, and Kirstin Hotelling Zona uses letters to chart the differences between Bishop's and Swenson's use of sexual language (Treseler, "Lyric" 111–153; Kent 6–17, 169–187; Zona 95–119). The virtual space of correspondence brings women together in relationships that are not easily defined – and are all the more creative for such ambiguity.

Did epistolarity model, in addition, a connection to readers of poems? The drafts that Treseler makes available point to a key question of Bishop's correspondence, that of its relation to her poetic composition. Several letters include material that became verse: description in a note to Lowell, for example, appears later in "The Bight" (*WIA* 23), and Ellis argues that Bishop generally wrote letters "with potential poems in mind" (*Art and Memory* 143). His analysis and others', however, rightly focus on form over content, arguing that Bishop took epistolarity as a stylistic model rather than an experiential fund. Joelle Biele, for example, uses unpublished material ("The Armadillo" was originally titled "From a Letter") to show how Bishop's verse adopts an epistolary sensibility. Correspondence demonstrates her preferred tone of indeterminate but presumed intimacy, an address that links writer and audience in a distant, considerate mutuality of ongoing compositional process. "I think I'll send you a poem I just this minute finished – ," Bishop writes to a friend at one point, for example, adding that "it will serve as a sort of letter; that's what it really is" (Biele, "Like Working" 95). And yet even in this sense, comparison of poetry and correspondence can only go so far, given that Bishop's poem will not retain its immediacy – or its particular address, or its expectation of response – beyond her epistolary enclosure. However "letterlike" a poem, it must nonetheless forgo a particular context of two-party exchange (Hammer 164). Abandoned drafts called "Dear Dr." and "Letter to Two Friends," now published in *Edgar Allan Poe & The Juke-Box*, attest to an unbridgeable difference between epistolary and poetic forms as much as a repeated desire to bring them together (*EAP* 77–78, 113–114).

That generic gulf, in turn, helps to explain Bishop's diffident reaction to publication, and her well-known discomfort with poetic "Business" (*OA* 202). Even though she sometimes regretted her limited fame, she was on the whole "very touched by the small but interested circle of readers I seem to have" (VC I.24.9), as she wrote to Bell in 1959; she looked back with longing, as she explains to Stevenson, to "the days when poems just got handed around among friends" (*NYr* viii). Coterie "handing round" would preserve the epistolary relationship that she preferred. Bishop's distribution of poems, papers, and paintings demonstrates this preference: she sent just-finished poems to Pauline Hanson, Lowell, Moore, Swenson, and others and she relished receiving unpublished verse from her friends. A large part of *Edgar Allan Poe* comes from notebooks she gave to Linda Nemer in Brazil (*EAP* xii; see also Goldensohn 27–29), and many of the paintings collected in *Exchanging Hats* were created and presented as gifts to friends in South and North America (*EH* viii). The rounds of correspondence were for Bishop the proper dissemination of all art. Her preference is clearest in a third major collection of Bishop's letters, *Elizabeth Bishop and The New Yorker*, which was published in 2011 and edited by Biele, and in which exchanges between Bishop and her editors reveal her efforts to turn commercial transactions into epistolary friendships. Bishop exaggerates a lack of publishing savvy, for example, when she asks Howard Moss to "enlighten" her about offprints "so I'll be more professional" (*NYr* 267); her insistence on dedications to her poems – against *New Yorker* policy – suggests a related desire to eschew professional economy for a friendly circuit (*NYr* 281, 283). At one point, Bishop even wished to dedicate a poem to Katharine White, who explained that "the *New Yorker* tries to avoid personal dedications and it would be particularly bad, of course, if the dedication were to an editor … too intramural" (*NYr* 212). It is just such intramuralism that Bishop hoped to dramatize. This latest collection of Bishop's letters thus supports and extends Hammer's earlier analysis of her ambivalent professionalism as it helps to explain the difference between Bishop's small number of poems and voluminous output of letters. Her scarce publication testifies to designs as well as difficulties. Bishop would reduce the unlimited purview of the mass market to the limited boundaries of an epistolary addressee.

Such epistolary narrowing – from the general to the specific, from the collective to the personal – might develop critical understanding of the poet's engagement not just in publishing, but also in politics – a theme of increasing interest to Bishop studies. Recent analysis has turned from the poet's opinion on particular issues to her position among various allegiances, particularly during her residence in South America (Gray 24–62; Hicok; White; McIntosh). Letters show Bishop's complicated attitude toward both the United States and Brazil, as she sends messages north that criticize American conditions but long for an American community (White 255–256; McIntosh 231–234) – and that complain about her adopted country while promoting its misunderstood ways. Form, however, might again be more important than content, since letters model Bishop's stance of testimonial participation: an expatriate whose romantic partner, Lota de Macedo Soares, was an upper-class, politically involved Brazilian, Bishop saw the political upheaval of 1960s Brazil with an insider's biased knowledge and an outsider's objective vision. Her correspondence enacts this position, often contrasting the inaccuracies of newspaper reportage with the truth of personal witness. She sends her account of the 1964 coup to Lowell, for example, "in a RAGE about what the US papers are quoted as saying ... What in HELL does the NY *Post* know about it?" and ends by imploring Lowell to "please try to see it fairly, and if you get the chance, make your liberal intellectual friends see it fairly, too" (*WIA* 532–533). The difference is one of affect as much as fact; from one friend to another, Bishop's epistolary intervention would work through invested relationship rather than abstract policy.

To recognize this is to perceive some easily overlooked political implications in her poems, as works like "Cootchie," "Faustina," and "Manuelzinho" approach the vexed sociology of race, class, and gender through the vexed sociability of particular pairs. Bishop's preference for epistolary citizenship contains a progressive potential even if her reaction to specific policies did not (her letter to Lowell, for example, dismisses civil rights violations that were supported by her friend Carlos Lacerda). Correspondent politics emphasize the particular position of the writer and the particular position of the audience; correspondent politics, moreover, enforces a transitivity that makes both parties agents of evolving meaning. To take epistolary composition as a model of political participation is thus to refuse abstract terms and hegemonic discourse for specific instances and mutually determined implication. Gillian White's recent work on the "interpretive space" of Bishop's poems shows how these emphases can turn even apolitical passages of description into scenes of social critique (258–263). When Bishop composes the provisionally titled "Letter to Two Friends," for example, she concludes her unfinished draft with a quoted sign-off, "Brazil, 'where the nuts come from'" (*EAP* 113–114). The ironic distance of that phrase suggests the sociopolitical self-consciousness that epistolarity fosters, in this writer "with a visa about to expire" – as Bishop writes, also, to ask Moore and Lowell for help with her poetry ("please cable a verb!") and to cure her anxious loneliness ("I am slightly sick of myself").

Even though that "Letter" remains unfinished, correspondence helps to specify the art in many of Bishop's completed poems as well. Consider "Santarém," for example, a late work of seemingly meandering, subtly cumulative progress that takes formlessness as a principle of composition, and a poem that Bishop may have written in part using letters she sent to Macedo Soares during a trip on the Amazon (Biele, "Like Working" 96). "Santarém" moves by means of questioning, associative observation, enforcing Bishop's refusal of "literary interpretations" and preference for the less absolute "dialectic" of experience. In so doing, the poem fosters indeterminacy through its very precision – a paradox implicit in the content of Bishop's "Darwin letter," with its aesthetic-scientific ideal, and resulting from its form, with its epistolary meditation. Bishop relished the way that correspondence could bring writer and reader together in an attentive immanence that is both productive and receptive, that is neither intentional nor meaningless. A similar sense pervades poems like "A Monument," which opens its observations with a question, or "A Cold Spring," the descriptions of which culminates in "your shadowy pastures," or even "North Haven," with its attentive, elegiac address – as well as many letters: her witty messages to Moore about European travels, when she would like "to describe many infinitely described things to you," or her precise accounts to Swenson of Brazilian birds, revising "our bird poem," or her late dispatches from that Maine island where she was learning names of flowers (*P* 25, 56, 210–211; *OA* 65, 418).

"Santarém" also indicates a respect for otherness that arises from the "self-forgetful" ideal in Bishop's epistolary writing. The poem concludes with a Brazilian pharmacist offering Bishop the "wasps' nest" she admires on his shelf. A Dutch tourist then scorns the present as "ugly" – challenging the reader, in conclusion, to perceive the worth of the object *and* the cross-cultural link it fostered. In this and other respects, the papery nest manifests an artistry akin to that of a letter – both dubiously aesthetic, inescapably humble, and potentially perishable, but both marked with a setting, attentiveness, and connection to be valued. One might equally compare the painting in "Poem," which Hammer analyzes in his consideration of Bishop's epistolary rhetoric, and which describes a small, descriptive artwork passed among friends (Hammer 175–176). The title emphasizes Bishop's recognition of these qualities in all sorts of art, even as she recognized the limitations, too, of epistolary writing – and wrestled with its distinct possibilities in both poems and letters. As she writes in a 1955 letter, "communication is an undependable but sometimes marvelous thing" (*OA* 312). Her lifelong trust in its chancy marvels help to describe the possibilities of the letter form as they help to deepen the profundities in her entire body of work.

11

PEGGY SAMUELS

Bishop and Visual Art

In interviews, Elizabeth Bishop repeatedly remarked that she would have loved to have been a painter (Brown 296; Johnson 100; Spires 129). The very trajectory of Bishop's work – from an early interest in Surrealism to one that altered the ratio between the natural and the oneiric – took place at least partly by an engagement with debates and trends within modern visual art about the role of the unconscious, geometric abstraction versus the biomorphic, the interlacing of the subjectivity of the painter in perception of the object, experiments with surface and depth, the elimination of narrative, and the move toward a "pure" and more sensual materiality. These issues constituted the conversations about art to which Bishop had access via exhibition catalogues, art books, articles in periodicals, and people – among them, the painters Loren MacIver and Kit Barker; the art patron Louise Crane; the art historian, researcher, and curator Margaret Miller; as well as Bishop's partner, the urban designer Lota de Macedo Soares and her circle of friends. Bishop's response to the visual arts and to criticism of the arts becomes a significant part of the story of her composition of poems. In this respect, she participates in what Charles Altieri has called the "dialectic between painterly achievements, writerly appropriations and painterly responses" in the twentieth century (*Painterly* 179). For Bishop, visual art served as a stimulus, a source of liberating permissions, a means of skirting dead ends or limitations, and a route for more clearly imagining the possibilities for her own linguistic medium.

The depth of her relationship to the visual was powerfully articulated early on by David Kalstone, who wrote that "objects hold radiant interest for her precisely because they help her absorb numbing or threatening experiences" (220). This "radiant interest" in the visual and its relation to deflection of emotion can be felt intensively in both her story, "In the Village," and her poems, "First Death in Nova Scotia" and "Sestina," works that centered on extreme grief experienced from the point of view of a child. Many of the unpublished poems contain autobiographical material eliminated from the published poems (Ellis *Art and Memory* 21–53; Schwartz "Finished"; Cleghorn "Wiring"), and Bishop had to invent a poetics that would neither fall into the place of loss nor become mere evasion (Ellis 71, 82, 91). As Bonnie Costello has argued in a crucial essay for Bishop studies, Bishop's lyrics have a far more complex relationship to the autobiographical than simply serving as metaphors or pointers (whether coded or deflected) for the poet's personal experience (Costello, "Impersonal"). Visual art became crucial for Bishop's ability to imagine how voice and subjectivity could be structured in poems.

In this lifelong project, Bishop used the visual arts to generate models for poetry. From the fact of her ownership of hundreds of art books, from her notebooks and from correspondence with Margaret Miller, we know that Bishop read extensively in commentaries on visual art and sometimes used art historians to help her to think about her poetics. For example, she worked on a draft poem on Charlemagne (now lost) that responded to issues of composition in Cézanne, regarding the mind's relationship to objects. She made notes about Alfred Barr's book on Picasso, reflecting on the composition of wholes, and insisting that they should not be based merely on multiple visual perspectives, but had to include the linguistic, memory, and both physical and emotional feeling. She thought about Venetian glass in relation to issues of surface and depth and illusion. She audited the German art historian Erwin Panofsky's course at New York University (NYU) and, in "Roosters," used some of his ideas about the way that conceptual and emotional meanings could be poured into or removed from visual images. Commentators on visual art took up the question of the artist's subjectivity in relation to the sensory world and provided Bishop with ways to think through the issue in addition to what she could see in literary exemplars.

The very beginning of her career took place in a context in which poets found each other's work in what Susan Rosenbaum has called "the little galleries" of the literary magazines that "set the terms for understanding surrealist poetry as an interdisciplinary endeavor" ("Exquisite" 271). A strong scholarly consensus has developed that Bishop's early poetry both uses and adapts Surrealist techniques and subject matter; that by the late 1930s, she alters her relationship with Surrealism, adapting it to pursue what she herself termed, "the always-more-successful surrealism of everyday life" (*PPL* 861); that she had significant doubts about Surrealism and strove to disassociate her own work from becoming overly identified with Surrealist painting (*EAP* 272; *OA* 135; *PPL* 859); and that nevertheless, she continued to deploy Surrealistic elements throughout her career (Mullen, Goldensohn, MacArthur, Vendler, Suarez-Toste; see Susan Rosenbaum in this collection for a fuller account of Bishop's relationship to Surrealism).

By late 1937, perhaps partly because of the sobering experience of a car accident in France in which Margaret Miller (Bishop's former college roommate and close friend) lost her right arm, Bishop alters her aesthetic. The wildness of personal memory and imagination in relation to the exterior world that the poet explores in "The Weed," or "Paris 7 A.M.," becomes far more subdued in "Quai d'Orléans." The poet executes precise and restrained demarcations as the mind turns from nature toward its own creations: a wake in water that the speaker says looks *like* a "giant oak-leaf of gray lights / on duller grey" is set delicately, slowly, against a real leaf ("real leaves [that] are floating by"). The movement of real "ripples / [that] make / for the sides of the quai, [and] extinguish themselves / against the walls" are given the gentle comparison: "as softly as falling-stars come to their ends / at a point in the sky" (*P* 29). The gentle modesty of this mind's flight into metaphor, into the imagination of "like," carries the mildness of nature's own movements. Water to leaf to star, the speaker's mental creations cling closely to nature's own materials. Humility reigns, a modesty restraining the giddy liberty of swooping and whirling mental flights in "Paris, 7 A.M." The close of "Quai d'Orléans," in which the speaker reflects on the impossibility of forgetting, or rather the impossibility of a painful event "forget[ting] us," gestures toward the depths of an interior life about which the speaker is ultimately reticent, as if a poem could close or turn away as well as open to the interior life of its speaker. All through the rest of Bishop's poems in *North & South* and *A Cold Spring*, we find her probing how the relations between inner and outer will be structured in poems, and this probing situates her as contemplating the relations between the visual (what can be seen) and the linguistic (what the mind thinks and feels) and crafting a means of arranging their "touch" through the materiality of verse. Part of her solution involves drawing on the way that visual images themselves incorporate "inferred touch" and emotional resonance close to physical sensation (Scarry 17).

Meyer Schapiro, a cult figure in the artistic community who had served as the master's thesis advisor for Margaret Miller and who Bishop much admired, wrote about the Impressionists as "represent[ing] the exterior world through a reacting sensibility" ("Fromentin" 29). But that formulation was rather vague to be of much use for structuring the relation between inner and outer. Schapiro also described the necessity of modern artists abandoning classical perspective and its stable relationship between the mind and objects. As Charles Altieri explains, the modernist work has to "orient itself to how the world appears when one is within the scene" ("Why" 10). Bishop explicitly shows the impossibility of using classical perspective in "Twelfth Morning; or What You Will," a poem in which the narrative follows her acts of visual perception and a series of decisions, inconclusive finally, about what to privilege. The focal point is claimed by culture (the company that owns the dunes), a fence, a horse, a house, nature (the sea) and finally by Balthazar ("the four-gallon can / approaching on the head of Balthazár / keeps flashing that the world's a pearl, *and I, / I am / its highlight!*"). The speaker never pronounces whether or not she accepts this center – this joyous sparkle of a poor boy singing the central celebratory moment in a folk nativity popular all over Brazil – a center that implies the world is a pearl not a "housewreck." In contrast, the last two stanzas of a draft poem about her mother poignantly reveal why the mind must be located *within* the scene. Mother and child are intimately rendered: "Hair being brushed at night / and brushed / 'Did you see the spark?' / Yes, I saw the spark / and the shadow of the elm / outside the window" ("A mother made of dress-goods ... ," *EAP* 156). The child-speaker's mind is held suspended among the compressed visual image of the spark, the physical movements of brushing, the mother's and child's floating voices, the rich and tangible atmosphere of a partially known exterior landscape. The sensation of background, of impending forces or places offstage or off-center and figures only partially known, becomes emotionally crucial: she overhears her mother's voice, "a voice heard still / echoing / far at the bottom somewhere / of my aunt's on the telephone – / coming out of blackness – the blackness all voices come from" (*EAP* 156). Visually, her mother is partially glimpsed, receding into a background: "A naked figure standing / in a wash-basin shivering half crouched / a little ... in the sloping-ceilinged bedroom / with the striped wallpaper" (*EAP* 156). Shifting foregrounds and backgrounds become crucial in thinking about relations of present to past, self to others, and trajectories of knowledge; hence her attraction to Édouard Vuillard, with whose aesthetics she experimented (*OA* 312). Vuillard's figures sometimes melted back into the substratum or into the un-visible. He depicted women incompletely known, fading into the wallpaper (not able to stand out and speak), like voices that come indistinctly out of blackness. In *A Cold Spring*, Bishop invents a poetics that inhabits the back-and-forth between all the levels of self – from deep to offhand, in all degrees of interaction with a world that has its own multiple degrees of surface and depth (see, for example, "Insomnia," "The Prodigal," "At the Fishhouses," and "The Shampoo").

The draft poem about early memories of her mother shows Bishop composing by setting the mind feelingly within the materials of the world. When we consider Bishop's relationship to visual art, it helps to consider not only her famous visual clarity and accuracy of observation, but also the way that her poems bring the visual, the emotional, and the linguistic close to the sensation of touch, incorporating the world with, in Phoebe Putnam's term, "caressive attention." We can sense, not only in Bishop's own poetry, but in her advice to other poets as well, that Bishop felt tactility to be a crucial constituent of seeing and feeling. In teaching May Swenson to feel the emotional valence of "physical words," Bishop sounds almost short-tempered and sets her a homework task of reading Hopkins's "Harry Ploughman" (*OA* 361). And, in a notebook jotting about Baudelaire, Bishop gives an asterisk to the first two stanzas of "Chant d'Automne," in which the speaker is plunged into foreboding about the dark and cold of winter by hearing firewood clattering on the paving stones of a courtyard, viscerally sensed as akin to the sharp and heavy blows used in the construction of a gallows or coffin. The materiality of the words "catches" the materiality of the world and holds it for the mind/heart/body to see it feelingly. The subjective feel of the world in the poet's mind is conveyed by drawing the materiality of the world into the poem's body. Like the Impressionists and Postimpressionists in their use of the canvas, Bishop uses the poetic text itself as a surface or field in which to arrange the divergent and decentered meeting of the materials of mind and world.

We can see the beginning of her solution in the early poem, "To be Written on the Mirror in Whitewash." The written text of a poem, appearing as a figure/text on a mirror, is granted a distinct material existence ("Above all I am not that staring man," the words on the mirror say) that differs from the writing "I" and from the "real" world, hovering *between* the eye of the visual beholder and the "I" of the mind that presumably can reflect on and is partially distinct from what the eye sees (*P* 273). The poetic text is defined as a reflective material surface mediating between the eye and the "I." Bishop later uses her poems as that kind of surface: a fluid, mobile meeting place where the mind, the heart, the eye, and the world can converge and diverge in a puzzling, open-ended, but contained and shaped encounter. That conception of a poem's status could explain why Bishop writes an extraordinary number of poems that engage either with works of visual art or with reflective surfaces: "The Map," "Wading at Wellfleet," "The Gentleman of Shalott," "Large Bad Picture," "Love Lies Sleeping," "The Weed," "The Unbeliever," "The Monument," "Quai d'Orléans," "Sleeping on the Ceiling," "Cirque d'Hiver," "Pleasure Seas," "Florida," "Roosters," "Seascape," "Over 2,000 Illustrations and a Complete Concordance," "At the Fishhouses," "The Bight," "Insomnia," "View of the Capitol from the Library of Congress," "Brazil, January 1, 1502," "Twelfth Morning; or What You Will," "Sestina," "First Death in Nova Scotia," "Sunday, 4 A.M.," "In the Waiting Room," "Poem," and "Sonnet." Visual art (whether maps, wallpaper, photographs, postcards, engravings, tapestries, chromographs, mechanical toys, sculptures, or paintings) and reflective surfaces (whether water or mirrors) are especially mobile and are more able to include the ephemerality, tentativeness, and temporality that structure the entanglement between subjectivity and the natural object (see Costello, *Questions* 14–45, 181–242). She tends to use a surface that can act as a mobile mirror because it reflects or can accommodate the mobility of mind as it alters in feeling and knowledge, seeking only provisional meaning retrospectively from a world that is always receding in both directions: forward and backward (Longenbach 22–34).

In this way, Bishop was able to put to rest doubts that she had in the late-1930s about her turn toward nature, which had the potential of deflating poetry to the merely picturesque. In looking at visual artists' relations to nature, she loved Vermeer, whose freshness, clarity, and accuracy of observation she valued in her own work and whose paintings' nacreous surfaces recorded the painter's own loving caress of the world. She loved the little Seurat, "Evening at Honfleur," in which the materials of water, rock, sky, land, and even the frame of the painting itself had elements that intermingled or interlaced in tiny notes of resemblance and difference (*PPL* 859). Nevertheless, neither of these artists would be able to offer her a means of imagining the position of the agent of that seeing, the seer, inside the work in a way that could position a lyric voice. Instead, Bishop turned to mid-century visual artists who stretched the visual to include embodied seeing, closely aligned with the tactile, where the material of the world and the subjectivity of the always-in-motion seer became most entangled (Samuels). These artists brought movement and temporality into their work, crossing closer to the features of the linguistic medium in which Bishop was working. At mid-century, Pierre Bonnard and Willem de Kooning both began to experiment with the look of objects when the mind is in motion, glimpsing them; however, to her early biographer, Anne Stevenson, Bishop singles out Paul Klee and Kurt Schwitters as of special interest (*PPL* 844, 859).

At mid-century, artists often situated themselves within crucial divides, including, in the 1930s, Surrealism and Postimpressionism versus a Realism that celebrated American regionalism. In the late 1930s and 1940s, when Bishop was most occupied with inventing her own poetics that diverged from Moore's, visual artists divided between abstraction (including geometric abstraction associated with Mondrian, tending toward the flattening of space) and biomorphism (irregular shapes sometimes reminiscent of the biological world and more accommodating of depth). Bishop sometimes contemplated these oppositions inside her poems. The oppositions between the geometric and the biomorphic could be translated or thought of as analogous to poetry, an apparently flat form that contains dynamic psychological material and often gives order to a fluent natural or social world (see, for example, "Pleasure Seas" or "Over 2,000 Illustrations and a Complete

Concordance"). Cornell, Schwitters, Klee, and Calder all experimented with bringing geometric abstraction closer to the three-dimensional material or biological world and bringing surface in dynamic relationship to depth. Cornell used grids that orchestrated fluid relations among the materials of life, arranging objects and the mind's encounter with them. His works simultaneously intensified a sense of the stability of the visual image and awareness of the fluidity of mental movements of personal association and cultural history that swirl toward and are evoked by those objects. Bishop called attention to the affinities between Cornell's work and her own poems by translating Octavio Paz's tribute poem to Cornell, including it as the only translation that she ever published with her own poems ("Objects & Apparitions"). As Bishop's translation puts it, in his "hexahedrons of wood and glass ... memory weaves, unweaves the echoes" (*P* 201). To the extent that both personal and cultural memory involve visual images as gravitational focal points that language resignifies, Cornell's art allows one way of imagining the relationship between visual imagery of objects and language's arranging and rearranging the meaning of those visual objects in poems. As Heather Treseler has shown, some of Bishop's drafts are concerned quite explicitly with the "insidious" "fluences" that "manufacture" those meanings (Bishop, quoted in Treseler 100–102).

Mid-century critics of Klee's work emphasized that the viewer of a Klee painting became immersed in a deep space, having to find his way with all his senses, including hearing and touch. Critics drew attention to the "psycho-physical" feeling of Klee's miniscule subject wandering, tactilely, among floating motifs in a field that had no defined frame (Samuels 63–68). To float among motifs in an edgeless space, without orientation or ground, felt as if it expressed the epistemological tentativeness, the seeing closely aligned to touch, and the embodied lyric "I" that characterized Bishop's work. The Klee paintings that Bishop mentions to Moore in 1938 (*OA* 96–97), and to Lowell in 1961 (*WIA* 364) have this feeling of "modesty, care, *space*, a sort of helplessness but determination at the same time"; qualities that Bishop listed in a letter to Lowell in 1958 as ones that appealed to her in Modernist writers, painters, and musicians (*WIA* 250). In notebook drafts, we can see that Bishop's compositional practice frequently begins by situating a nearly effaced or submerged speaker, who arises only gradually and gently to speak the "I" from within a multitude of acts of visceral, visual, and somatic perception. In poems like "Faustina, or Rock Roses," Bishop suspends the lyric speaker in a deep fluid space of floating shapes and materials that open into or drift across that speaker. She creates a dynamic sense of subjectivity intensely vulnerable to an environment that can diffuse across its boundaries and yet also a subjectivity held in suspension among variable objects.

Alexander Calder's work made a long-lasting impression on Bishop (letter to Stevenson, March 6, 1964) and the poet most likely discussed Calder's work with both Margaret Miller (who worked with the American curator James Johnson Sweeney on the 1943 Museum of Modern Art exhibition catalogue) and Lota de Macedo Soares (who played a significant role in the reception of Calder in Brazil and who owned a Calder mobile, hung in Bishop's and her home in Samambaia). As small movement machines, Calder's mobiles led to conceptualizing a poem as composed of the arrangement of moving parts of syntax, rhythms, rhymes, words, and thematic or natural objects that come into view, move or impact one another, and recede. Calder's work gave Bishop one way of imagining the dynamics of poems. Lyrics become systems for orchestrating the drift and weight of one interior thought or emotion as it arises from, is weighed against, or replaces another – all orchestrated within the moving environment of the exterior world. In "A Cold Spring," "The Armadillo," "Arrival at Santos," "The Moose," "Five Flights Up," and the draft poem "Gypsophilia," natural and man-made objects float, ascend, descend, cross, recede, unfurl, lift, open, threaten or give a sense of weight or weightlessness to a lyric speaker who responds discursively and emotionally to the moving environment with the release, cascade, uplift or "downdraft" of her own mental movements.

Bishop also turned to the aesthetics of Kurt Schwitters, who combined the visual with a visceral sense of the tactile, incorporating the bodily and ephemeral material of the world – often worn papers and textiles – into his compositions. In turning to Schwitters, Bishop shared in Margaret Miller's enthusiasm for this artist. Miller included many of his pieces in the MoMA collage exhibition that she curated from 1946–1948; she served as an advocate for Schwitters in his relations with the museum administration; she owned a Schwitters collage and selected another for Bishop to give to Lota as a birthday gift. Schwitters orchestrated sequences of like and unlike so that dense materiality (for example, cardboard) could gradually segue into airy nothingness (airmail letter paper or tissue paper). And he used materials that were soaked in historical and personal association, but also lifted the associations from the objects turning toward the sheerly sensory and material. These compositional techniques gave Bishop another way of conceiving of lyric as a meeting place for the fluid crossing between the sensory material of the world, cultural meanings, and the more airy realm of thought and feeling – the mind of the poet. A good example is "Cape Breton," where Bishop moves from "mist" to "rotting-snow-ice sucked away" to "spirit" to "ghosts" and then modulates back to the density of the natural world with its tinier or "closer" distinctions in color and texture: "those folds and folds of fir: spruce and hackmatack" (*P* 65). As in Schwitters's collages, the poet moves toward the cultural or the discursive and fluidly lets it go, moving back to mere sensory touch. Klee, Cornell, Calder, and Schwitters, while leaving behind classical perspective, had all gone beyond the Impressionists' use of the surface of a painting to record their subjective response to the natural world; they invented ways of giving form or structure to the fluidity and tentativeness of a mobile I/eye encountering a world always in flux. The depth of the encounter was not located in the personal psychology of a "deep" self but in the intricacy, density, and mobility of a desiring mind's encounter with the materials of a moving world; an encounter that took place by means of the tactile materials of an aesthetic medium.

Bishop's tributes to two contemporary painters, her memorial essay for the folk artist Gregorio Valdes and her deeply sympathetic "Gallery Note for Wesley Wehr," are her most extended descriptions of any painter's work. She values Wehr's paintings for granting her an opportunity to enter a more contemplative mode that, far from abandoning the natural object, arranges access to the tactile and visceral feeling of the visual. In Wehr's paintings, she feels different kinds of coldness in the landscape ("the coldness of the Pacific Northwest coast in the winter, its different coldness in the summer"), the tactile wearing away of materials ("the snow had worn off the low hills almost showing last year's withered grasses"), and the subdued timbre of a movement physically remote from the viewer ("the white line of surf was visible but quiet, almost a mile away") (*Pr* 352). The art object magically opens "space" (she is transported "far off," feels inside of "so much space, so much air, such distances and loneliness"), experiencing an alternative orientation to the geography of the three-dimensional world in which one usually lives (*Pr* 352). This is why Bishop refuses to call Wehr's paintings "small scale," although they are of small size. Wehr's paintings with their sense of privacy are not only important to her because "intimate, low-voiced, and delicate things" constitute a revolt against and invention of an alternative to the values of contemporary American culture: a "mostly huge and roaring, glaring world," "addicted to the gigantic" (*Pr* 352; see White, "Words"). They are important to her because they orchestrate relations *between* the vast and the private. Many poems in her oeuvre set up startling arrangements between vast and intimate scales: from the early career in which peninsulas become women taking whole seas "between thumb and finger," "my crumb" becomes "my mansion," and an unbeliever "curled / in a gilded ball on the mast's top" faces "the spangled sea" to the mid-career "moon in the bureau mirror," "equinoctial tears," and the sandpiper's "grains" next to the Atlantic, to the late-career's "my legs dangling down familiarly / over a crater's edge" and an "I" "falling off / the round, turning world / into cold, blue-black space" (*P* 5, 21, 24, 68, 121, 129, 183, 180). In her engagement with visual art, Bishop seems to have experienced another medium's powerful evocation of these spectacular and odd perspectival relations, perhaps in a less threatening mode. In discussing her experience of Wehr's paintings, she renders the pleasure of a fall into an act of visceral contemplation where an embodied, floating self is enlivened and absorbed by wandering in an expanse of infinite and quiet relations. "Rothko in a whisper," she says (*Pr* 353).

While the paintings of the folk artist Gregorio Valdes can seem almost the opposite (objects rendered with "flatness and remoteness"), Bishop takes delight in the "freshness" of his images (*Pr* 31). This pleasure derives partly from his escape from conventions (he has not been "trained to do 'oils'" like her landlady) and does not hide that his works are artifacts, homemade by an artist's hand (*Pr* 26). Partly, her delight in his work attaches to his rendering of objects that are allowed to flourish on their own, with a kind of privacy surrounding them: "who could fail to enjoy and admire those secretive palm trees in their pink skies" (*Pr* 31). The Valdes essay continuously veers into descriptions of the objects and decorations of Gregorio's house and work places, and when she commissions a painting from him, she tells him to throw in all kinds of beloved objects: "more flowers, a monkey that lived next door, a parrot, and a certain type of palm tree, called the Traveller's Palm" (*Pr* 27). In this respect, Bishop takes pleasure in art as a collection of other objects, allying her sense of both visual art and poetry to the kind of collecting that she engaged in with Marianne Moore (elephant hair, nautilus shell, the "sting" of a Stingray fish) and the way that her own poems collect objects, both natural and homemade. "Questions of Travel" is as much about the delight of collecting as it is about larger questions: "trees along this road / really exaggerated in their beauty, / ... gesturing / like noble pantominists, robed in pink," "the sad, two-noted, wooden tune / of disparate wooden clogs," and a bird cage like "a bamboo church of Jesuit baroque: / three towers, five silver crosses" (*P* 91–92). Ultimately in this poem, however, Bishop's delight in the objects derives from their ability to connect to history in its beauty, plenitude, and unpredictability: "history in / the weak calligraphy of songbirds' cages" (*P* 92). Like the "mongrel" and "casual" collection of objects, people, sights, actions in "Santarém" – exemplified most surprisingly by the oars brought to the Amazon by the serendipity of emigrating Southern families from the American Civil War – each item carries the trace of the currents that brought it to its present location. Delight, for Bishop, emerges from contemplation of the "embarking, / disembarking" of all this particularity, just as her departure from Santarém carries away one particular white wasp's nest (*P* 208).

Scholars have looked at Bishop's own visual art works mostly as revelatory of the poet's sensibility, seeing affinities between strategies and images in paintings and poems (Goldensohn, "Written"; Chiasson, "Tea"; Schwartz, "Two Arts"; Biele, "Three-Fourths Painter"). Lorrie Goldensohn has written the most extensive, nuanced descriptions of the paintings, noting among other qualities their strange, skewed perspectives, "swift skittering lines and joky sketchiness" ("Homeless" 106), and the "peculiar and captivating freshness, flatness, and remoteness" that Bishop herself admired in the paintings of Valdes (*Pr* 31). The paintings have been considered akin to folk art; however, Dan Chiasson thinks of Bishop's paintings as portraying a "calculated simplicity" and "an impersonation of naïvité" (20), which distinguishes them from Bishop's own view of Valdes's folk art that she characterizes as unsophisticated if charming (*Pr* 27, 29, 31).

Foremost, the paintings, like the poems, and like the art works that Bishop chose to describe in her ekphrastic poems, live on a modest and intimate scale. She created them on inexpensive brittle papers that would not endure (and, in fact, some of the works are beginning to alter). Giving one of the paintings to her doctor, Anny Baumann, Bishop even jokingly remarked that the painting was "big enough so that if you like any section of it you can cut that part out" (*OA* 246). Often given away as gifts, these artworks allowed Bishop to participate in the kind of "publication" that she wished was available for poetry. Indeed, she told May Swenson that she "would have preferred the days when poems just got handed around among friends" (letter to Swenson, February 18, 1965; see also *OA* 431). The small scale of the work accords with her stated preference in poetry for small uncommodified art with a low-keyed voice (White, "*Words*"). As she once said in an interview: "I'm not interested in big-scale work as such. Something needn't be large to be good" (*Conversations* 24). Although reproductions of many of these works have become readily accessible through the work of William Benton, who tracked down the scattered works, annotating and dating them where possible, as is usual with visual art, the reproductions cannot deliver the materiality of the object. Face-to-face, much of the feel of these works emerges in the sense of fragility and ephemerality of the paper and the "announcement" that the work is only a tentative, humble, and inexact attempt, which also has the effect of making the objects that are pictured seem as slight and vulnerable as the materials. Many of the buildings appear almost lonely, as if they were so unremarkable that no one else would ever have chosen them, certainly not that "side" of them. Yet, as in her poetry, *her* looking becomes part of the paintings' subjects. In "County Courthouse," one encounters the leaning instability and palpable fragility of radio towers seemingly almost embarrassingly (comically?) made of tiny matchsticks (*EH* 23). In "Palais du Senat" (*EH* 9), the serious and noble sculptures perched on the roof are humorously inexact: the squiggly Chinese white on the building's edges produce a wobbly "solidity" in the stone columns and the skylights are slightly bent – all conveying the artist's delight in the slightly askew or accidental. The accident is not only in the objects, but in the act of mind and hand that renders them. Bishop's paintings enlace the artist's subjectivity – her look, her making – as also the subject of the piece. To include attentiveness to the medium and to the making as part of the work accords with her poetics that made the medium's (language's) touch of the world a crucial part of her poetic project (Putnam). A patch of color is liberated from and hovers alongside a mimosa tree (*EH* 31), the line of an electric cord wanders up and across the ceiling in a joke about the materiality of an artist's drawn line (*EH* 43), the Harris School just happens to look as thin and flat as a piece of paper (*EH* 21). These works never forget what they are made of. Like the poems, they orchestrate the meeting of the material of the medium and subjectivity in order to enact the feeling mind's touch of world through artistic medium.

Bishop's poems on paintings allow us to watch the poet thinking about the nature of poetry via reflections on visual art. As Bonnie Costello shows, in these poems Bishop portrays the artwork as a "meditative center" able to "activate memory," to "commemorate, designate, evoke" in a "dynamic space" that holds a "multiplicity of durations" for both creator and beholder (*Questions* 215, 218, 225, 232–233). "The Monument" (1937) describes an imaginary drawing of a sculpture based on a frottage by Max Ernst (*PPL* 842; Costello, *Questions* 220). Frottages are created by physically rubbing a graphite pencil over an actual articulated surface, such as wood, so that the tactile features of the surface are captured in the drawing and impel the invention of other images. The technique may have appealed to Bishop because it literally brings the materiality of the world into the art object. Bishop's poem is a dialogue between a guide or curator and a more naïve spectator as they confront and respond to a drawing of a pile of boxes, arranged catty-cornered on one another, on a beach. The poem unveils Bishop's early reflections on the ontology of art. The artwork is a made object that becomes unnatural and partially remote or reticent, and therefore draws partly away from the sensory world: "Why does that strange sea make no sound?" (*P* 25). Nevertheless, the poem is based in nature and in fact takes up the "grain" of nature into its own material ("the sky looks wooden, grained with cloud"). It is assuredly not monumental, grandiose, or perfected. Instead, it is homely, plain, crude, handmade, and subject to deterioration ("It's piled-up boxes, / outlined with shoddy fret-work, half-fallen off, / cracked and unpainted"). And yet it is ornamented and contains a sort of odd or awkward (therefore humane and touching) beauty and charm ("on the topmost cube is set / a sort of fleur-de-lys of weathered wood, / long petals of board, pierced with odd holes, / four-sided, stiff, ecclesiastical"). Its materials are drawn from the history of art ("fleur-de-lys"), daily life ("fishing-poles"), and community culture ("flag-poles"). The ornament, although not grandiose or succeeding in creating perfect adornment or beauty, betrays the art work as "having life" and "wishing" "to cherish something" so that the desire of the artist to commemorate becomes part of the object. Although crude, decaying, and, in its artificiality, more "cramped" and arid than life, the art work is also more enduring and more cohesive than nature ("wood holds together better / than sea or cloud or sand could by itself"). It does not escape history (the paint is "flaked off" and is falling apart), nor does it escape the historical contingency of the viewer's misunderstanding or projection and it can become a focal point for that audience's own emotional life. It cannot exhibit in any fully available sense its creator or the creator's intention, but it is able to "roughly but adequately" give "shelter" to that creator, even though the artist has altered, disappeared from view, or perhaps deceased: "The bones of the artist-prince may be inside / or far away on even drier soil. / But roughly but adequately it can shelter / what is within" (*P* 26–27). Here, we can see that reflecting on visual art liberated Bishop to produce an aesthetic theory that she felt unable to articulate in the form of a prose essay. She abandoned essays on the aesthetics of Gertrude Stein and W. H. Auden and mentioned to Moore that she was unsuccessful in crafting a poetic theory (*OA* 73).

By the time she again uses a work of visual art to establish her own aesthetics in "Poem" – a description of her encounter with a small painting made by her uncle, George Hutchinson – Bishop drops into a less intellectualized, more humane, warmer declaration of the ontology of art. The poem brings into crisper view the way that the materiality (tangibility) of an art form occurs as a kind of connecting mechanism for mind and world and for the sensations of physical and emotional touch:

> Up closer, a wild iris, white and yellow,
> fresh-squiggled from the tube.
> The air is fresh and cold; cold early spring
> clear as gray glass; a half inch of blue sky
> below the steel-gray storm clouds. (*P* 196)

The materiality of the paint, its tangibility and freshness, elicits the tangibility of a feeling response that touches the viewer who can thereby sense the materiality of the world, that the "air is fresh and cold." Then the mind – the responding mind, the play of mind – is let in or let loose, always clinging closely to the materials of world; the cold spring day is "clear as gray glass" – another reflecting surface in which the eye and the "I" can have their mobile encounter, the mind always "touching" the world and becoming touched by it. It is fitting that in summing up her theory of art and life, the poet uses as subject matter a work of visual art, which so often in her career became her means of imagining ways for mind to feelingly touch world. The verbal text of this poem establishes a screen, a reflecting surface, at which the materials of mind, materials of the world, and the tangibility of the visual and verbal arts are brought into view and quietly, humbly encounter one another. Bishop's characteristic restraint functions to allow the world and the mind to touch without either overwhelming the other. Learning from visual artists, she invents a kind of poetry that creates a middle realm – a meeting place where mind and world can register each other's activities.

12

LORRIE GOLDENSOHN

Bishop's Posthumous Publications

In 1983, when Elizabeth Bishop's *The Complete Poems: 1927–1979* was posthumously issued, the style, shape, and focus of a Bishop poem appeared to have settled. In 2006, Alice Quinn, denying that the canon had been completed in 1983, cracked it open with unfinished drafts and previously uncollected poems for her *Edgar Allan Poe & The Juke-Box*. By 2008, when Lloyd Schwartz and Robert Giroux edited *Elizabeth Bishop: Poems, Prose, and Letters,* the idea of her significant work had swollen to some 900 printed pages. By 2011, Bishop's longtime publisher, Farrar, Straus and Giroux, separated poetry and prose into two immensely plain volumes, their covers shorn of Bishop's own delightful paintings. *Poems* 2011 appears in dark navy; *Prose* 2011 in gold, dressed in a cheap, inelegant paper. The visual style could not be balder. But Farrar, Straus and Giroux's answer to the problem of completing the Bishop canon alongside the irrepressible growth of the unpublished and uncollected work was to stuff a modest twenty-seven additional poems into "Appendix I: Selected Unpublished Manuscript Poems." In one improvement over Quinn's *Edgar Allan Poe & The Juke-Box*, however, *each* of the appended poems comes with a neat facing of manuscript facsimile. I hazard that these will be interim editions.

Responding to the massive injection of work taken from notes and papers, Lloyd Schwartz answered those who were indignant at the publication of Bishop's drafts and who deemed it a conspicuous violation of the poet's choice to show only "finished" poems. Bishop, says Schwartz, never repudiated her drafts; her will "actually gives her literary executors 'the power to determine whether any of my unpublished manuscripts and papers shall be published, and if so, to see them through the press'" ("Finished" 54). Those of us who began writing about her unpublished papers early in the 1980s can attest that various poems from these papers, sold by Bishop herself to Vassar, show drafts, phrases, stanzas, and lines surviving for years in notebooks and journals. Most famously, Bishop revised and rewrote "The Moose," in drafts that straddled over decades. The "new" stories and memoirs are studded with many glittering fragments that the poet had obviously looted for poems. Whatever Bishop wrote always came from its own integrated universe of crisp, inimitable description, odd-angled perspective, and its own light poise of elements, however tragic the underlying material. But her own wish was to make plain the complex origins, as well as the scope and continuity, of her work.

Simple images – a limp lashing of wires, the line of surf seen as a curling string, the burden of a day "too heavy to lift," the erratic movements of a sandpiper (a bird dear to Elizabeth Bishop's identity) – all have an earlier genesis than the poems in which they later appeared. Most of Bishop's finished poems were matters of slow and steady accretion, and represented, in words by Charles Baudelaire with which she was familiar, a "profonde unité" of symbols. Elizabeth Bishop understood the long and binding timeline of her work.

On August 12, 1963, Bishop's great friend, Robert Lowell, remarked of her unfinished and unpublished work: "You *never* write junk, seldom write anything that isn't a kind of landmark, so your slow pace must be the one that wins the race. Still I brood about all those rich unfinished fragments, such a fortune in the bank" (*WIA* 489). Nevertheless, as the decades begin their slow, volcanic accumulation over this body of poetry, so must our critical reception of it heave and realign.

Years having elapsed since the time that Bishop's friend, Linda Nemer, first put new poems and a fresh trove of papers into my hands in Brazil, I have become aware of my own shifting assessment of the newer unearthed material. Ruefully, I see that I fit Bishop's acid description of the critic quite well, only the job of assigning merit I move from poets to the poetry itself: "Critics," Bishop decided, "can't rest easy until they have put poets in descending order of merit; they change the lists every night before they go to bed." It is clear that night has come – and a number of my opinions have indeed changed since last writing. Or, as Bishop herself wrote as a Vassar undergraduate at the very onset of her career, "the *recognition* itself of what is being written must be kept fluid" (*PPL* 676). Good advice for both writer and reader.

But certain formal manners stay constant – and their emerging definition from her newly released drafts gives a time-lapse photograph of the mind at work: Bishop's apparently scattershot process is incremental and augmentative. The transactions that lie visibly within the drafts are firmly within Bishop's aesthetic. Although late in life she forgot the name of the scholar who brought to her attention the Baroque practice, she still found herself affirming what was, in George Herbert and others, "new" and "quick." "Their purpose," says M. W. Croll, speaking of Baroque poets, and quoted by an undergraduate Bishop, "was to portray, not a thought, but a mind thinking" (*PPL* 666). This was the paradox of what Bishop came to call "the unnatural act of writing poetry," an act which produces a necessarily fixed order of words and yet remains an act that embodies the naturally living and changing (*PPL* 702, 706).

Elizabeth Bishop was never anything other than a formal writer, by her own practice and her own repeated admission. To Anne Stevenson, in 1963, she wrote: "I've always been an umpty-umpty poet with a traditional 'ear'" (*PPL* 842). In the last years of her writing life, we see how much the latest, even the tardiest revisions, were governed by questions of form. Unusually, in September 1974, Bishop sent Robert Lowell a copy of "The End of March" prior to its publication in *The New Yorker* and asked his advice: "Suggestions welcome – even to tearing it up. (No – I can't – I've already spent the *N Yorker* check)" (*WIA* 767). Lowell answered cautiously: "I am troubled by one thing, a sort of whimsical iambic Frost tone to the last five lines or so, tho I think they are needed. New lines might make a fine poem into one of your finest" (*WIA* 769). If we look at what Bishop sent Lowell, and check the final version in print, we see that Bishop dissipated any unease about the poem's ending not by adding new lines, but by subtly altering those that set up her ending.

As Joelle Biele compares the poem pre- and post-Lowell (*NYr* xlix–liii), what strikes one about the changes is not just how the syntax tightened. When Bishop dropped in the late-developing figure, moving "the embedded stones" to stones "set in their bezels of sand," the new metaphor of the jewel setting allowed a whole stanza to reconfigure: "For just a minute, set in their bezels of sand, / the drab, damp, scattered stones / were multi-colored, / and all those high enough threw out long shadows, / individual shadows, then pulled them in again" (*P* 200). Sweating through yet another draft, the poet critically repositioned sun, stones, and sand, and an apparently prosy, even "umpty-umpty" narrative took on a rhythmic, miniature sculpting – and a luminous dramatic force. Five lines before the five lines Lowell queries, Bishop now repeats the last half of a line, and repeats it in the first half of the next, rocking it back on its heels: "for just a minute / For just a minute," lightly mimicking the flickering sun. The rocking repeats again at the turn of another pair of lines: "long shadows, / individual shadows." With characteristic spatial sensitivity, Bishop writes that only those stones "high enough" threw out shadows, and she coordinates the fleeting, teasing motion of these effects with the high/low stones, the left/right, out-and-back pace of the beach walkers, whose faces on the way back "froze on the other side."

The anti-ending of "The Prodigal" runs: "But it took him a long time / finally to make his mind up to go home" (*P* 69). "The End of March" concludes with similar flatness: " – a sun who'd walked the beach the last low tide, / making those big, majestic paw-prints, / who perhaps had batted a kite out of the sky to play with" (*P* 200). The preposition arrived early and remains the daring terminal word for the playful, distinctly antiheroic lion-sun. Lowell ultimately wrote to Bishop: "My suggestions for the end of your poem must have been troublesome ... you were probably right all along" (*WIA* 776). Yet she made grand use of the nudge he gave her. All the papers we now have in print show the great delicacy of her adjustments.

Even in initial stages, the drafts show the recursive and incremental way in which Bishop's mind worked. A bare phrase appears and then without pause repeats itself in a line, with a slight change in syntax, then will come in again beside the old phrase with an additional adjective, and then once more, in a kind of fertile stammer, will repeat with the changes incorporated. This movement is visible in all of the initial drafts that Alice Quinn reproduces. "On the Amazon" (*EAP* 124) contains these lines: "The water moves faster / a thin [glaze] of blue skin blue skin / reflects, reflects – nothing," and then at the right – "thin loose blue skin." And a little later, "A [sudden] line of birds / [flung up] like beads," and again at the margin, "flings out." In many repetitions, beside the additional modifiers introduced for clarity and precision, you can see Bishop shaking out the syntactically extra syllables, as she strategically loads what on several occasions she called her characteristic "umpty-umpty" to be ready to soar. Stanzas or sections of longer poems were set aside to work on with particular concentration. In "On the Amazon," you can almost glimpse the confident brilliant speech unwrapping from its stutter of repetition, and from the page-cluttering parentheses and brackets with which Quinn supplemented her record. A bit like "The Monument" (*P* 25), it is "the beginning of a painting, / a piece of sculpture, or poem, or monument." And all of paper. "Watch it closely."

The mechanically nimble typewriter has made it possible to track these metamorphoses in the twentieth century. Our twenty-first century practice, in which a trace of hesitation disappears in a blink of the electronic keyboard, will block this traffic for future scholars. But in Bishop's drafts, her mental progress is legible. The recursive, circling, looping movement is there – but also, curiously enough, it is conserved in the observations she made of her Aunt Maude Shepherdson's speech, which she transcribed into a Key West notebook. I have copied one of several passages that fascinated Bishop, containing Aunt Maude's cycle of advance, retreat, retrieve, advance: "Well now wait. I'm just telling you. Oh! She's the *worst* woman. The wretch; she's a wretch. She's [etc.] downright *mean* that woman. Oh – oh. What I could [?] her. She's a B. It's an awful thing to say; but it's the truth. She's the meanest wretch of a woman. That's what she is. She's a regular B. I never said that before but I thought it. Yes. *Oh* she is mean" (VC 75.113).

Bishop wrote about Maude as a figure of devotion in "Salem Willows," whose good effect on her upbringing and education she remarked on elsewhere with great fondness. Among the drafts fortunately scooped up by both the editors of *Poems, Prose, and Letters* (234) and *Edgar Allan Poe* (98) is a small, tender elegy for Maude, "For M.B.S., buried in Nova Scotia." Maude lies "in a little, slightly tip-tilted graveyard / where all of your childhood's Christmas trees are foregathered / with the present they meant to give, / and your childhood's river quietly curls at your side / and breathes deep with each tide." Bishop conflates Maude's and her own Nova Scotian childhood with a teasing and deeply resonant affection.

Both the thrust of Elizabeth Bishop's understated, conversational verse – which in its meter follows both literary and familial tradition as it carries forward "the family voice" heard in the dentist's waiting room – and Bishop's open attention to autobiographical narrative in the prose of the 1960s define what is most novel in the picture we now have of Bishop in poetry. Many of the poems included in *Edgar Allan Poe & The Juke-Box* and *Poems, Prose, and Letters*, along with a few from *Poems* 2011 – which feature sex, gender, sexual shame, and alcoholism – suggest that Bishop's hold on the subjects touching her personal history was apparently more biographical throughout her writing life than we had imagined. In *Geography III*, Bishop's amplifying engagement with autobiographical narrative was striking: and yet, even if the limits had loosened, she was still mindful of what could or could not be written involving lovers and relationships. Reluctantly, with many caveats against perpetuating what she called "The School of Anguish," Bishop had begun taking her narrative into that troubling personal territory in which she saw her friend and fellow poet, Robert Lowell, perform so compellingly. Description deepened into narrative space, objects turned more to people planted in active memory, and new narrators waded into greater turbulence of feeling on riskier terrain.

Their selections an edge more controversial than those of *Poems*, the editors of *Edgar Allan Poe & The Juke-Box* and *Poems, Prose, and Letters* include a number of brief love lyrics from the New York and Key West periods. These pieces lack the natural descriptive detail of the poems published during that time like "The Bight" (*P* 59) or "The Fish" (*P* 43) or fail to exert the magical authority of a poem like "At the Fishhouses" (*P* 62). Nevertheless, the short, stabbing arc of these newly published poems show how Bishop kept trying short lyric as her answer to the stretchy flatness of narrative poetry. "We hadn't meant to spend so much time ..." (*EAP* 41) is saturated with the melancholy evidence of Bishop's chaotic emotional life bouncing from one lover to the other in the 1930s and 1940s, and has the telegraphic immediacy, the bone-on-bone jar of painful reality, that we associate with more "confessional" poets. After the speaker watches her partner play desultorily all afternoon with three green leaves, the reader is startled when in line five the poet says, "I can't stand your arrangements anymore." What has been the hitherto unvoiced dialogue of this pair? But the page is swept clean of these images, and the poem moves to another venue, "a little booth," placed "On the outskirts of a sad suburban fair." "Now," we are asked, "look behind the dirty curtain where / Harlequin lies drunk in his checquered clothes." "Harlequin," not yet a less studied, less formally costumed protagonist, occupies this bed with its scene of thwarted love, in the alcoholic stupor hinted at in other poems – a condition with which a struggling Bishop was altogether too familiar.

These veiled, ragged scenes are similar to the suggestive squalor of "Varick Street" (*P* 73) and "The Soldier and the Slot-Machine" (*P* 287), two poems that were politely but firmly rejected by Katharine White at *The New Yorker*, who apparently preferred something less disheveled from a lady poet. "A lovely finish I have seen …" (*EAP* 11) is an even earlier draft from 1929: in sharply occluded terms, the second of the poem's two stanzas ends: "When in the dawn you turned to speak / & waited for my teeth to touch / the sugared coolness on that cheek, / – the other cheek – I found in such / deliberation of caress / the utmost of your worldliness." The final lines present a lover whose demure self-possession is utterly infuriating. What kept the poem buried in a notebook? Was it the obstinate failure of the first stanza to fall into the elegant *ababcc* rhyme scheme of the second?

"Gypsophilia" (*EAP* 128) is another interesting case of a draft in which the poet seems to wait for the right rhymes. (Bishop acquired the misspelling, "Gypsophilia" from a botanical mistake of her friend Alexander Calder's, who had called a mobile, with which Bishop was familiar, by this title – it should be "Gypsophila.") In the drafts recently published, each stanza falls into the onionskin rhyme Bishop favored elsewhere, in which a stanza is meant to be something like *abccba*. The first two stanzas do this well – and then the third wobbles. The order of the rhyme words in the first stanza – *noises, sunset, barks, hatchet, sparks* and *houses* – is nearly there. In the second – *nursery, bar, farriers, flowers, are, sea* – meet the challenge triumphantly. But by the third – *thinner, blue, in, dew, dinner, thin* – it is straining – not in itself unforgivable or incurable – but by the fourth, the rhyme scheme is off the rails. What remains is beguiling, but too sketchy in both form and substance. The poem's fate might have duplicated other occasions, like the end of "One Art," where what the poet wanted more readily came to mind.

Over a period of many years, Bishop was fortunate in keeping a first-read contract at *The New Yorker*, one of the most coveted and relatively lucrative arrangements then possible in publishing poetry. *The New Yorker* brought Bishop a certain financial security, as well as the broad exposure and the prestige of its readership, but how much this may have cost her is not quite easy to determine. In 1953, she protested the journal's editorial policies to Pearl Kazin, but ended an outburst in resignation: "The idea underneath it all seems to be that the N Yorker reader must never have to pause to think for a single second – be informed and re-informed comfortingly all the time ... but then if one does attempt to publish there I guess one has no earthly right to complain" (*PPL* 783). Whatever *The New Yorker* rejected was quickly published elsewhere in journals of smaller circulation, also paying less, like *Partisan Review*; yet as Joelle Biele demonstrates, White's "emphasis on gentle irony and observation," or "what James Thurber called 'playing it down,'" plus William Shawn's dislike of "functional references" (meaning bodily function), influenced what Bishop felt she could place there and finally anywhere else. Regardless of how these pressures may have been successfully or unsuccessfully exerted, they did shape the public perception of Bishop's poetry as finished, cool, and elegant – always a poetry with distinctive phrasing, inventive figuration, and firm structure. But at least on one occasion Bishop lamented in private on the emotional distance of her poetry: "I think myself," she said to May Swenson in 1955, "that my best poems seem rather distant ... I don't think I'm very successful when I get personal, – rather, sound personal – one always is, of course, one way or another" (*PPL* 810).

In 1953, Katharine White also rejected "The Shampoo" (*P* 82), Bishop's discreet celebration of an intimate occasion, a poem that ends in the tender washing of Lota de Macedo Soares's hair. After this rejection, Joelle Biele notes that Bishop sent no more love poems to *The New Yorker* until Howard Moss, the poetry editor after Katharine White, accepted "One Art" for publication in 1976. Two earlier notebook poems, "Dear, my compass" (*EAP* 140) and "Close, close all night" (*EAP* 141), were written in the 1960s for other lovers, and were never submitted anywhere. A poem of the 1970s, "Breakfast Song," was only rescued from oblivion by Lloyd Schwartz through surreptitious copying when Bishop's attention was elsewhere occupied. All three of these poems either take place in bed or wind up there, either in appreciation of the nightly nestle with a beloved body or, as in "Breakfast Song" (*EAP* 158) – the last of these pieces, in apprehension of the shadow of the last sleep: "Today I love you so / how can I bear to go / (as soon I must, I know) / to bed with ugly death / ... without the easy breath / and nightlong, limblong warmth / I've grown accustomed to?" The earlier two poems are pleasing, but the third has the blunt force of other late poems like "Sonnet" (*P* 214) and "Pink Dog" (*P* 212).

Two more love poems from the 1940s, again absent from *Poems*, are bedroom scenes: "In a cheap hotel" (*EAP* 83) and "I had a bad dream" (*EAP* 79) both display anxiety and shame; in the latter, the burdensome fear of exposure and sexual shame. "I had a bad dream" describes a protagonist's desperate need to hold a lover in her arms, even though "'a load of guests' might come in … & see us lying / with my arms around you / & my cheek on yours." It is a "loneliness like falling on / the sidewalk in a crowd / that fills [one with shame], some / slow elaborate shame." "In the golden early morning" (*EAP* 80), another 1940s poem not in *Poems*, fills with the pain and confusion of separation.

All of these poems are haunting – in part, because of their provocative fragmentation. If we revert to the very young Bishop who was beginning to write in 1934, here is how, as cited by Brett Millier (65), she came to define the poet's "proper materials": "immediate, intense physical reactions, a sense of metaphor and decoration in everything – to express something not of them – something I suppose, spiritual." She identifies a shortcoming in Romantic poetry as the betrayal of spiritual content by an automatic and routine application. For a young Bishop, this "easy" use of the material to produce the spiritual "could also explain the dangers of love poetry."

In 1951, noting this danger in a short review of Emily Dickinson's letters, Bishop explained her qualified admiration by saying: "To her, little besides love, human and divine, was worth writing about, and often the two seemed to fuse." Castigating the narrow range of Dickinson's interests, she says: "there is a constant insistence on the strength of her affections, an almost childish daring and repetitiveness … that must have been very hard to take" (*PPL* 689). The taking, Bishop surmises, was owing to the prevailing "bad taste and extreme sentimentality of the times." More than a dozen years later, in her January 1964 letter to Anne Stevenson (*PPL* 855–865), Bishop completes her indictment of Dickinson: "I never really liked Emily Dickinson much, except a few nature poems … I still hate the oh-the-pain-of-it-all poems" (*PPL* 858). But almost grudgingly in her 1951 review, she concedes that Dickinson's letters nonetheless evince "structure and strength. It is the sketchiness of the water-spider, tenaciously holding to its upstream position by means of the faintest ripples, while making one aware of the current of death and the darkness below" (*PPL* 689–690). A contrarian spirit has mastered Bishop; yet in a more generous and reflective turn, she then leaps to that strong figure of the water-spider. Writing literary criticism rarely interested Bishop, and except for the astonishing 1933–1934 papers written at Vassar, with their astute and original formal analysis and penetrating insight into writers as varied as Gerard Manley Hopkins and Gertrude Stein, little of the criticism Bishop published says nearly as much as her letters do about her mature practice and aesthetic principles.

Love poetry was a minefield for Bishop. Throughout her correspondence she deplores an indiscriminate spill of feeling, whether commenting on Mary McCarthy's "sex-language" or on Anne Sexton's public crises of sanity, the "confessional" impulse is held away from her like a bad-smelling object. Whether or not she was primarily constrained in the submission of love poems by editorial predilection or by her own self-doubts about how or even whether to approach the subject, her options for writing and publishing with depth and candor were few: only the rather occluded passion of poems like "Insomnia," "Argument," and "Four Poems," ever made it into the periodicals of the time.

It was not merely that the subject of women loving women openly, passionately, and sexually was forbidden in mainstream culture, but that this *dictu* undoubtedly fused with Elizabeth Bishop's pride in stoicism and detachment of self in pursuit of truth. The dangers of courting self-pity were too great. Quoted on "Confessional Poetry" in June of 1967, she said: "Now the idea is that we live in a horrible and terrifying world, and the worst moments of horrible and terrifying lives are an allegory of the world ... The tendency is to overdo the morbidity. You just wish they'd keep some of these things to themselves" (Cory and Lee 68). For a woman whose early life had been marked by a virtual orphaning, whose childhood had been plagued by asthma and eczema, and who from late adolescence had dispersed the panic of homelessness with alcohol, hope was crucial – a beleaguered and displaced body had to be surmounted. Engagement with a foundering physical self was something to be fought off: its sufferings too combustible for the mind to dwell on ethically or at length.

Bishop indirectly explored these psychic dilemmas in the monologues of "Rainy Season: Sub-Tropics" (*P* 163–164), published in 1967 in *The Kenyon Review* – the very year in which her outburst against "Confessional" poetry took place. In these prose pieces, Elizabeth Bishop speaks as the Giant Toad, the Strayed Crab, and the Giant Snail – all the poignance and turbulence of her own placelessness in world and body come to the fore. In an almost non-gender-specific, slippery balance of animal and human, frightful and funny, terrible and pitiful, she satirizes innocent self-importance and disrupts our ideas of the beautiful and the ugly, the natural and the distorted. In no other poems does she make a more pointed response to the treacheries of self-representation.

Typically, it is through the engagement of correspondence that Bishop gives her most comprehensive answers to questions of craft, and about her sense of herself as poet. Both *Poems, Prose, and Letters* and *Prose* published Bishop's October 1963 letter to Anne Stevenson (851, 424). Bishop writes of those she admires: "They are usually stoical, unsentimental, and physically courageous." Brett Millier remarks on Bishop's occasional blackouts after hysterical, confessional rants to friends during periodic binge drinking; rants that were never remembered afterward (Millier 504–506). Perhaps partly from that experience, she cultivated reticence for very life and pride.

In Elizabeth Bishop's admiring remarks on Darwin, she concludes with the image of a young scientist "sinking or sliding giddily off into the unknown." Many critics have noticed the resemblance of the sliding and sinking Darwin to Bishop's own giddy moment of discovering connection – of her "I," her "Elizabeth," to "*them*" – from "In the Waiting Room" (*P* 179): "I said to myself: three days / and you'll be seven years old. / I was saying it to stop / the sensation of falling off / the round, turning world / into cold, blue-black space." About Darwin, Bishop continues, her single sentence abrupt and stunning in its casual lift into supreme eloquence: "What one seems to want in art, in experiencing it, is the same thing necessary for its creation, a self-forgetful, perfectly useless concentration." The morality of this "self-forgetful, perfectly useless concentration" stands behind Bishop's insistence on transcending what is merely the obsessive, or "morbid" release of the "confessional."

When it came to dealing with alcoholism, rather than love for women, Bishop found the direct approach much harder to sustain. She tried out the topic of drunkenness in a variety of poems, sometimes in glancing allusion and sometimes head on – with mixed success. "The Prodigal" (*P* 69) was a poem eventually accepted at *The New Yorker*; its inception she described to May Swenson "suggested by my stretch with psychoanalysis – that, and the actual incident of being offered a drink of rum in a pig-pen in Nova Scotia at 9 o'clock one morning" (*PPL* 806). The experience had trailed into one draft included in a Key West notebook, "The Ark of the Covenant" – a piece of innocence that took the barn atmospherics, added childhood, and eliminated the rum. But the moment, finally taking shape in "The Prodigal," blazed into a double sonnet in which the autobiographical Elizabeth Bishop disappears completely behind the biblical figure of the prodigal son. Similarly, the Key West poem, "The Soldier and the Slot-Machine" (*P* 287), which Katharine White rejected for *The New Yorker*, uses a male protagonist as its inebriate – a gender switch with which Bishop was always comfortable. This is a very funny poem and its vivid battle between man and machine, both somewhat diminished in their human capacities, draws credibly and with real affection from the servicemen Bishop might have encountered in a wartime Key West.

In *The Georgia Review*, Thomas Travisano gives the full historical background behind another poem, posthumously published as "A Drunkard" (*P* 317) and written in the 1970s, or roughly at the time of "Vague Poem (*Vaguely love poem*)" (*P* 323). "A Drunkard" is interesting not just because of its effort to deal with the uncomfortably personal, but because of its narrative emphasis, an emphasis sharply different from the generally tighter, more formal lyrics with which Bishop began her writing life. There is no hint of rhyme. If we compare the preparation for this poem to other unpublished pieces, it is not merely a missing substrate of rhyme that weakens "A Drunkard," but the comparative lack of the distinctive description or the poised, psychological acuity so deftly and precisely marking the memories of the child speaker of "In the Waiting Room." The full tracking of sensation that marked the six-year-old in that poem, the patient reworking that added stars "astringent as white currants," to "Apartment in Leme," (*P* 307) and that put the "bezels" beneath the drab and damp stones of "The End of March" (*P* 199) – another one of Bishop's late revisions; none of these traits govern "A Drunkard."

Critical narrative details – the darkness, the heat, the flying cinders, the red sky – accompanied by the emotional panic and hurry of a great disaster seen through the gapped perspective of a child – strongly establish the setting. But only the repeated black, and the final emergence of the trope – feathers – signal Bishop's customary intensity. Yet "Blackened boards, shiny black like black feathers – / pieces of furniture, parts of boats, and clothes – " lead to no further vital invention. "Clothes" sparks something: "I picked up a woman's long black cotton / stocking. Curiosity. My mother said sharply / *Put that down!*" And then the poem yields to a kind of smirking comedy. "But since that night, that day, that reprimand / I have suffered from abnormal thirst – " the poet avers. "I swear it's true – " the poem continues, then dissolves into a rough denial, in which neither the poet nor the half-hearted poem develops its subject with full conviction: " – and by the age / of twenty or twenty-one I had begun / to drink, & drink – I can't get enough / and, as you must have noticed, / I'm half-drunk now ... // And all I'm telling you may be a lie..." (*P* 319). This is an awkward narrator. So often, Bishop's swerves – her abrupt changes in register – are pure gifts. This is true of the Baptist seal in "At the Fishhouses" (*P* 62); in "One Art" (*P* 198), the final injunction to the speaking self, "*Write* it!" is a brilliant gesture, crystallizing the poem. That is not the case for the narrative feint in "A Drunkard."

The terse urgency and fear of the ubiquitous red suffuses air, sky, and even out on the lawn it colors "my mother's white dress ... rose-red"; the reflected red also spreads to "my white enamelled crib ... and my hands holding to its rods – / its brass knobs holding specks of fire – " all of these opening details render the poem's setting as terrifying. As Thomas Travisano fills in the background (*The Georgia Review* 612–616), he notes that the Great Salem Fire of June 1914 was called by Frances Diana Robotti, "the greatest disaster in Salem's history." Travisano summarizes: "Fire devastated 252 acres, destroyed 1,800 buildings, and rendered 15,000 people homeless." But then Bishop begins to neutralize what she has summoned up: "I felt amazement not fear / but amazement may be / my infancy's chief emotion" (*P* 317). This little drop into a kind of dry and knowing adult sotto voce makes no attempt to wring pathos out of the circumstances (a pathos Bishop would have detested as a sentimental abomination), but the unfortunate alternative she chose inopportunely echoes the drunken Edwin Boomer in her 1937 story, "The Sea and Its Shore" (*Pr* 11). "Boomer" was the vernacular adaptation of Bishop's maternal family name, "Bulmer"; "A Drunkard," however, streams another Boomer/Bulmer voice onto another remembering – this one outside of fable and onto an intractably mournful piece of history. The poem's forced explanation of "abnormal thirst" superimposes farce uneasily on tragedy, and is unpersuasive even to itself.

Perhaps the puzzle of this narrative voice belongs to Bishop's lingering resistance to reductive psychoanalyses. Herself a brief analysand, she may have been mocking those simplified chains of causation that deal badly with a complex and multi-layered psychic history. Or, she may have been trying to imitate the ruses by which clients evade explanation and responsibility. "I loathe explanation," she once wrote to Robert Lowell: "To hell with explainers" (*WIA* 465). Whatever a "correct" psychological or genre reading of "A Drunkard" might have been, Bishop never quite got it in focus.

Tapping into burlesque was far more effective in the poem, "The Soldier and the Slot-Machine." In the voice of the soldier, Bishop's natural distrust of explanation in favor of dramatic embodiment resulted in a comic display of drunken opposition to mechanical law. The soldier declares, "I will not play the slot-machine, / Don't force the nickel in my hand." He growls, "I will not ask for change again. / The barkeeper can see me dead / Before I'll try to meet those eyes / That move like money in his head." And more darkly: "The slot-machine is who is drunk / And you're a dirty nickel, too ... // Its notions all are preconceived ... / The workings of its metal heart, // The grinding of its metal brain, / The bite of its decisive teeth. / Oh yes, they decorate the top / But not the awful underneath" (*P* 287–289). That "awful underneath" exactly balances and precisely signals the large and light elements of Bishop's uncomfortable topic. The poem is very surefooted. Comic farce or biblical myth, as in "The Prodigal," proved to be safer vehicles for a topic containing the shaming losses of control, the humiliations and distortions of character that alcohol could bring about. If we contrast the brave little mechanical horse of the better-known poem, "Cirque d'Hiver" (*P* 32), a poem accepted by *The New Yorker*, with the mean-minded slot-machine, perhaps we can see why one was stomached by the editor whereas the other's more louche reality was not.

"It is marvellous to wake up together ..." (*P* 283) exhibits no formal deficit. It is not just a love poem, but an openly erotic one. Its central image – the electrical storm as a great cage of wires wakening lovers in bed to kissing – shares a great deal with "Rain Towards Morning," a poem first published in 1951 in *The Partisan Review.* "Rain Towards Morning," probably written after "It is marvellous ...," was then added as part of a sequence of "Four Poems" included in A *Cold Spring* (*P* 74–77). In the printed poem, it is "The great light cage" that breaks up in the air and frees about a million birds "whose wild ascending shadows will not be back," so that "all the wires come falling down." But in "It is marvellous ...," the rain suddenly clears, "As if electricity had passed through it / From a black mesh of wires in the sky. / All over the roof the rain hisses, / And below, the light falling of kisses." One kiss is reserved for the published, many kisses for the unpublished poem. While the closing of "Rain Towards Morning" is brightened by a mysterious face bestowing "an unexpected kiss," those birds in the more somber published poem are "frightening."

In the leisurely frame of "It is marvellous ...," probably written in the 1940s to invoke Bishop's relationship with Marjorie Stevens, there is more safety than threat. The roof of the house is specifically protected from lightning by "four blue china balls," and the speaker says: "we imagine dreamily / How the whole house caught in a bird-cage of lightning / Would be quite delightful rather than frightening." Playing with the conclusions of the sister poem, the more candid poem points out that at night "lying flat on one's back / All things might change equally easily." Within the benevolent enclosure of the wires, "It is marvellous ..." continues and concludes: "Without surprise / The world might change to something quite different, / As the air changes or the lightning comes without our blinking, / Change as our kisses are changing without our thinking" (*P* 283). Its gerunds insisting on the marvelous present, the poem moves into its serene erotic climax. "It is marvellous ..." is not a draft, nor adrift; it is lovely, strong, and complete.

One might ask, what did the word "homosexuality" really connote to Bishop? What wayward detraction, what dangerously partial truth might this word represent to her? Alice Quinn notes that Bishop had attended lectures by Gertrude Stein at Vassar in 1934 and in Paris in 1935 (*EAP* 287). Quinn teases a crossed-out entry from a Key West notebook, peers at the handwriting underneath, still fully visible, and quotes from it: "G. Stein's reason for 'concealment' of the 'automatic' nature of her writings = or, is another form of, her 'concealment' of the 'homosexual' nature of her life – False Scents we all give off" (VC 75.4a, pp. 2–3). False Scents black with x's and prickly with off-putting and ostentatious orthography, designed to ward off not only captivity within a censorious conventionality, but also a stereotypic identity? Was this dilemma wholly resolved by Bishop's late and guarded adoption of the liberating shades within the word "gay"?

An organic vitality pulses through Bishop's "Vague Poem (*Vaguely love poem*)" – one of the least-vague love poems ever written. The central metaphor brings together rock roses and the vagina – substances initially quite far apart: the one emblematic of a hard crystalline structure, the other a living softness, yet both joined by Bishop in that enigmatic, finally incantatory rose. Out of the rock rose, rising from the rock, the narrator moves, in a repetitive rock-a-bye from looking at the rock rose to looking at her naked lover: "Rose, trying, working to show itself, / forming, folding over . . . / Rose-rock, unformed, flesh beginning, crystal by crystal, / clear pink breasts and darker, crystalline nipples, / rose-rock, rose-quartz, roses, roses, roses, / exacting roses from the body, / and the even darker, accurate, rose of sex – " (*P* 325). The rock-rose is an old prop. Bishop used the botanical rather than the mineral rose to quite different emotive effect in "Faustina, or Rock Roses," where the rock roses of the visitor's gift decay, helplessly proliferate, and are hopelessly ambiguous – malign or benevolent – in what they signify. Although Elizabeth Bishop treated rhyme and meter with all of the daring of the trapeze artist, nearly always landing brilliantly within the rhyme no matter what may have been the original launch – she was, as she said often, in favor of the craftsman who knowingly used, even in modification, traditional tools. But in the rhyme-free "Vague Poem," the rock rose rises to new heights, not just an emblem of the source of the female beloved's innate generativity, but glinting with the creative process of poetry itself, as worked by powerful craft, freshly defined as both human and natural – "new" and "quick."

BIBLIOGRAPHY AND GUIDE TO FURTHER READING

For primary sources, please see the List of Abbreviations at the front of the book. The Bibliography and Guide to Further Reading in this section is not exhaustive – such a booklist would require its own volume – but it does contain the main critical studies and collections of essays on Bishop's writing, together with all the primary and secondary sources cited in this book. Readers should also consult Candace MacMahon's *Elizabeth Bishop: A Bibliography, 1927–1979* (Charlottesville: University Press of Virginia, 1980). The main Elizabeth Bishop archives are held at Vassar College.

Abrams, M. H. "Structure and Style in the Greater Romantic Lyric." *Romanticism and Consciousness: Essays in Criticism*. Edited by Harold Bloom. New York: Norton, 1970. 201–229.

Altieri, Charles. *Painterly Abstraction in Modernist American Poetry*. Cambridge: Cambridge University Press, 1989.

"Why Modernist Claims for Autonomy Matter." *Journal of Modern Literature* 32.3 (2009): 1–21.

Altman, Janet Gurkin. *Epistolarity: Approaches to a Form*. Columbus: Ohio State University Press, 1982.

Arendt, Hannah. *The Human Condition*. Chicago: University of Chicago Press, 1958.

Ashbery, John. "*The Complete Poems*" (1969). *Elizabeth Bishop and Her Art*. Edited by Lloyd Schwartz and Sybil P. Estess. Ann Arbor: University of Michigan Press, 1983. 201–205.

Axelrod, Steven Gould. "Elizabeth Bishop and Containment Policy." *American Literature* 75.4 (December 2003): 843–867.

Bannet, Eve Tavor. *Empire of Letters: Letter Manuals and Transatlantic Correspondence, 1688–1820*. Cambridge: Cambridge University Press, 2005.

Barry, Sandra. *Elizabeth Bishop: An Archival Guide to Her Life in Nova Scotia*. Hantsport, Nova Scotia: Lancelot Press, 1996.

Elizabeth Bishop: Nova Scotia's "Home-Made" Poet. Halifax: Nimbus, 2011.

Bate, Jonathan. *The Song of the Earth*. Cambridge: Harvard University Press, 2000.

Beards, Richard D. "Introducing Elizabeth Bishop." *Times Literary Supplement* 25 March 2011: 15.

Benton, William. "Introduction." *Exchanging Hats: Elizabeth Bishop Paintings*. New York: Farrar, Straus, and Giroux, 1996. vii–xx.

Berger, Charles. "Bishop's Buried Elegies." *Elizabeth Bishop in the Twenty-First Century: Reading the New Editions*. Edited by Angus Cleghorn, Bethany Hicok,

and Thomas Travisano. Charlottesville: University of Virginia Press, 2012. 41–53.
Bergmann-Loizeaux, Elizabeth. *Twentieth-Century Poetry and the Visual Arts*. Cambridge: Cambridge University Press, 2008.
Bernard, April. "A Genius Ill-Served." *The New York Review of Books* 24 March 2011: 16–18.
Bernlef, J. "A Conversation with Elizabeth Bishop." *Conversations with Elizabeth Bishop*. Edited by George Monteiro. Jackson: University Press of Mississippi, 1996. 62–68.
Biele, Joelle. "Introduction." *Elizabeth Bishop and The New Yorker: The Complete Correspondence*. New York: Farrar, Straus, and Giroux, 2011. vii–lx.
"'Like Working Without Really Doing It': Elizabeth Bishop's Brazil Letters and Poems." *Antioch Review* 67.1 (2009): 90–98.
"Three-Fourths Painter." *Elizabeth Bishop: Objects & Apparitions*. [New York]: Tibor de Nagy Gallery in association with James S. Jaffe Rare Books, 2011. 33–42.
Bishop, Elizabeth. *The Complete Poems*. New York: Farrar, Straus, and Giroux, 1969.
The Complete Poems: 1927–1979. New York: Farrar, Straus, and Giroux, 1983.
The Diary of "Helena Morley." Translated and Introduced by Elizabeth Bishop. New York: Farrar, Straus, and Cudahy, 1957.
Letter to May Swenson, 5 June 1959. May Swenson Papers, Department of Special Collections, Washington University Library in St. Louis (I.103.4003).
Letters to Pearl Bell (1954, 1959), Dorothee Bowie (1968), and Pauline Hanson (1951). Elizabeth Bishop Papers, Special Collections, Vassar College Libraries (I.24.4; I.24.9; I.27.3; I.32.1).
"On *Life Studies*" (1959). *Elizabeth Bishop and Her Art*. Edited by Lloyd Schwartz and Sybil P. Estess. Ann Arbor: University of Michigan Press, 1983. 285.
"On 'The Man-Moth.'" *Poet's Choice*. Edited by Paul Engle and Joseph Langland. New York: Dial, 1962. 102–104.
Bishop, Elizabeth and the Editors of *Life*. *Brazil*. New York: Time-Life Books, 1962.
Bishop, Elizabeth and Emanuel Brasil, eds. *An Anthology of Twentieth-Century Brazilian Poetry*. Hanover: Wesleyan University Press, 1972.
Blasing, Mutlu Konuk. "From Gender to Genre and Back: Elizabeth Bishop and 'The Moose.'" *American Literary History* 6.2 (Summer 1994): 265–286.
"'*Mont D'Espoir or Mount Despair*': The Re-Verses of Elizabeth Bishop." *Contemporary Literature* XXV.3 (1984): 341–353.
Politics and Form in Postmodern Poetry: O'Hara, Bishop, Ashbery, and Merrill. Cambridge: Cambridge University Press, 1995.
Bloom, Harold. "Foreword." *Elizabeth Bishop and Her Art*. Edited by Lloyd Schwartz and Sybil P. Estess. Ann Arbor: University of Michigan Press, 1983. ix–xi.
Boland, Eavan. "That the Science of Cartography is Limited." *In a Time of Violence*. Manchester: Carcanet, 1994. 5.
Boschmann, Robert. *In the Way of Nature: Ecology and Westward Expansion in the Poetry of Anne Bradstreet, Elizabeth Bishop, and Amy Clampitt*. Jefferson, NC: McFarland and Company, 2009.

Bossis, Mireille. "Methodological Journeys Through Correspondences." Translated by Karen McPherson. *Yale French Studies* 71 (1986): 63–75.

Breton, André. *Manifestoes of Surrealism*. Translated by Richard Seaver and Helen Land. Ann Arbor: University of Michigan Press, 1969.

Britto, Paulo Henriques. "Elizabeth Bishop as a Cultural Intermediary." *Brazil 2000–2001: A Revisionary History of Brazilian Literature and Culture*. Edited by João Cezar de Castro Rocha. *Portuguese Literary & Cultural Studies* 4/5 (Spring/Fall 2000): 489–497.

Brown, Ashley. "An Interview with Elizabeth Bishop" (1966). *Elizabeth Bishop and Her Art*. Edited by Lloyd Schwartz and Sybil P. Estess. Ann Arbor: University of Michigan Press, 1983. 289–302.

Bryson, J. Scott, ed. *Ecopoetry: A Critical Introduction*. Salt Lake City: University of Utah Press, 2002.

Buell, Lawrence. *The Environmental Imagination: Thoreau, Nature Writing, and the Formation of American Culture*. Cambridge: Harvard University Press, 1995.

Castro, Fernando de. "Paternalism and Antiamericanism." *Correio da Manhã* (28 March 1965).

Caws, Mary Ann, Rudold Kuenzli, and Gwen Raaberg, eds. *Surrealism and Women*. Cambridge, MA: MIT Press, 1991.

Chadwick, Whitney. *Women Artists and the Surrealist Movement*. Boston: Little, Brown, 1985.

Chiasson, Dan. "Works on Paper: The Letters of Elizabeth Bishop and Robert Lowell." *The New Yorker* 8 November 2008: 106–110.

"Tea for One: Elizabeth Bishop's Art." *Elizabeth Bishop: Objects & Apparitions*. [New York]: Tibor de Nagy Gallery in association with James S. Jaffe Rare Books, 2011. 17–25.

Cleghorn, Angus. "Bishop's 'Wiring Fused': 'Bone Key' and 'Pleasure Seas.'" *Elizabeth Bishop in the Twenty-First Century: Reading the New Editions*. Edited by Angus Cleghorn, Bethany Hicok, Thomas Travisano. Charlottesville: University of Virginia Press, 2012. 69–87.

"The Politics of Editing Bishop's 1962 *Brazil* Volume for Life World Library." Berfrois. 20 September 2011. http://www.berfrois.com/2011/09/angus-cleghorn-elizabeth-bishops-brazil/. Web.

Cleghorn, Angus, Bethany Hicok and Thomas Travisano. "Introduction." *Elizabeth Bishop in the Twenty-First Century: Reading the New Editions*. Edited by Angus Cleghorn, Bethany Hicok, and Thomas Travisano. Charlottesville: University of Virginia Press, 2012. 1–7.

Clifford, James. *Routes: Travel and Translation in the Late Twentieth Century*. Cambridge: Harvard University Press, 1997.

Colwell, Anne. *Inscrutable Houses: Metaphors of the Body in the Poems of Elizabeth Bishop*. Tuscaloosa: University of Alabama Press, 1997.

Cory, Chris, and Alwyn Lee. "Poets: The Second Chance." *Time* 89.2 (2 June 1967): 67–74.

Costello, Bonnie. "Attractive Mortality." *Elizabeth Bishop: The Geography of Gender*. Ed. Marilyn May Lombardi. Charlottesville: University of Virginia Press, 1993. 126–152.

"Elizabeth Bishop's Impersonal Personal." *American Literary History* 15.2 (2003): 334–366.

Elizabeth Bishop: Questions of Mastery. Cambridge: Harvard University Press, 1991.

Cucinella, Catherine. *Poetics of the Body: Edna St. Vincent Millay, Elizabeth Bishop, Marilyn Chin, and Marilyn Hacker.* New York: Palgrave Macmillan, 2010.

Cunha, Euclides da. *Os Sertões* (*Rebellion in the Backlands*). Trans. Samuel Putnam. Chicago: University of Chicago Press, 1975.

Curran, Stuart. "The I Altered." *Romanticism and Feminism.* Ed. Anne Mellor. Bloomington: Indiana University Press, 1988. 185–207.

ed. *The Poems of Charlotte Smith.* New York: Oxford University Press, 1993.

Curry, Renée R. *White Women Writing White: H.D., Elizabeth Bishop, Sylvia Plath, and Whiteness.* Connecticut and London: Greenwood Press, 2000.

Dallek, Robert. "How Not to End Another President's War (L.B.J. Edition)." *New York Times,* 12 March 2009. http://100days.blogs.nytimes.com/2009/03/12/how-not-to-end-another-presidents-war-lbj-edition/. Web. Accessed 21 September 2012.

Davidson, Michael. *Guys Like Us: Citing Masculinity in Cold War Poetics.* Chicago: Chicago University Press, 2004.

Derrida, Jacques. *The Post Card: From Socrates to Freud and Beyond.* Trans. Alan Bass. Chicago: University of Chicago Press, 1987.

Dickey, Frances. "Bishop, Dewey, Darwin: What Other People Know." *Contemporary Literature* 44.4 (2003): 301–331.

Dickie, Margaret. "Race and Class in Elizabeth Bishop's Poetry." *The Yearbook of English Studies* (24), 1994: 44–58.

Stein, Bishop & Rich: Lyrics of Love, War, & Place. Chapel Hill: The University of North Carolina Press, 1997.

Diehl, Joanne Feit. *Women Poets and the American Sublime.* Bloomington: Indiana University Press, 1990.

Doreski, C. K. *Elizabeth Bishop: The Restraints of Language.* Oxford: Oxford University Press, 1993.

DuPlessis, Rachel Blau. *Blue Studios: Poetry and its Cultural Work.* Tuscaloosa: University of Alabama Press, 2006.

Dworkin, Craig. "Against Reading." University of Georgia. Athens, GA. Fall 2001. Address.

Earle, Rebecca. "Introduction." *Epistolary Selves: Letters and Letter-Writers, 1600–1945.* Ed. Rebecca Earle. Aldershot: Ashgate, 1999. 1–12.

Edelman, Lee. "The Geography of Gender: Elizabeth Bishop's 'In the Waiting Room.'" *Elizabeth Bishop: The Geography of Gender.* Edited by Marilyn May Lombardi. Charlottesville: University Press of Virginia, 1993. 91–110.

Eliot, T. S. *Selected Essays of T. S. Eliot.* New York: Harcourt, Brace & World, Inc., 1960.

Ellis, Jonathan. *Art and Memory in the Work of Elizabeth Bishop.* Aldershot: Ashgate, 2006.

"Aubade and Elegy: Elizabeth Bishop's Love Poems." *English* 60.229 (2011): 161–179.

"'Between Us': Letters and Poems of Stevenson and Bishop." *Voyages Over Voices: Critical Essays on Anne Stevenson.* Edited by Angela Leighton. Liverpool: Liverpool University Press, 2010. 28–54.

"'Mailed Into Space': On Sylvia Plath's Letters." *Representing Sylvia Plath*. Edited by Sally Bayley and Tracy Brain. Cambridge: Cambridge University Press, 2011. 13–31.

Engelhardt, Tom. *The End of Victory Culture: Cold War America and the Disillusioning of a Generation*. Amherst: University of Massachusetts Press, 2nd ed., 2007.

Erkkila, Betsy. "The Emily Dickinson Wars." *The Cambridge Companion to Emily Dickinson*. Edited by Wendy Martin. Cambridge: Cambridge University Press, 2002. 11–27.

Esdale, Logan. "Gertrude Stein, Laura Riding and the Space of Letters." *Journal of Modern Literature* 29.4 (2006): 99–123. Web. 26 June 2010.

Fountain, Gary and Peter Brazeau, eds. *Elizabeth Bishop: An Oral Biography*. Amherst: University Press of Massachusetts, 1994.

Flynn, Richard. "*Words in Air*: Bishop, Lowell, and the Aesthetics of Autobiographical Poetry." *Elizabeth Bishop in the Twenty-First Century*. Edited by Angus Cleghorn, Bethany Hicok, and Thomas Travisano. Charlottesville: University of Virginia Press, 2012. 204–222.

Gilcrest, David. *Greening the Lyre: Environmental Poetics and Ethics*. Reno: University of Nevada Press, 2002.

Gill, Jo. "Bestiary USA: The Modern American Bestiary Poem." *A Companion to Poetic Genre*. Edited by Erik Martiny. Oxford: Blackwell, 2012. 555–567.

Giroux, Robert. "Introduction." *One Art: Letters*. By Elizabeth Bishop. New York: Farrar, Straus, and Giroux, 1994. vii–xxii.

Goldensohn, Lorrie. "The Body's Roses: Race, Sex, and Gender in Elizabeth Bishop's Representations of Self." *Elizabeth Bishop: The Geography of Gender*. Edited by Marilyn May Lombardi. Charlottesville: University of Virginia Press, 1993. 70–90.

"Elizabeth Bishop's Drafts: 'That Sense of Constant Readjustment.'" *Elizabeth Bishop in the Twenty-First Century: Reading the New Editions*. Edited by Angus Cleghorn, Bethany Hicok, and Thomas Travisano. Charlottesville: University of Virginia Press, 2012. 104–116.

Elizabeth Bishop: The Biography of a Poetry. New York: Columbia University Press, 1992.

"The Homeless Eye." *Divisions of the Heart: Elizabeth Bishop and the Art of Memory and Place*. Edited by Sandra Barry, Gwendolyn Davies and Peter Sanger. Wolfville: Gaspereau Press, 2001. 103–111.

"Written Pictures, Painted Poems." *"In Worcester, Massachusetts": Essays on Elizabeth Bishop: From the 1997 Elizabeth Bishop Conference at WPI*. Edited by Laura Jehn Menides and Angela G. Dorenkamp. New York: Peter Lang, 1999. 167–176.

Gray, Jeffrey. *Mastery's End: Travel and Postwar American Poetry*. Athens: University of Georgia Press, 2005.

"Postcards and Sunsets: Bishop's Revisions and the Problem of Excess." *Elizabeth Bishop in the Twenty-First Century: Reading the New Editions*. Edited by Angus Cleghorn, Bethany Hicok, and Thomas Travisano. Charlottesville: University of Virginia Press, 2012. 26–40.

Halpern, Nick, Jane Hedley and Willard Spiegelman, eds. *In the Frame: Women's Ekphrastic Poetry from Marianne Moore to Susan Wheeler*. Newark: University of Delaware Press, 2009.

Hammer, Langdon. "Useless Concentration: Life and Work in Elizabeth Bishop's Letters and Poems." *American Literary History* 9.1 (1997): 162–180.

Haraway, Donna. *Simians, Cyborgs and Women: The Reinvention of Nature*. New York: Routledge, 1991.

Harrison, Victoria. *Elizabeth Bishop's Poetics of Intimacy*. Cambridge: Cambridge University Press, 1993.

Hartman, Geoffrey. "Romanticism and Anti-Self-Consciousness." *The Geoffrey Hartman Reader*. Edited by Geoffrey Hartman and Daniel T. O'Hara. Edinburgh: Edinburgh University Press, 2004.

Heaney, Seamus. *The Redress of Poetry*. London: Faber and Faber, 1995.

Hemans, Felicia Dorothea. *The Poetical Works of Felicia Dorothea Hemans*. Oxford: Oxford University Press, 1914.

Herbert, Bob. "This Is Bush's Vietnam." *New York Times*, 17 September 2004. www.nytimes.com/2004/09/17/opinion/17herbert.html. Web. Accessed 21 September 2012.

Hicok, Bethany. "Bishop's Brazilian Politics." *Elizabeth Bishop in the Twenty-First Century: Reading the New Editions*. Edited by Angus Cleghorn, Bethany Hicok and Thomas Travisano. Charlottesville: University of Virginia Press, 2012. 133–150.

Hofmann, Michael. "The Linebacker and the Dervish." *Poetry* 193.4 (2008): 357–367.

"Mostly Middle." *London Review of Books* 8 September 2011: 14–16.

Huang, Iris Shu-O. "Landscapes, Animals and Human Beings: Elizabeth Bishop's Poetry and Ecocentrism." *Intergrams* 10.2–11.1 (2010): n. pag. Web. 20 August 2012.

Jackson, Virginia. *Dickinson's Misery: A Theory of Lyric Reading*. Princeton: Princeton University Press, 2005.

Jarrell, Randall. "The Poet and His Public." *Partisan Review* 13 (1946): 488–500.

"Poets." *Poetry and the Age*. New York: Knopf, 1953. 220–236.

Johnson, Alexandra. "Geography of the Imagination." *Conversations with Elizabeth Bishop*, ed. George Monteiro. Jackson: University Press of Mississippi, 1996. 98–104.

Johnson, Lyndon B. "We Will Stand in Viet-Nam" (July 28, 1965). Presidential address. www.history.navy.mil/library/special/stand_vietnam.htm. Web. Accessed August 24, 2012.

Kalstone, David. *Becoming a Poet: Elizabeth Bishop with Marianne Moore and Robert Lowell*. New York: Farrar Straus, and Giroux, 1989.

Five Temperaments. New York: Oxford University Press, 1977.

Kaplan, Caren. *Questions of Travel: Postmodern Discourses of Displacement*. Durham, NC: Duke University Press, 1996.

Keller, Lynn. *Re-Making It New: Contemporary American Poetry and the Modernist Tradition*. Cambridge: Cambridge University Press, 1987.

"Green Reading: Modern and Contemporary American Poetry and Environmental Criticism." *The Oxford Handbook to Modern and Contemporary American Poetry*. Edited by Cary Nelson. Oxford: Oxford University Press, 2012. 602–623.

Kennedy, Stetson. *Grits & Grunts: Folkloric Key West*. Sarasota: Pineapple Press, 2008.

Kent, Kathryn R. *Making Girls into Women: American Women's Writing and the Rise of Lesbian Identity*. Durham: Duke University Press, 2003.

Lensing, George, "Elizabeth Bishop and Flannery O'Connor: Minding and Mending a Fallen World." *Elizabeth Bishop in the Twenty-First Century: Reading the New Editions*. Edited by Angus Cleghorn, Bethany Hicok and Thomas Travisano. Charlottesville: University of Virginia Press, 2012. 186–203.

Leviston, Frances. "Spectacle and Speculation: Reflecting on *Elizabeth Bishop in the Twenty-First Century: Reading the New Editions*." *Edinburgh Review* 136 (2012): 43–51.

Lispector, Clarice, "The Smallest Woman in the World," "A Hen," "Marmosets," trans. Elizabeth Bishop. *Kenyon Review* 26 (Summer 1964): 500–511.

Lombardi, Marilyn May. *The Body and the Song: Elizabeth Bishop's Poetics*. Carbondale: Southern Illinois University Press, 1995.

"The Closet of Breath: Elizabeth Bishop, Her Body and Her Art." *Elizabeth Bishop: The Geography of Gender*. Ed. Marilyn May Lombardi. Charlottesville: University of Virginia Press, 1993. 46–69.

Longenbach, James. *Modern Poetry after Modernism*. New York and Oxford: Oxford University Press, 1997.

Lowell, Robert. *Collected Poems*. Edited by Frank Bidart and David Gewanter. New York: Farrar, Straus, and Giroux, 2003.

"Elizabeth Bishop's *North & South*." *Collected Prose*. Edited by Robert Giroux. New York: Farrar, Straus, and Giroux, 1987. 76–80.

MacArthur, Marit J. "'In a Room': Elizabeth Bishop in Europe, 1935–1937." *Texas Studies in Literature and Language* 50.4 (2008): 408–442.

McCabe, Susan. *Elizabeth Bishop: Her Poetics of Loss*. University Park: Pennsylvania State University Press, 1994.

"Stevens, Bishop, and Ashbery: A Surrealist Lineage." *The Wallace Stevens Journal* 22.2 (Fall 1998): 149–168.

"Survival of the Queerly Fit: Darwin, Marianne Moore, and Elizabeth Bishop." *Twentieth-Century Literature* 55.4 (Winter 2009): 547–571.

McCarthy, Mary. "Symposium" (1981). *Elizabeth Bishop and Her Art*. Edited by Lloyd Schwartz and Sybil P. Estess. Ann Arbor: University of Michigan Press, 1983. 267.

McClatchy, J. D. "Letters From A Lonely Poet." *The New York Times Book Review* 17 April 1994. Web. 27 June 2010.

McGann, Jerome. *The Romantic Ideology: A Critical Investigation*. Chicago: University of Chicago Press, 1983.

McIntosh, Hugh. "Conventions of Closeness: Realism and the Creative Friendship of Elizabeth Bishop and Robert Lowell." *PMLA* 127.2 (2012): 231–247.

Mellor, Anne. *Romanticism and Gender*. New York: Routledge, 1993.

Menides, Laura Jehn, and Angela G. Dorenkamp. *"In Worcester, Massachusetts": Essays on Elizabeth Bishop: From the 1997 Elizabeth Bishop Conference at WPI*. New York: Peter Lang, 1999.

Merrill, James. "Elizabeth Bishop, 1911–1979" (1979). *Elizabeth Bishop and Her Art*. Edited by Lloyd Schwartz and Sybil P. Estess. Ann Arbor: University of Michigan Press, 1983. 259–262.

Merrin, Jeredith. *An Enabling Humility: Marianne Moore, Elizabeth Bishop, and the Uses of Tradition*. New Jersey: Rutgers University Press, 1990.

"Elizabeth Bishop: Gaiety, Gayness, and Change." *Elizabeth Bishop: The Geography of Gender*. Edited by Marilyn May Lombardi. Charlottesville: University of Virginia Press, 1993. 153–172.

Millier, Brett C. *Elizabeth Bishop: Life and the Memory of It*. Berkeley: University of California Press, 1993.

Mindlin, Henrique E. *Modern Architecture in Brazil*. New York: Reinhold, 1956.

Monteiro, George, ed. *Conversations with Elizabeth Bishop*. Jackson: University of Mississippi Press, 1996.

Elizabeth Bishop in Brazil and After: A Poetic Career Transformed. Jefferson, North Carolina and London: McFarland, 2012.

Moore, Marianne. *Selected Letters*. Edited by Bonnie Costello, Celeste Goodridge and Cristanne Miller. New York: Viking, 1997.

Morton, Timothy. "John Clare's Dark Ecology." *Studies in Romanticism* 47.2 (Summer 2008): 179–193.

Mullen, Richard. "Elizabeth Bishop's Surrealist Inheritance." *American Literature* 54.1 (March 1982): 63–80.

Nickowitz, Peter. *Rhetoric and Sexuality: The Poetry of Hart Crane, Elizabeth Bishop, and James Merrill*. New York: Palgrave Macmillan, 2006.

Niebuhr, Reinhold. *The Irony of American History* (1952). Chicago: University of Chicago Press, 2008.

Oliveira, Carmen L. *Rare and Commonplace Flowers: The Story of Elizabeth Bishop and Lota de Macedo Soares*. Trans. Neil K. Besner. New Brunswick and London: Rutgers University Press, 2002. [Translation of *Floras raras e banalíssimus: A história de Lota de Macedo Soares e Elizabeth Bishop*, 1995.]

Orr, David. "Elizabeth Bishop's Rough Gems." *The New York Times Book Review* 2 April 2006: 1, 10–11.

Ortner, Sherry B. "Is Female to Male as Nature is to Culture?" *Woman, Culture, and Society*. Edited by M. Z. Rosaldo and L. Lamphere. Stanford: Stanford University Press, 1974. 68–87.

Page, Barbara. "Off-Beat Claves, Oblique Realities: The Key West Notebooks of Elizabeth Bishop." *Elizabeth Bishop: The Geography of Gender*. Edited by Marilyn May Lombardi. Charlottesville: University of Virginia Press, 1993. 196–211.

Parker, Robert Dale. *The Unbeliever: The Poetry of Elizabeth Bishop*. Urbana and Chicago: University of Illinois Press, 1988.

Paton, Priscilla. *Abandoned New England: Landscape in the Works of Homer, Frost, Hopper, Wyeth, and Bishop*. Hanover and London: University Press of New England, 2003.

"Landscape and Female Desire: Elizabeth Bishop's 'Closet' Tactics." *Mosaic* 31.3 (September 1998): 133–151.

"'You are not Beppo': Elizabeth Bishop's Animals and Negotiation of Identity." *Mosaic* 39.4 (December 2006): 197–214.

Paulin, Tom. "Dwelling without Roots: Elizabeth Bishop." *Grand Street* 36 (1990): 90–102.

"Newness and Nowness." *Times Literary Supplement* 4752 (1994): 3–5.

"Writing to the Moment: Elizabeth Bishop." *Writing to the Moment*. London: Faber and Faber, 1996. 215–239.

Paz, Octavio. "Elizabeth Bishop, or the Power of Reticence" (1975). *Elizabeth Bishop and Her Art*. Edited by Lloyd Schwartz and Sybil P. Estess. Ann Arbor: University of Michigan Press, 1983. 211–213.

Phillips, Siobhan. *The Poetics of the Everyday: Creative Repetition in Modern American Verse*. New York: Columbia University Press, 2010.

Pickard, Zachariah. "The Attack on Surrealism in Elizabeth Bishop's Darwin Letter." *Studies in the Humanities* 31.2 (December 2004): 121–137.

Elizabeth Bishop's Poetics of Description. Montreal: McGill-Queen's University Press, 2009.

"Natural History and Epiphany: Elizabeth Bishop's Darwin Letter." *Twentieth-Century Literature* 50.3 (Fall 2004): 268–282.

Pound, Ezra. *Make It New*. London: Faber and Faber, 1934.

Pugh, Christina. "'A Lovely Finish I Have Seen': Voice and Variorum in *Edgar Allan Poe & The Juke-Box*." *Elizabeth Bishop in the Twenty-First Century: Reading the New Editions*. Edited by Angus Cleghorn, Bethany Hicok and Thomas Travisano. Charlottesville: University of Virginia Press, 2012. 274–288.

Putnam, Phoebe. "'I could open your belly with my claw': Touch and the Erotics of Panorama in Elizabeth Bishop." Draft to Peggy Samuels, June 2012.

Quinn, Alice. "Introduction." *Edgar Allan Poe & The Juke-Box: Uncollected Poems, Drafts, and Fragments*. By Elizabeth Bishop. New York: Farrar, Straus, and Giroux, 2006. ix-xv.

Rasula, Jed. *This Compost: Ecological Imperatives in American Poetry*. Athens: University of Georgia Press, 2002.

Ribeiro, Léo Gilson. "Elizabeth Bishop: The Poetess, the Cashew, and Micuçu." *Conversations with Elizabeth Bishop*. Edited by George Monteiro. Jackson: University of Mississippi Press, 1996. 14–17.

Rich, Adrienne. "The Eye of the Outsider: The Poetry of Elizabeth Bishop." *Boston Review* 8 (April 1983): 16–17.

Riggs, Sarah. *Word Sightings: Poetry and Visual Media in Stevens, Bishop, and O'Hara*. New York: Routledge, 2002.

Rognoni, Francesco. "Reading Darwin: On Elizabeth Bishop's Marked Copies of *The Voyage of the Beagle* and *The Autobiography of Charles Darwin*." *Jarrell, Bishop, Lowell, & Co*. Edited by Suzanne Ferguson. Knoxville: University of Tennessee Press, 2003. 239–248.

Roman, Camille. *Elizabeth Bishop's World War II–Cold War View*. New York: Palgrave, 2001.

Roselle, Jan. "Corporeal Sovereignty: The Territory of American Feminism." Diss. University of California, Riverside, 2012.

Rosemont, Penelope, ed. *Surrealist Women: An International Anthology*. Austin: University of Texas Press, 1998.

Rosenbaum, Susan. "Elizabeth Bishop and the Miniature Museum." *Journal of Modern Literature* 28.2 (2005): 61–99.

"Exquisite Corpse: Surrealist Influence on the American Poetry Scene, 1920–1960." *The Oxford Handbook to Modern and Contemporary American Poetry*. Edited by Cary Nelson. Oxford: Oxford University Press, 2012. 268–300.

Professing Sincerity: Modern Lyric Poetry, Commercial Culture, and the Crisis in Reading. Charlottesville: University of Virginia Press, 2007.

Rotella, Guy. *Reading and Writing Nature: The Poetry of Robert Frost, Wallace Stevens, Marianne Moore, and Elizabeth Bishop*. Boston: Northeastern Press, 1991.

Samuels, Peggy. *Deep Skin: Elizabeth Bishop and Visual Art*. Ithaca: Cornell University Press, 2010.

Scarry, Elaine. *Dreaming by the Book*. New York: Farrar, Straus, and Giroux, 1999.

Schapiro, Meyer. "Fromentin as Critic." *Partisan Review* 16 (January 1949): 25–51.

Paul Cézanne. New York: Abrams, 1962 [1952].

Schiller, Beatriz. "Poetry Born Out of Suffering." *Conversations with Elizabeth Bishop*. Edited by George Monteiro. Jackson: University of Mississippi Press, 1996. 74–81.

Schor, Naomi. *Reading in Detail: Aesthetics and the Feminine*. New York: Methuen, 1987.

Schulze, Robin G. "Marianne Moore's 'Imperious Ox, Imperial Dish' and the Poetry of the Natural World." *Twentieth-Century Literature* 44.1 (Spring 1998): 1–33.

Schwartz, Lloyd. "Annals of Poetry: Elizabeth Bishop and Brazil." *The New Yorker* (30 September 1991): 85–97.

"Elizabeth Bishop's 'Finished' Unpublished Poems." *Elizabeth Bishop in the Twenty-First Century: Reading the New Editions*. Edited by Angus Cleghorn, Bethany Hicok and Thomas Travisano. Charlottesville: University of Virginia Press, 2012. 54–65.

"Elizabeth Bishop: Two Arts." *Elizabeth Bishop: Objects & Apparitions*. [New York]: Tibor de Nagy Gallery in association with James S. Jaffe Rare Books, 2011. 5–10.

Schwartz, Lloyd and Sybil P. Estess, eds. *Elizabeth Bishop and Her Art*. Ann Arbor: University of Michigan Press, 1983.

Schweik, Susan. *A Gulf So Deeply Cut: American Women Poets and the Second World War*. Madison: University of Wisconsin Press, 1991.

Scully, James. *Line Break: Poetry as Social Practice*. Willimantic, CT: Curbstone Press, 2005.

Simic, Charles. "The Power of Reticence." *The New York Review of Books* 27 April 2006: 17–19.

Soper, Kate. *What is Nature? Culture, Politics and the Non-Human*. Oxford: Blackwell, 1995.

Stanley, Liz. "The Epistolarium: On Theorizing Letters and Correspondences." *Auto/Biography* 12.3 (2004): 201–235.

Starbuck, George. "'The Work!' A Conversation with Elizabeth Bishop" (1977). *Elizabeth Bishop and Her Art*. Edited by Lloyd Schwartz and Sybil P. Estess. Ann Arbor: University of Michigan Press, 1983. 312–330.

Stevens, Wallace. *Collected Poetry & Prose*. New York: Library of America, 1997.

Stevenson, Anne. *Elizabeth Bishop*. New York: Twayne Publishers, 1966.

Five Looks at Elizabeth Bishop. Newcastle: Bloodaxe Books, 2006.

Suárez-Toste, Ernesto. "Dream Logic and Multiple Metamorphoses in Elizabeth Bishop's Early Poetry." *Revista de Estudios Norteamericanos* 9 (2003): 111–121.

"Empathy vs. Surrealism in Elizabeth Bishop's Animal Poems." *Animal Magic: Essays on Animals in the American Imagination*. Joensuu: University of Joensuu Press, 2004. 112–123.

"Une Machine a Coudre Manuelle: Elizabeth Bishop's 'Everyday Surrealism.'" *Mosaic* 33.2 (June 2000): 143–161.

Tomlinson, Charles. "Elizabeth Bishop's New Book." *Shenandoah* 17 (Winter 1966): 88–91.

Travisano, Thomas. *Elizabeth Bishop: Her Artistic Development*. Charlottesville: University of Virginia Press, 1988.

"The Elizabeth Bishop Phenomenon." *Gendered Modernisms: American Women Poets and Their Readers*. Edited by Margaret Dickie and Thomas Travisano. Philadelphia: University of Pennsylvania Press, 1996. 217–244.

"'The Flicker of Impudence': Delicacy and Indelicacy in the Art of Elizabeth Bishop." *Elizabeth Bishop: The Geography of Gender*. Edited by Marilyn May Lombardi. Charlottesville: University of Virginia Press, 1993. 111–125.

"Geography IV, or the Death of the Author Revisited: An Essay in Speculative Bibliography." *Elizabeth Bishop in the Twenty-First Century: Reading the New Editions*. Edited by Angus Cleghorn, Bethany Hicok, and Thomas Travisano. Charlottesville: University of Virginia Press, 2012. 223–238.

Mid-Century Quartet: Bishop, Lowell, Jarrell, Berryman and the Making of a Postmodern Aesthetic. Charlottesville: University of Virginia Press, 1999.

"With an eye of Flemish accuracy: An Afterword." *The Georgia Review* (Winter 1992): 612–616.

Travisano, Thomas with Saskia Hamilton, eds. *Words in Air: The Complete Correspondence Between Elizabeth Bishop and Robert Lowell*. New York: Farrar, Straus, and Giroux, 2008.

Treseler, Heather. "Dreaming in Color: Bishop's Notebook Letter-Poems." *Elizabeth Bishop in the Twenty-First Century: Reading the New Editions*. Edited by Angus Cleghorn, Bethany Hicok, and Thomas Travisano. Charlottesville: University of Virginia Press, 2012. 88–103.

"Lyric Letters: Elizabeth Bishop's Epistolary Poems." Diss. University of Notre Dame, 2010.

Tyler, Carole-Anne. *Female Impersonation*. New York: Routledge, 2003.

Tyler, Meg. "'Named Airs': American Sonnets (Stevens to Bidart)." *A Companion to Poetic Genre*. Edited by Erik Martiny. Oxford: Blackwell, 2012. 220–233.

Veloso, Caetano. *Tropical Truth: A Story of Music and Revolution in Brazil*. Trans. Isabel de Sena. Ed. Barbara Einzig. New York: Knopf, 2002. [Originally published in Brazil as *Verdade tropical* in 1997.]

Vendler, Helen. "The Art of Losing." *New Republic* 3 April 2006: 33–37.

"Domestication, Domesticity, and the Otherworldly" (1977). *Elizabeth Bishop and Her Art*. Edited by Lloyd Schwartz and Sybil P. Estess. Ann Arbor: University of Michigan Press, 1983. 32–48.

"'Long Pig': The Interconnection of the Exotic, the Dead, and the Fantastic in the Poetry of Elizabeth Bishop." *The Art of Elizabeth Bishop*. Eds. Sandra Regina Goulart Almeida, Gláucia Renate Gonçalves, Eliana Lourenço de Lima Reis. Belo Horizonte, Brazil: Universidade Federal de Minas Gerais, 2002. 25–38.

Wagley, Charles. *Amazon Town: A Study of Man in the Tropics*. New York: Macmillan, 1953.

Walker, Cheryl. *God and Elizabeth Bishop: Meditations on Religion and Poetry*. New York: Palgrave, 2005.

"Metaphysical Surrealism in Bishop." *Poetry and the Sense of Panic: Critical Essays on Elizabeth Bishop and John Ashbery*. Edited by Lionel Kelly. Amsterdam: Rodopi, 2000. 145–168.

Warner, Michael. *Publics and Counterpublics*. New York: Zone, 2002.

Wehr, Wesley. "Elizabeth Bishop: Conversations and Class Notes." *Conversations with Elizabeth Bishop*. Edited by George Monteiro. Jackson: University of Mississippi: 1996. 38–46.

White, Gillian. "*Words in Air* and 'Space' in Art: Bishop's Midcentury Critique of the United States." *Elizabeth Bishop in the Twenty-First Century: Reading the New Editions*. Edited by Angus Cleghorn, Bethany Hicok and Thomas Travisano. Charlottesville: University of Virginia Press, 2012. 255–273.

Williams, William Carlos. "Reply to Questionnaire." *View* 1.11–12 (February-March 1942): 10.

Wilson, Woodrow. "First Inaugural Address." Miller Center, University of Virginia. http://millercenter.org/scripps/archive/speeches/detail/3566. Web. Accessed 24 August 2012.

Zona, Kirstin Hotelling. *Marianne Moore, Elizabeth Bishop, and May Swenson: The Feminist Poetics of Self-Restraint*. Ann Arbor: University of Michigan Press, 2002.

INDEX

Cambridge Companions to...

AUTHORS

Edward Albee edited by Stephen J. Bottoms
Margaret Atwood edited by Coral Ann Howells
W. H. Auden edited by Stan Smith
Jane Austen edited by Edward Copeland and Juliet McMaster (second edition)
Beckett edited by John Pilling
Bede edited by Scott DeGregorio
Aphra Behn edited by Derek Hughes and Janet Todd
Walter Benjamin edited by David S. Ferris
William Blake edited by Morris Eaves
Brecht edited by Peter Thomson and Glendyr Sacks (second edition)
The Brontës edited by Heather Glen
Bunyan edited by Anne Dunan-Page
Frances Burney edited by Peter Sabor
Byron edited by Drummond Bone
Albert Camus edited by Edward J. Hughes
Willa Cather edited by Marilee Lindemann
Cervantes edited by Anthony J. Cascardi
Chaucer edited by Piero Boitani and Jill Mann (second edition)
Chekhov edited by Vera Gottlieb and Paul Allain
Kate Chopin edited by Janet Beer
Caryl Churchill edited by Elaine Aston and Elin Diamond
Coleridge edited by Lucy Newlyn
Wilkie Collins edited by Jenny Bourne Taylor
Joseph Conrad edited by J. H. Stape
H. D. edited by Nephie J. Christodoulides and Polina Mackay
Dante edited by Rachel Jacoff (second edition)
Daniel Defoe edited by John Richetti
Don DeLillo edited by John N. Duvall
Charles Dickens edited by John O. Jordan
Emily Dickinson edited by Wendy Martin
John Donne edited by Achsah Guibbory
Dostoevskii edited by W. J. Leatherbarrow
Theodore Dreiser edited by Leonard Cassuto and Claire Virginia Eby
John Dryden edited by Steven N. Zwicker
W. E. B. Du Bois edited by Shamoon Zamir
George Eliot edited by George Levine
T. S. Eliot edited by A. David Moody
Ralph Ellison edited by Ross Posnock
Ralph Waldo Emerson edited by Joel Porte and Saundra Morris
William Faulkner edited by Philip M. Weinstein
Henry Fielding edited by Claude Rawson
F. Scott Fitzgerald edited by Ruth Prigozy
Flaubert edited by Timothy Unwin
E. M. Forster edited by David Bradshaw
Benjamin Franklin edited by Carla Mulford
Brian Friel edited by Anthony Roche
Robert Frost edited by Robert Faggen
Gabriel García Márquez edited by Philip Swanson
Elizabeth Gaskell edited by Jill L. Matus
Goethe edited by Lesley Sharpe
Günter Grass edited by Stuart Taberner
Thomas Hardy edited by Dale Kramer
David Hare edited by Richard Boon
Nathaniel Hawthorne edited by Richard Millington
Seamus Heaney edited by Bernard O'Donoghue
Ernest Hemingway edited by Scott Donaldson
Homer edited by Robert Fowler
Horace edited by Stephen Harrison
Ted Hughes edited by Terry Gifford
Ibsen edited by James McFarlane
Henry James edited by Jonathan Freedman
Samuel Johnson edited by Greg Clingham
Ben Jonson edited by Richard Harp and Stanley Stewart
James Joyce edited by Derek Attridge (second edition)
Kafka edited by Julian Preece
Keats edited by Susan J. Wolfson
Rudyard Kipling edited by Howard J. Booth
Lacan edited by Jean-Michel Rabaté
D. H. Lawrence edited by Anne Fernihough
Primo Levi edited by Robert Gordon

Lucretius edited by Stuart Gillespie and Philip Hardie

Machiavelli edited by John M. Najemy

David Mamet edited by Christopher Bigsby

Thomas Mann edited by Ritchie Robertson

Christopher Marlowe edited by Patrick Cheney

Andrew Marvell edited by Derek Hirst and Steven N. Zwicker

Herman Melville edited by Robert S. Levine

Arthur Miller edited by Christopher Bigsby (second edition)

Milton edited by Dennis Danielson (second edition)

Molière edited by David Bradby and Andrew Calder

Toni Morrison edited by Justine Tally

Nabokov edited by Julian W. Connolly

Eugene O'Neill edited by Michael Manheim

George Orwell edited by John Rodden

Ovid edited by Philip Hardie

Harold Pinter edited by Peter Raby (second edition)

Sylvia Plath edited by Jo Gill

Edgar Allan Poe edited by Kevin J. Hayes

Alexander Pope edited by Pat Rogers

Ezra Pound edited by Ira B. Nadel

Proust edited by Richard Bales

Pushkin edited by Andrew Kahn

Rabelais edited by John O'Brien

Rilke edited by Karen Leeder and Robert Vilain

Philip Roth edited by Timothy Parrish

Salman Rushdie edited by Abdulrazak Gurnah

Shakespeare edited by Margareta de Grazia and Stanley Wells (second edition)

Shakespeare on Film edited by Russell Jackson (second edition)

Shakespeare and Popular Culture edited by Robert Shaughnessy

Shakespeare on Stage edited by Stanley Wells and Sarah Stanton

Shakespearean Comedy edited by Alexander Leggatt

Shakespearean Tragedy edited by Claire McEachern

Shakespeare's History Plays edited by Michael Hattaway

Shakespeare's Last Plays edited by Catherine M. S. Alexander

Shakespeare's Poetry edited by Patrick Cheney

George Bernard Shaw edited by Christopher Innes

Shelley edited by Timothy Morton

Mary Shelley edited by Esther Schor

Sam Shepard edited by Matthew C. Roudané

Spenser edited by Andrew Hadfield

Laurence Sterne edited by Thomas Keymer

Wallace Stevens edited by John N. Serio

Tom Stoppard edited by Katherine E. Kelly

Harriet Beecher Stowe edited by Cindy Weinstein

August Strindberg edited by Michael Robinson

Jonathan Swift edited by Christopher Fox

J. M. Synge edited by P. J. Mathews

Tacitus edited by A. J. Woodman

Henry David Thoreau edited by Joel Myerson

Tolstoy edited by Donna Tussing Orwin

Anthony Trollope edited by Carolyn Dever and Lisa Niles

Mark Twain edited by Forrest G. Robinson

John Updike edited by Stacey Olster

Mario Vargas Llosa edited by Efrain Kristal and John King

Virgil edited by Charles Martindale

Voltaire edited by Nicholas Cronk

Edith Wharton edited by Millicent Bell

Walt Whitman edited by Ezra Greenspan

Oscar Wilde edited by Peter Raby

Tennessee Williams edited by Matthew C. Roudané

August Wilson edited by Christopher Bigsby

Mary Wollstonecraft edited by Claudia L. Johnson

Virginia Woolf edited by Susan Sellers (second edition)

Wordsworth edited by Stephen Gill

W. B. Yeats edited by Marjorie Howes and John Kelly

Zola edited by Brian Nelson

TOPICS

The Actress edited by Maggie B. Gale and John Stokes

The African American Novel edited by Maryemma Graham

The African American Slave Narrative edited by Audrey A. Fisch

Allegory edited by Rita Copeland and Peter Struck

American Crime Fiction edited by Catherine Ross Nickerson

American Modernism edited by Walter Kalaidjian

American Realism and Naturalism edited by Donald Pizer

American Travel Writing edited by Alfred Bendixen and Judith Hamera

American Women Playwrights edited by Brenda Murphy

Ancient Rhetoric edited by Erik Gunderson

Arthurian Legend edited by Elizabeth Archibald and Ad Putter

Australian Literature edited by Elizabeth Webby

British Literature of the French Revolution edited by Pamela Clemit

British Romantic Poetry edited by James Chandler and Maureen N. McLane

British Romanticism edited by Stuart Curran (second edition)

British Theatre, 1730–1830, edited by Jane Moody and Daniel O'Quinn

Canadian Literature edited by Eva-Marie Kröller

Children's Literature edited by M. O. Grenby and Andrea Immel

The Classic Russian Novel edited by Malcolm V. Jones and Robin Feuer Miller

Contemporary Irish Poetry edited by Matthew Campbell

Creative Writing edited by David Morley and Philip Neilsen

Crime Fiction edited by Martin Priestman

Early Modern Women's Writing edited by Laura Lunger Knoppers

The Eighteenth-Century Novel edited by John Richetti

Eighteenth-Century Poetry edited by John Sitter

English Literature, 1500–1600 edited by Arthur F. Kinney

English Literature, 1650–1740 edited by Steven N. Zwicker

English Literature, 1740–1830 edited by Thomas Keymer and Jon Mee

English Literature, 1830–1914 edited by Joanne Shattock

English Novelists edited by Adrian Poole

English Poetry, Donne to Marvell edited by Thomas N. Corns

English Poets edited by Claude Rawson

English Renaissance Drama edited by A. R. Braunmuller and Michael Hattaway (second edition)

English Renaissance Tragedy edited by Emma Smith and Garrett A. Sullivan Jr.

English Restoration Theatre edited by Deborah C. Payne Fisk

The Epic edited by Catherine Bates

European Modernism edited by Pericles Lewis

European Novelists edited by Michael Bell

Fantasy Literature edited by Edward James and Farah Mendlesohn

Feminist Literary Theory edited by Ellen Rooney

Fiction in the Romantic Period edited by Richard Maxwell and Katie Trumpener

The Fin de Siècle edited by Gail Marshall

The French Novel: From 1800 to the Present edited by Timothy Unwin

Gay and Lesbian Writing edited by Hugh Stevens

German Romanticism edited by Nicholas Saul

Gothic Fiction edited by Jerrold E. Hogle

The Greek and Roman Novel edited by Tim Whitmarsh

Greek and Roman Theatre edited by Marianne McDonald and J. Michael Walton

Greek Lyric edited by Felix Budelmann

Greek Mythology edited by Roger D. Woodard

Greek Tragedy edited by P. E. Easterling

The Harlem Renaissance edited by George Hutchinson

The Irish Novel edited by John Wilson Foster

The Italian Novel edited by Peter Bondanella and Andrea Ciccarelli

Jewish American Literature edited by Hana Wirth-Nesher and Michael P. Kramer

The Latin American Novel edited by Efraín Kristal

The Literature of the First World War edited by Vincent Sherry

The Literature of London edited by Lawrence Manley

The Literature of Los Angeles edited by Kevin R. McNamara

The Literature of New York edited by Cyrus Patell and Bryan Waterman

Literature on Screen edited by Deborah Cartmell and Imelda Whelehan

The Literature of World War II edited by Marina MacKay

Medieval English Culture edited by Andrew Galloway

Medieval English Literature edited by Larry Scanlon

Medieval English Mysticism edited by Samuel Fanous and Vincent Gillespie

Medieval English Theatre edited by Richard Beadle and Alan J. Fletcher (second edition)

Medieval French Literature edited by Simon Gaunt and Sarah Kay

Medieval Romance edited by Roberta L. Krueger

Medieval Women's Writing edited by Carolyn Dinshaw and David Wallace

Modern American Culture edited by Christopher Bigsby

Modern British Women Playwrights edited by Elaine Aston and Janelle Reinelt

Modern French Culture edited by Nicholas Hewitt

Modern German Culture edited by Eva Kolinsky and Wilfried van der Will

The Modern German Novel edited by Graham Bartram

Modern Irish Culture edited by Joe Cleary and Claire Connolly

Modern Italian Culture edited by Zygmunt G. Baranski and Rebecca J. West

Modern Latin American Culture edited by John King

Modern Russian Culture edited by Nicholas Rzhevsky

Modern Spanish Culture edited by David T. Gies

Modernism edited by Michael Levenson (second edition)

The Modernist Novel edited by Morag Shiach

Modernist Poetry edited by Alex Davis and Lee M. Jenkins

Modernist Women Writers edited by Maren Tova Linett

Narrative edited by David Herman

Native American Literature edited by Joy Porter and Kenneth M. Roemer

Nineteenth-Century American Women's Writing edited by Dale M. Bauer and Philip Gould

Old English Literature edited by Malcolm Godden and Michael Lapidge

Performance Studies edited by Tracy C. Davis

Popular Fiction edited by David Glover and Scott McCracken

Postcolonial Literary Studies edited by Neil Lazarus

Postmodernism edited by Steven Connor

The Pre-Raphaelites edited by Elizabeth Prettejohn

Renaissance Humanism edited by Jill Kraye

The Roman Historians edited by Andrew Feldherr

Roman Satire edited by Kirk Freudenburg

Science Fiction edited by Edward James and Farah Mendlesohn

Scottish Literature edited by Gerald Carruthers and Liam McIlvanney

The Sonnet edited by A. D. Cousins and Peter Howarth

The Spanish Novel: From 1600 to the Present edited by Harriet Turner and Adelaida López de Martínez

Travel Writing edited by Peter Hulme and Tim Youngs

Twentieth-Century British and Irish Women's Poetry edited by Jane Dowson

The Twentieth-Century English Novel edited by Robert L. Caserio

Twentieth-Century English Poetry edited by Neil Corcoran

Twentieth-Century Irish Drama edited by Shaun Richards

Twentieth-Century Russian Literature edited by Marina Balina and Evgeny Dobrenko

Utopian Literature edited by Gregory Claeys

Victorian and Edwardian Theatre edited by Kerry Powell

The Victorian Novel edited by Deirdre David

Victorian Poetry edited by Joseph Bristow

War Writing edited by Kate McLoughlin

Writing of the English Revolution edited by N. H. Keeble